The History of the Green Bay Packers
Book II
The Lambeau Years
Part Two

by

Larry D. Names

Angel Press of WI   Berlin, Wisconsin

1989

Angel Press of WI
P.O. Box 643
Wautoma, WI 54982

Copyright © 1987 by Larry D. Names
ISBN: 0-939995-01-8

All rights reserved, including the right
to reproduce this book or any portion thereof in
any form whatsoever. For information,
address inquiries to:
Angel Press of WI
P.O. Box 643
Wautoma, WI 54982

First Printing May 1989

Printed by
Bookcrafters
Chelsea, Michigan

Photographs courtesy of
The Green Bay Packers Hall of Fame
Pro Football Hall of Fame

Front cover photograph courtesy of
Pro Football Hall of Fame

Publisher............................Joseph H. Schlaefer
Editor ....Gregory K. Scott
Cover Art..............................Julie Schinle

Table of Contents

Acknowledgements   9

Introduction   11

Chapter 1
   Aloha, Green Bay   17
      End of the 1932 season. Johnny Blood arranges trip to Hawaiian Islands for Packers. Charity games to be played in Hawaii. Blood given newspaper assignment to cover team on trip. Packers sail to Hawaii. Packers beat locals in two contests. Games broadcast back to Green Bay. Return to Mainland to play games in San Francisco and Los Angeles against local all-star teams. Red Grange playes for Packers in California. Lambeau gets his first taste of Hollywood.

Chapter 2
   The Game That Changed the Game   26
      Chicago Bears and Portsmouth Spartans tie for 1932. Playoff game arranged to be played in Chicago. Bad weather forces game indoors at Chicago Stadium. Cramped quarters of Chicago Stadium force rule changes. Bears win title. Winter meetings. NFL divided into divisions. New teams admitted to league. Rule changes make pro game distinctive from college game.

Chapter 3
   The New Era Begins — On The Wrong Foot   32
      Packers have big financial loss in 1932. Joannes re-elected president of corporation. Lawsuit against Packers by injured fan. Insurance company fails, leaving Packers to pay off suit. Corporation put into receivership. Jonet appointed receiver.

Chapter 4
   The First Losing Season   38   Several new faces join Packers for 1933. Five veteran players report late for camp, upsetting Lambeau. How Johnny Blood got to Green Bay one year. Lambeau designs new offense to take advantage of Herber's passing ability. Packers get off to bad start. Ollie

Kuechle arranges for Packers to play against Giants in Milwaukee. Big crowd turns out to see Packers lose to Giants. Portsmouth franchise similar to Packers in ownership. Pittsburgh's first game against Packers. Eagles first game against Packers. Season ends on sour note.

Chapter 5
Excuses, Excuses   56
Lambeau tries to explain away Packers first losing season. Herber's automobile accident at beginning of season. NFL President Carr mishandles incident involving Cal Hubbard and referee George Lawrie. Blood tells of being fired by Lambeau at critical time of season.

Chapter 6
Back on Track   63
Hubbard and Comstock give up playing and take up coaching. Lambeau signs several new players, including Joe Laws. Most regulars back from previous year. More rule changes by NFL to make game more exciting for fans. Bears win first NFL title game. Packers get season off to good start, then run into Bears. Packers play Giants at State Fair Park in Milwaukee, then play exhibition game there against Bears in October. Lions nip Packers in Motor City. Champ Seibold declared ineligible by NFL. Tiny Engebretsen joins Pack late in year. Cincinnati franchise sold and moved to St. Louis. Bears win West Division title, then lose to Giants in championship game.

Chapter 7
The Green Bay Packers Incorporated   73
Joannes tells public that a new corporation must be formed or the team will have to move to Milwaukee. Green Bay Business Association solicits money city-wide. New corporation formed. Packers saved again.

Chapter 8
Lightning Comes to Green Bay   78
Lambeau scouts a future Hall-of-Famer at Rose Bowl. The signing of Don Hutson. New players for 1935. Most veterans return, including Cal Hubbard. Stockholders meeting elects executive committee. Bear game prices raised. Packers report to first camp outside of Green Bay. Packers sweep series of exhibition games against amateur teams. Blood gains release from Pittsburgh, resigns with Packers. Carr given new contract.

Pack gets new uniforms. Cardinals ruin opener. Hutson catches first NFL pass and beats Bears. Hutson Legend is born. Another loss to Cards in Milwaukee. Packers in thick of title chase. Packers go on road and season goes down tubes. Detroit wins division and NFL championship.

Chapter 9
A New System, A New Title   93
NFL magnates devise a plan to draft college players. Jay Berwanger, first draft choice, priced himself out of the market. First Packer draft. Russ Letlow, first Packer choice. Packers play exhibitions in California against Lions and local all-star teams. Packers face another court case and win. Red Smith becomes assistant coach. Packers open with win over Cards, then get slammed by Bears. Blood wins salary dispute and signs with Packers. Packers begin long winning streak that culminates in division title and NFL championship.

Chapter 10
To Repeat Or Not To Repeat   109
Lambeau makes Wisconsin's Ed Jankowski Packers first round draft pick for '37. Bud Wilkinson passes on pro ball with Packers for coaching career. Packers barnstorm to West Coast. Herber punched out by Bear player in Los Angeles. Packers get in the movies. Redskins move to Washington. Cleveland Rams admitted to NFL from AFL. Packers wilt in College All-Star game and lose. New seats for City Stadium. New members added to board of directors. Blood and Kiesling become coaches for Pittsburgh. Cards spoil opener. Hutson has big day against Rams in Cleveland. Injuries put Packers out of title chase in last two weeks of season. Redskins win playoff against Giants, then beat Bears for NFL championship.

Chapter 11
Best Man at the Wedding   120
NFL changes college draft rules. Packers draft Cecil Isbell in first round. Lambeau takes usual scouting trip to West Coast. Pittsburgh trains at Two Rivers. Packers and Pirates play pair of exhibitions. Lambeau signs Baby Ray. Several veterans hold out for more pay. Seating capacity at City Stadium increased. Packers play Cards in Buffalo. Herber breaks hand in fight on train during trip home. Despite two early losses, Packers in thick of title chase. Rooney cancels Pirate game against Rams to prepare better for

Packers. Pack wins easily anyway as Isbell has big day. Lambeau puts white jerseys on Packers when they play Rams in Cleveland. Bears fade in mid-season. Lions only threat to Packers' division title hopes. Eagles defeat Lions to give Packers western division crown. Packers lose thriller to Giants in NFL title game at Polo Grounds.

Chapter 12
The Cream Also Rises   134

Lambeau drafts Charley Brock in second round. Lambeau makes longer scouting trip to West, then Midwest, and finally East to see his son at Fordham before going to Europe for vacation. Dick Zoll acquired from Cleveland. NFL President Joe Carr dies of heart attack. Hollywood movie has team called Chicago Packers. 24 roster spots up for grabs when camp opens. Pirates train in Two Rivers again and play Packers a doubleheader. Packers go to Dallas to play Southwest All-Stars before season. Packers upset by Rams in third game of season, then don't lose again until they play Bears in Chicago. Hinkle scores winning TD at Detroit to give Pack division crown over Bears. Joannes causes furor in Green Bay by moving NFL title game to Milwaukee. Packers whitewash Giants to win fifth NFL championship in 11 years.

Chapter 13
Resting on Laurels   152

Draft grows longer. Only three draftees make squad. New AFL formed; Milwaukee gets franchise. Packer trainer dies of heart attack. Marshall tries to oust Storck as league president. Lambeau signs several free agents. Bud Svendsen traded to Brooklyn for Beattie Feathers. Stockholders reward Lambeau by making him "second" vice-president. Long-time Packer Hank Bruder traded to Pittsburgh. Packers demolish College All-Stars. Pack plays exhibition against Redskins in Milwaukee, then host little AFL Kenosha Cards. Herm Schneidmann retires. Frank Balazs suspended for "insubordination". Packers win opener against Eagles. Bears give Packers worst ever beating in Green Bay. Lions drub Packers in Green Bay. Packers continue domination of Steelers. Packers crush Lions in Detroit, but lose division title to Bears.

Chapter 14
Close But No Cigar   166

Sportswriters start using war terms to describe football players and games. Bears annihilate Redskins in NFL title game. Packer draft list for 1941. Hinkle retirement rumored. Elmer Layden replaces Storck at top of NFL, becomes first commissioner. Many teams unhappy about going all the way to Green Bay to play instead of playing in Milwaukee. Milwaukee Chiefs drawing away Packer fans. Packers make working agreement with Long Island Indians of American Football Association. Hinkle signs record Packer pact. Herber released. Packers win opener from Detroit. Balazs sold to Cardinals. Engebretsen retires. Packers lose to Bears, then trail Chicago till mid-season when Packers get revenge in Chicago and retake first. Packers and Bears tie for first, but Bears when division playoff.

Chapter 15
Year with an Asterisk   182

World War II starts for U.S. Many college players drafted on graduation. Several Packer players enlist in military or navy. Most of Packer draftees never play pro ball. Travel restrictions prevent Lambeau from making usual West Coast scouting tour. Four other NFL teams train in Wisconsin in '42. Lambeau signs several local products to meet wartime work restrictions. More problems concerning Green Bay's location and travel. Packers lose opener to Bears, trail Bears rest of season. Hutson racks up record numbers for games and season.

Chapter 16
The Year of Uncertainty   193

George Halas and Dan Reeves enlist in armed forces. Halas names Anderson and Johnsos as co-coaches of Bears. Reeves suspends operation of Rams. Packer draft nets only a few players. Roster limits cut to 28. Eagles and Steelers merge for '43 season. Isbell retires, takes coaching reins at Purdue. Season ticket sales drive keeps Packers going. Hutson's brother killed in war and father dies at same time. AFL suspends operations for duration. Bears still loaded with talent. Investigation of Chicago players war-time duties. Packers tie Bears in opener. Redskins massacre Packers in Milwaukee. Bears knock Pack out of race.

Chapter 17
Lambeau's Last Hurrah   202

Hutson becomes coach at end of '43 season. Red Smith quits Packers, takes assistant job with Giants. Canadeo called into Army. NFL takes first *step to football war by denying Don Ameche a franchise for Los Angeles. Steelers merge with Cards for '44 campaign. Boston given franchise. Rams resume operations. First meeting of AAC. Lambeau hires former Bear George Trafton as assistant coach. Packers win opener from Brooklyn now renamed the Tigers. Packers beat Bears in Green Bay for first time in five years. Packers win six straight before losing to Bears in Chicago. Packers back into division title in controversial loss to Giants. Lambeau and Red Smith have brouhaha in print. Packers win NFL title in New York.*

Chapter 18
  One War Ends . . .   220
  Owners leary about expansion. Snubbed applicants form AAC. Lambeau fires Trafton. Dan Topping has trouble with Branch Rickey over lease of Ebbetts Field. Brooklyn Tigers merge with Boston Yanks for '45. Lambeau makes speech about Andy Turnbull. Lambeau hires Walt Kiesling as assistant. Packers win opener from Bears. Hutson sets single game and quarter scoring records against Detroit. Rams hand Packers first loss. Packers never catch up again. Rams win division and NFL titles. Lambeau given new contract thru "49 season.

Summary   233

Bibliography   239

Index   240

§ § §

Acknowledgements

The first person I wish to thank is my wife Peggy who isn't a football fan. She displayed the patience of a saint for several months as I bombarded her with every little bit of information about the Green Bay Packers I gleaned from various sources. Also, she was an invaluable research assistant. I couldn't have done this book without her.

This book may never have gotten off the ground if my close friend and confidant Fr. Joesph Schlaefer hadn't given me the confidence to write it. He knows how grateful I am for this opportunity, but I would like the whole world to know what a truly remarkable man he is. It's a great honor to be his friend.

My friend Greg Scott provided some invaluable editorial assistance. His suggestions and prodding kept me digging for the facts.

Craig Cramer at the Wisconsin State Historical Society in Madison put me on the right track in researching the old newspapers.

The librarians at the Brown County Public Library and the Berlin (Wisconsin) Public Library were very kind and helpful to me when I used their excellent facilities.

Jethrow Kyles took time out from his busy schedule at Notre Dame University to answer my questions and do a little a research for me.

Pat O'Connell took the time to help in the selection of photographs, and he was ill at the time, too. He showed the real spirit of Packer people.

The late Clark Hinkle gave me some invaluable information about the team when he was with them.

Abe Abrohams was a fountain of information about Nate Abrams and his family's contribution to Packers history.

Many thanks to the staff of the Green Bay Packers Hall of Fame for their assistance and co-operation.

Last but not least, once again I want to thank my good friend Jim Ford for all of his research assistance, advice, encouragement, and compliments on this book. As I wrote in the first book, so often Jim pointed me in the right direction to find some detail or he confirmed information I had uncovered through another source. Jim also talked to several people who provided answers to a myriad of questions about the Packers and Curly Lambeau in the early years. Without his contacts in Green Bay, this book wouldn't have all those little known details that separate it from others publications. I can't begin to express my gratitude to Jim and do him justice, so I'll put it simply. Thanks, Jim.

§ § §

Introduction

While researching the history of the Green Bay Packers, it was amazing to discover so much about the era detailed in this volume. In all other works on the Packers, the years after the first triple championship team are called the Hutson era or something similar, as if Don Hutson were the only star on the team. There is no doubt that Hutson was the first great receiver in National Football League history, but he was not the only great player to wear a Packer uniform between 1932 and 1950. In fact, he was but one of several great Packers that other writers seem to have overlooked.

Another fault I found with other works covering this time period was how they handled Curly Lambeau. Most of them only saw him as the coach of an NFL team that did well over a number of seasons. A few saw a part of the man, the good part in every case. None of them wrote a discouraging word about Lambeau. None of them portrayed him as the very complex individual that he was.

Beyond the Packers was the NFL itself. The 1930s marked the beginning of change in the league and its game. For the first time, the professionals had their own brand of football. No longer was it just like the college version of running on first and second down and punting on third down if a first down wasn't made or wasn't even close. The pro game became an offensive show, and the fans loved the wide open style; their attendance proved it.

Of course, the Packers prospered during this time, overcoming several incredible obstacles placed in their way. One of these stumblingblocks was bankruptcy. For some reason the story of how the Packers went into receivership was glossed over by every previous writer of Packer history and many of them had the facts wrong, beginning with the dates. In fact, the *Green Bay Packers Media Guide* for 1987 even has the wrong years.

The media guide has several other facts incorrect as well. Most of them concern the years various men played for the Packers. These are trivial errors but errors all the same, and it appears that they were made by the man who originally helped breathe life into the Packers, George Whitney Calhoun. As a publicity man, he was among the best. But as an historian, he was a failure because he relied too heavily on his own memory.

Calhoun was not alone with this problem. Arch Ward, Chuck Johnson, John Torinus, and others failed to check their facts before offering them as gospel. Greatly disappointing are the works of authors whose primary subject is not the Packers but some other team or the NFL. Nearly every one of them fails to portray the beginnings of the Packers accurately, then they compound their initial mistakes by glossing over other important events in Packer history that had a great impact on the history of the NFL.

It was these inaccuracies which spurred this writer to check and double check all the information presented within these pages before committing it to print. Of course, as with the first volume in this series, there will be those who will disagree with what it is written here. Some reviewers disputed the argument about George Halas being the man behind the expulsion of the Packers from the league after the 1921 season, and another wrote that the cause of that incident was not a game in Chicago against the Bears but a later game against the Racine Legion in Milwaukee. None of them came forth with any proof to the contrary.

Mrs. Colleen Barnett, from Boscobel, Wisconsin, expressed her gratitude for someone finally giving her father, Attorney Gerald Clifford, his proper due in Packer history, but she objected to the word "diminutive" in the description of him. Mr. Neil M. Murphy, from Ukiah, California, told Jim Ford how much he enjoyed the first volume, then offered some additional information about the early years of the Packers. Mr. Murphy gave evidence of how deeply involved his father, C.M. Murphy, was with the Packers when the team was supported by the Indian Packing Corporation, then the Acme Packing Company.

Others who wrote, called, or spoke to me at the several public appearances I made in conjunction with the first volume expressed their gratitude for finally giving credit where credit was due, for getting the names right on the pictures (or at least as right as possible), and for telling the whole story of the Packers and not just part of it.

When the first volume came onto the market, I busied myself with radio and television programs and autograph parties all over Wisconsin and northern Illinois. On these occasions, I was grilled by sportscasters, talk show hosts, and Packer fans who really are everywhere. The best part of it all was meeting so many wonderful people. The one I think I enjoyed the most was a clergyman from Chippewa Falls who drove down to Eau Claire to meet me at a Waldenbooks store. We shared a really nice visit that went so long that his wife almost had to drag him away from the table. Another gentleman in Eau Claire told me how his father had played for the Chippewa Falls Marines when they played the Packers in an exhibition game. At Conkey's Book Store in Appleton, I met Jeff Everson from Clintonville who told me he had heard me on Jack Baker's sports talk show over WTMJ radio in Milwaukee. Jeff questioned me about writing a history and told me he was working on one. The next time I saw Jeff I was getting his autograph in a copy of his history of the Milwaukee Brewers.

There were some tense moments, too. One in particular when a fellow in Manitowoc walked up to me and told me in no uncertain terms that the Packers were ★*!!!★#!!**#@@!! and then some. Of course, he was referring to the Packers of 1986, one of whom had slam-dunked the Bears quarterback the Sunday before and put him out of the lineup for the rest of the season. And then there was the night I was on Chet Coppoc's show over WMAQ in Chicago. It was the Wednesday before the Bears-Packers game in Chicago and I followed Bears' wide receiver Willie Gault on the air. What a tough act to follow! But Mr. Coppoc got me through it.

It was all of these experiences that drove me to fill in as many of the blank spots in Packer history between 1932 and 1946 that I could. I know there are some stories about this player or that one that have been left out, but those will have to wait for another day. There got to be so many tales to tell and facts to report that I had to draw the line at some point. I was forced to remind myself — and now my readers — that this is the history of the *Green Bay Packers* team and organization and not a collection of biographies on individual players.

Which brings me to a point that I know will be brought up when this book reaches the market. I will be asked about — and criticized for — including so much of Curly Lambeau's personal life in this book. The reason for this is simple: A lot of what he did off the field and out of the office directly affected his relationships with his players and the officers of the corporation that paid his salary which in turn affected the team's play and thus the history of the Packers. Those episodes of his life — and the lives of others in Packer history — that have no direct bearing on the overall history of the Packers have been omitted here and left for other tomes.

So here is the history of how the Green Bay Packers survived the Great Depression, pressure to move the franchise to Milwaukee, and the great pro football war of the late 1940s during the second half of Curly Lambeau's tenure with the organization. Like the first half of his years in Green Bay, it is truly an amazing relation. The story of the men — and women — who kept the Packers in Green Bay is incredible, and I hope I've done them justice in recalling it here.

§ § §

The History of the Green Bay Packers
Book II
The Lambeau Years
Part Two

§ § §

*To my good
and great friend
Jim Ford
with love*

§ § §

1
Aloha, Green Bay

"Everything was just fine with the Packers until Lambeau went Hollywood." That was the saying in Green Bay in the late 1940s when Packer fortunes hit an all-time low under Lambeau. What most people didn't know was the seed of truth in that statement was sown in early 1933.

Although the Packers failed to win the National Football League title for the fourth straight year in 1932, Green Bay was still the darling of America's pro football fans. People everywhere wanted to see the team from the little town in Wisconsin. Even in places as far away as Hawaii, the Pack was in demand for postseason play.

Green Bay Football Corporation President Lee Joannes received an invitation from the *Honolulu Star–Bulletin* and the Bank of Hawaii December 6, 1932 to bring the Packers to the island territory for a pair of exhibition games to be played on Christmas and New Year's Day against a team of West Coast All–Stars and University of Hawaii players. A third game was set up by the Knights of Columbus in San Francisco for later in January. The Packers would be reimbursed for their expenses and paid a portion of the gate receipts. But before Joannes could accept, there was the little matter of the Chicago Bears.

The Packers–Bears game of December 11, 1932 was the final scheduled contest of the year in the NFL. Green Bay was mathematically eliminated the week before when the Portsmouth Spartans crushed Curly Lambeau's eleven, 19-0, and clinched a tie for the league championship. Chicago still had a chance to tie the Spartans for the top spot; all the Bruins had to do was beat the Packers.

Snow fell each of the three days before the game. Workers did their best to keep the field clear, but Mother Nature was determined to have the two pro aggregations fight it out in the flakes. It snowed the morning of the game and all through the contest. To make matters worse for Green Bay, several players were suffering from colds or cases of the flu. Although they were sick and weak and out of the title chase, the Packers showed 3,000 shivering spectators that they had pride. Green Bay lost, 9-0, but the Bears knew they had been given a real game.

The small turnout was a real problem for George Halas, the Bears' owner. He couldn't pay the Packers their guarantee of $2,500. Completely in sympathy with Halas, Joannes agreed to accept a partial cash payment and a promissory note for the balance. Halas handed over $1,000 in cash and the note for $1,500 which he promised to pay within six months. Halas said Joannes could take it out of his guarantee for the Bears' game in Green Bay the following season. Joannes found this to be acceptable at the time, and as it turned out, having the promissory note instead of the cash actually worked to the benefit of the Packers. But that's getting ahead of the story.

After the defeat in Chicago, Joannes announced that the Packers would accept the invitation to play in the tropics. Curly Lambeau and 17 players packed their bags and jumped on the train for Los Angeles on December 13. Staying behind were Tom Nash who was injured on the eastern trip, Hurdis McCrary who was still sick with the flu, Paul Fitzgibbons, Cal Hubbard, and Verne Lewellen whose job as Brown county district attorney precluded any lengthy stays away from Green Bay. *Press-Gazette* reporters Art Bystrom and George Whitney Calhoun vied for the privilege of accompanying the team on the western journey, but neither was allowed to go; the newspaper's business head, Andrew V. Turnbull, citing the enormous expense of covering an exhibition tour. But to make sure the home folks could read about the exploits of their gridiron favorites, Calhoun struck on the plan to have Johnny Blood send back reports. Blood agreed, and his byline began appearing in the publication at the end of the week when the "Vagabond Halfback" wrote about the team sailing on the *S.S. Mariposa* from San Pedro, California for the Hawaiian Islands.

Clarke Hinkle related this story to author Myron Cope for his book, *The Game That Was*:

"My rookie year we played twenty-two games, fourteen of them league games and eight exhibitions, and we were still playing in February, almost in March, and the reason we were was Johnny Blood. Now there's a guy! Let me tell you about him.

"He was a rangy halfback, about six-two and 190, and he had great speed. When he was about thirty-five and Don Hutson was about twenty-four, he raced Hutson a hundred yards. Hutson could outrun the wind, but he beat Johnny in that race by only a step. Johnny was the kind of guy who would read Shakespeare, Chaucer, and all those kind of people, although when he was drinking he would read filthy dime novels.

"Johnny's life was probably even more glamorous off the field than on. After a game he'd buy up whorehouses. He purchased them and closed them up. Yes, he'd close them up so he could stay with those girls all by himself. I doubt if he had relations with any of them, but that's just the way he was. He liked an unusual conversation. He just liked to do things like that. So during my rookie season he was corresponding with some people in Honolulu, and one day he came to us and said, 'Do you want to play a few postseason exhibition games in Honolulu? All you got to do is say yes, and I'll arrange it.'

"Nobody took him seriously. Lambeau said, 'Okay, John. I'll let you handle it. You make all the arrangements.'

"Well, darned if Johnny didn't get us all lined up for Honolulu."

Blood waxed poetic in his opening paragraph when he wrote: "When Green Bay and Wisconsin football fans read this, the Packers will be on the briny deep, bound for the Hawaiian Islands, the home of the hula hula dancer . . . " Then he told about the large crowd that was at the dock to see the ship off but admitted that it wasn't for the Packers. "Some movie actress was going to Honolulu for the holidays and many of her admirers and friends came down to the dock to bid her farewell." He then made a curious remark. "It looks like a pleasant trip." It was as if he was planning to meet this Hollywood starlet and have himself a good time.

The following paragraph was a smokescreen of words. "We

expect to arrive in Honolulu next Wednesday and will immediately begin working out for the contest with the University of Hawaii Christmas Day. The Packers will be 'strictly business' until this game and there will be no sightseeing until after Christmas." Blood knew there was no way he and his fun-loving friends would be "strictly business" up until game time. No sightseeing until after Christmas? Maybe not in the daylight when Lambeau was watching them like a hawk.

After a few remarks about escaping Wisconsin's winter winds for the balmy breezes of the Pacific, Blood colored his story nicely with a few personal notes.

"Arnie Herber has been barred from all future card games. He's too lucky. Mike Michalske is lonesome and is already pining for old Green Bay.

"Jug Earpe is also crying the blues. He was undecided whether he would get on the *S.S. Mariposa* or not tonight. It seems someone put a picture of a sinking ship in his berth Thursday night and he didn't sleep a wink — so he says. Jug is no sailor, and he says that if that ship sinks he can't walk back. Dry land will look good to him when he gets to Honolulu."

Blood failed to report who could have done that to a nice guy like Jug Earpe. Maybe it was Paul Burke, an avid supporter of the team who had come along on the trip. Blood reported that Burke complained that there was no chaplain accompanying the team. It was remarked in Green Bay that "the Lord Himself could have gone with the Packers and still couldn't have kept those boys on the straight and narrow."

As soon as the team landed in Hawaii, Lambeau was notified that Cal Hubbard, Nate Barrager, and Arnie Herber had been selected to the National Football League's All-Star team. Lavvie Dilweg and Clarke Hinkle were picked for the second team; and Tom Nash, Dick Stahlman, Mike Michalske, Joe Zeller, and Blood were honorable mentions. The Bears also had 10 men honored, and Portsmouth had eight.

In Blood's next installment for the folks back home, he raved about the beautiful weather and said all the players were glad to be off the ship and back on the practice field. Blood also stated that the players had had the run of the ship and that "there was considerable tux work from the time the big boat left the mainland until it docked here..." What Blood failed to mention was that the Prohibition Act didn't reach beyond the territorial waters of the United States. Not that it mattered a whole lot, but with drinking legal, Johnny and the boys took full advantage of the situation.

Lambeau knew how to handle his team. Hinkle told Cope that Lambeau was as tough a disciplinarian in the '30s and '40s as Vince Lombardi was in the '60s. As soon as the ship was tied up to the pier, he had the Packers get into their practice togs and had them taxied to the playing field at the University of Hawaii where he put them through some much needed exercise. After an hour of sweating out the booze, he took them down to Waikiki Beach and had them take a swim in the warm Pacific water. Finally satisfied that they were drying out, he took them to the Moana Hotel and checked in.

After three more days of practicing, it was game time. The opposition was supposed to be the University of Hawaii squad, a college team. In reality, the Hawaiian eleven was a combination of players from the university and from Kamehameha School, an institution that was established for educating children of Hawaiian descent.

The Kams, as the locals were called, were reported as planning to play barefoot. This was merely an advertising gimmick. They played in regular football shoes, the same as the Packers. For the most part, they were smaller than the Packers, but they made up for their lack of size by being much quicker. Their speed and local officials kept them in the game. Blood nicely explained that the reason the Packers had 175 yards in penalties and the Kams only 25 was the difference in interpretation of the rules by the Islanders. Even had the Packers lost, Blood would probably have said the same thing. A crowd of 13,362 fans turned out for the contest, and the Packers came away 19-13 winners.

WHBY, the St. Norbert College radio station in West De Pere, was engaged by Walkers Cleaners and Tailors to air the game. It was a huge success, so the second game of the Hawaiian series was also airwaved back to Green Bay.

The second team to face the Packers was called the Mickalums because it was backed by an alumni group from Honolulu's McKinley High School. Clarke Hinkle's former Bucknell coach Neil Blaisdell was the squad's mentor. Later in life, Blaisdell became mayor of Honolulu. The Mick–alums were pretty much an all–star aggregation from the Islands semi–pro league. Although the Mick-alums were supposed to be a better team than the Kams, Green Bay was favored by three touchdowns. The Packers lived up to their advance notices this time by crushing the Mick–alums, 32-0.

Then it was back to the Mainland for the Green Bayers on the luxury liner *S.S. Maui*. Hinkle told another story on Blood about the trip home:

"We were having a good time on the boat, when suddenly we couldn't find Blood. So Milt Gantenbein, who was my roommate at the time — Milt and I walked out on the main deck and went back toward the stern. The sea was a little rough, and that ship was pitching. But we walked back there toward the stern, and then we turned white. We froze.

"Johnny Blood was outside the safety railing, on the extreme stern end of that ship. He was hanging on to the flagpole. There he was, in the middle of that pitch–black night, with the ship pitching, and he was swinging around that flagpole. He didn't even know he was in any danger.

"He'd been drinking that Okole Hao, that native drink. Made from pineapple juice or tea roots or something. Hell of a drink, I'll tell you. Anyway, we eased out there and got him out of there, but if he'd have dropped off that stern, nobody would have ever found him. And that's just one of the things he did."

Another incident occured when the Packers arrived in San Francisco on January 17 and were met by Red Grange who had signed on to play with the Packers for two West Coast games. Lambeau and the boys were also greeted by San Francisco's Mayor Angelo Rossi who officially welcomed them to the city. Blood showed his gratitude by passing out in Rossi's office. Poor Johnny had done too much "tux work" on the voyage home. As he explained in his interview with Myron Cope, "Alcohol, you see, hangs on to me. I don't sober up real fast. It's a family characteristic — I have plenty of recuperative power, but alcohol doesn't fall out of me. It hangs on to me."

Ernie Nevers, the Packers' old nemesis from his days with the Duluth Eskimos and Chicago Cardinals, put together the Pacific Coast All–Star squad that was set to face Green Bay at Kezar Stadium. The Knights of Columbus sponsored the game, and all profits were to go to charity. A crowd of approximately 30,000 showed up for the Sunday afternoon affair, and Nevers' hand–picked eleven stuck it to the NFL bruisers, 13-6.

The following week the Packers headed south to Los Angeles to meet a team of mostly University of Southern California alumni. Former USC halfback Ernie Pinckert captained the squad, and Ernie Nevers was on hand to lend his name and reputation to the game. The contest was set for Sunday January 29, but a heavy downpour made the playing surface at Wrigley Field a quagmire, forcing postponement of the game until the following Saturday.

In the interim, the Packer players had a lot of time on their hands and not all of it was put to good use. In an interview with Myron Cope, Red Grange remembered a particular night he spent with the inimitable Johnny Blood.

"Talk about swingers, what about Johnny Blood? One year, I played a couple of post–season exhibition games for Green Bay and roomed with Blood. What a guy! I remember a couple of girls wanted Johnny to sign a program, and he said, 'I'll do better than that. I'll sign it in blood.' He cut his wrist with a knife and signed that program in blood, and he had to have about four stitches taken in the wrist.*

"He was a lovable guy, a very learned guy, and one whale of a football player. A long-legged guy who could kill you every way. Run, punt, pass, catch passes, a great football player. He used to drive Curly Lambeau crazy. We were staying in Los Angeles, and Johnny and I had a hotel room next to Coach Lambeau. Curly was in the corner room. Johnny knew that Curly had a case of whiskey in his room, so when Curly went out, Johnny climbed out on the ledge, which was on the ninth floor and must have been about a foot wide, and he walked along that ledge for about twenty feet and got through Curly's window and

---

* This story was told by others in print, but Cope was the only writer to credit Grange with originating it.

took a couple of bottles and came back. I don't think Curly ever did learn who stole his whiskey."

When Green Bay and the USC All–Stars were able to meet, the Packers were without the services of Michalske and Earpe who had returned to Green Bay during the week as originally planned. Earpe came back to see his new baby daughter who was born the Sunday before.

The game in San Francisco wasn't broadcast back to Green Bay, but WHBY got Bob Elson of radio station WGN in Chicago to do the play–by–play for the Los Angeles affair. Once again Walkers Cleaners and Tailors sponsored the broadcast.

If not for Red Grange, the game would have been just another exhibition of football. This particular contest was supposed to be Grange's last as a professional and was billed as such. But he changed his mind the next summer and signed on with the Bears again. He scored one touchdown as he and Herber led the Packers to a 19-6 win over the Southern California All–Stars.

With the football season finally behind them, most of the players headed home to enjoy well earned vacations. Roger Grove, Wuert Engelmann, Lavvie Dilweg, Hurdis McCrary, Red Bultman, Arnie Herber, Vern Lewellen, Claude Perry and Hank Bruder returned to Green Bay. Johnny Blood had taken a real liking to the *wahines* of Hawaii, so he decided to spend the rest of the winter in Honolulu. Nate Barrager went to his home in Southern California, and all of the others headed to their various homes throughout the Midwest. The only man who didn't hurry home was Curly Lambeau.

Much of Lambeau's time in Los Angeles was spent in conference with various Hollywood types who were interested in filming a movie about a football team. Lambeau lunched with George Lee, the famous screenplay writer who scripted *Little Caesar* and *Seventy Thousand Witnesses*. They discussed utilizing Lambeau as "football director." Curly also met with Champ Pickens, the famous promoter for Barney Oldfield, balloon races, Grange's southern trip in 1926, and other projects. Pickens wanted Lambeau to sponsor a motorcycle racing track in Green Bay.

All of this talk of motion pictures and big–time promotions

turned Lambeau's head away from what he knew best. Helping to scramble his thinking was a young starlet named Myrna Kennedy. A movie studio loaned Miss Kennedy to the Packers as a sort of tour guide. In return, Lambeau invited the lady to sit on the Packers' bench as an "honorary coach" for the LA game. Being seen in public with Lambeau was good for Miss Kennedy's career, and it was good publicity for the forthcoming game being played for charity. It also did wonders for Curly Lambeau. After all, the man had been away from home for the better part of six weeks. There's nothing like a young movie starlet to lift a man's spirits.

The Green Bay Press-Gazette finally reported in mid-February that "Coach E.L. Lambeau, of the Green Bay Packer professional football club, arrived in Green Bay last night after his extended trip with the club to the Pacific coast and Hawaiian Islands. The Packer mentor stopped in the southwest on business on his way back from the Pacific coast . . . " Lambeau was the last man to come back to Green Bay — almost two weeks after his players. Not everyone knew exactly what sort of business Lambeau had been conducting "in the southwest," although several wagging tongues in Green Bay were saying that it was probably monkey business. This was not a proven fact at the time, but in the years to come the rumormongers would be proven right for once.

Although the Green Bay Packers and their followers didn't know it then, Curly Lambeau had taken his first step toward "going Hollywood."

§ § §

2

The Game That Changed the Game

When history is being made, no one really knows the impact of the event for days, weeks, maybe even years after. That was exactly the case when the Chicago Bears met the Portsmouth Spartans for the 1932 National Football League title.

The Bears and the Spartans finished the regular season with six wins and one loss each. The four ties that Portsmouth had and the six that Chicago had meant nothing in the standings. If ties had counted as half a win and half a loss, the Packers would have won the title outright; but there's no need to go into that here because the subject was thoroughly covered in the *Summary* of the first book in this series.

Because of the tie between Chicago and Portsmouth, a play-off game was necessary to decide the championship. Chicago being the larger city and thus more apt to draw a bigger crowd, NFL President Joe Carr assigned the game to the Bears home park, Wrigley Field, denying a bid by a Cincinnati group to host the game in the Queen City of the Ohio. Portsmouth owner Harry Snyder didn't argue with Carr, giving his consent to play in the Windy City.

When the Packers visited Chicago for their final contest of the regular season, it snowed throughout the game and spectators had a difficult time following the ball. *The Chicago Tribune* photographers also had trouble identifying players in the pictures they took of the game. One caption below a game photo in the Windy City newspaper read: "Somewhere in there is Green Bay quarterback Roger Grove with the ball. Your guess is as good as ours."

Since it was December and weather forecasting wasn't as proficient as it would be in later decades, Bears owner George Halas asked Chicago Cubs President Bill Veeck, Sr., to release the Bears from their agreement to play all home games in Wrigley Field. Veeck was a great man who new the value of friendship. He let Halas out of their agreement for this one game, then Halas took the precaution of reserving Chicago Stadium as a possible playing site. Financial matters were bad enough already for the Chicago magnate. Just the week before, he'd paid the Packers a part of their $2,500 guarantee with a promissory note for $1,500 because attendance had been very low for the game and he had to use all his cash to pay his players and meet other immediate expenses. Fortunately for Halas, Lee Joannes and the rest of Green Bay's management were understanding, having been in similar predicaments a few times themselves. With his debt to the Packers already hanging over his head, Halas couldn't afford another big loss of ticket revenue, so he got Carr's permission to move the game into the Stadium and to play it on Sunday night.

It wasn't exactly a novelty for the Bears to play in the Stadium. They had played the Chicago Cardinals in the arena two years earlier in a post-season charity contest.

With the day and time set, Chicago Stadium had to be prepared for holding a football game. Several tons of earth had been brought into the arena earlier in the month for a circus that was playing there. More dirt was brought in to make a better playing surface and to cover up the telltale signs of elephants, horses, lions, and tigers having been there just the week before. Even so, some of the Chicago players remarked about how they weren't so sure that they wanted to play in a manure pile. Halas told them not to worry about it, but if they did find a particularly offensive spot, then that was where they should rub the Spartans' noses in the dirt.

The field was only 60 yards long from goal to goal and 45 yards wide. With the abbreviated distances, the game was played with a few rule changes.

Because the Bears and Spartans had played to ties in their two previous encounters, Halas proposed an overtime period of 10 minutes if the playoff game ended knotted up. In the charity game with the crosstown Cardinals in 1930, the referee was instructed to move the ball back 20 yards with each change of possession. This only served to confuse the fans as well as the teams. So moving the ball back was ruled out.

Football fields didn't have hash marks in 1932 because the next play started where the last play ended unless the ball was carried out of bounds. In that case, the ball was moved in 15 yards from the sideline. Most teams would intentionally waste a down by running the ball out of bounds in order to get it moved toward the middle of the field. For the title game, both teams agreed to move the ball in 15 yards at any time it was downed closer than 10 yards to the sideline; but for moving it toward the middle of the field, the possession team was penalized a down. All the penalty did was replace the time lost running a wasted play.

Also by agreement, placekicking and dropkicking, except for points after touchdown, were banned from play because neither coach wanted to turn the game into a field goal kicking contest, which would have happened considering the short distance between goals. But punting was allowed.

The game was played almost like any other game of the day, but it had some highlights.

Red Grange was knocked cold in the first period and sat out until the final quarter. Keith Molesworth of the Bears and Ace Gutowsky of the Spartans punted the ball frequently and always into the end zone, preventing any runbacks. A crowd of 11,198 watched each team put on a goal line stand and fight to a 0-0 tie after three quarters of play. Then Grange returned in time to catch a five-yard pass from Bronko Nagurski for six points with 10 minutes remaining to be played. Paul Engebretsen converted the extra point, and the Bears led, 7-0. A safety in the dying moments of the contest made the final score, 9-0, and the Bears won their first title since 1924.

With a champion finally decided upon, the powers-that-be in the NFL took time to reflect on the season just completed and came to the conclusion that some changes had to be made in the way the game was played and in how the standings were figured.

The foremost topic of study was the tie game; what to do about it when figuring the standings. Before the professional moguls could reach a decision, the leaders of the collegiate Southern Conference announced that starting in 1933 a tie game would count as a half game won and a half game lost when figuring the standings. C.P. Miles, athletic director at Virginia Polytechnic Institute, had asked newspapermen to use the system in 1932, and the journalists gave their wholehearted endorsement of it at the end of the 1932 campaign.

When the league magnates met in Pittsburgh in late February, they discussed the problem of ties but did nothing about it. Instead, they instructed Lambeau and Halas to get together and work out the wording for a rule that would be presented to the convention in July.

The club owners did make a few significant rule changes. Just as the college coaches had done the month before, they made passing from anywhere behind the line of scrimmage legal instead of making the passer stand at least five yards behind the line while throwing the ball. Again they followed the example of the collegiate rule makers when they adopted the regulation allowing the referee to move the ball from any point within 10 yards of the sideline to a point 10 yards from the sideline. Finally, the leaders of the pro game decided it was time to make their game a bit different than the college system of play, and Carr said it was high time that the foot was put back in football. So the pros moved their goal posts from the end line to the goal line.

President Carr was empowered to make out a schedule for the entire league and present it to the owners at the summer meeting. Even so, he still allowed the teams to choose their own playing dates and who they wanted to play. This was complicated by the fact that the NFL owners decided expansion was in order for 1933. They admitted teams from Pittsburgh and Cincinnati and allowed Staten Island to withdraw for the 1933 season with the promise of returning in 1934, while Philadelphia returned to the fold as the Eagles instead of the Frankford Yellowjackets. This set the league at 10 teams. The two Pennsylvania teams were still handicapped in scheduling by the Keystone State's blue law prohibiting the playing of football on Sunday, but there was promise that this would change after the fall elections.

The year before George Preston Marshall, a Washington, D.C., laundry magnate and first-class promoter, enticed four partners to join him in establishing a pro franchise in Boston. Marshall was able to rent the Boston Braves' baseball park for a home field, so he called his team the Braves. New Englanders were yet to appreciate the professional game; they stayed away from the Braves in droves. Marshall and friends lost $40,000 that first year, so his partners gracefully bowed out of the organization, leaving Marshall on his own.

Fortunately for pro football, Marshall was a tenacious man who refused to accept defeat. He knew there was plenty of money to be made in the gridiron game but only if some changes were made — and made soon.

At the winter meeting in Pittsburgh, Marshall suggested that the league divide into two divisions: one in the East and one in the West. There was a lot of opposition to this plan, especially from the three great powers of the NFL: Lambeau in Green Bay, Halas in Chicago, and Mara in New York. This was only natural because those were the three most financially successful franchises in the league. Marshall backed off and waited until a better time like the summer meeting in Chicago where he argued that one of the most attractive parts of professional baseball, as far as fan appeal went, was the World Series. The National Football League should have its own version of a championship series, said Marshall; if not a series, then a title game like the one Chicago and Portsmouth had played the winter before. Look at all the national press coverage that game got.

No one could dispute this, but the three super powers still opposed his plan to split into east and west divisions. Their opposition was based on Marshall's design on the schedule; each team would play every team in its own division twice and play only one game against teams in the other division. Halas, Mara, and Lambeau didn't like this idea because that would mean the Giants would only play the Bears and Packers once each instead of twice. Then the argument would be over which western team would be host to the Giants and which one would have to travel to New York. Also, the other magnates disliked this idea because they wouldn't be getting their chance to play the Bears, Giants, and Packers.

Marshall continued to argue that fans were more likely to support a third-place team in a five-team division than they were to support an sixth-place team in 10-team league. He pointed to the National Baseball League as the perfect example when it had 12 teams in the 1890s. Every team that was in the second division by July 4 was doomed to a financial loss because the attendance dropped to practically nothing in the second half of the season. The same was true in the NFL. Once a team was close to being mathematically eliminated its attendance faded rapidly until it seemed that the only people at the games were the players, officials, coaches, owners and family, and a few vendors who passed the time eating their own goodies.

There was no arguing that point, so the magnates agreed to split the league into two divisions: New York, Brooklyn, Boston, Philadelphia, and Pittsburgh in the East; and Cincinnati, Green Bay, Portsmouth, Chicago Bears, and Chicago Cardinals in the West. This was contingent upon Joe Carr coming up with an agreeable schedule for everyone. No problem! Carr was at his best under pressure. He met their challenge superbly, and the National Football League was split into two divisions for the 1933 campaign.

§ § §

3

The New Era Begins — On The Wrong Foot

Professional football had become a real business by 1933, but not all of the National Football League's franchises had their foundations built on solid ground by good businessmen with sufficient capital and resources to last beyond the decade. Among the strong were relatively new owners George Marshall of the Boston Redskins and Charlie Bidwill of the Chicago Cardinals; new owners Bert Bell of the Philadelphia Eagles and Art Rooney of the Pittsburgh Pirates (which he later renamed the Steelers); and established owners George Halas of the Chicago Bears, Tim Mara of the New York Giants, and the people of northeastern Wisconsin and their Green Bay Packers.

At the annual stockholders' meeting at the Brown County Courthouse supervisors' room in July, President Leland H. Joannes practically ignored the fact that the corporation had lost $6,000 the year before in spite of the fact that expenses had been cut by $26,000. The stockholders were so confident and secure with previous results and excited about the forthcoming campaign that they re-elected the entire board of directors who in turn re-elected the officers and the executive committee. Besides Joannes as president, Gerald F. Clifford was once again the vice-president; C.J. O'Connor, treasurer; and George W. Calhoun, secretary. Joannes and Clifford were joined on the executive committee by Andrew B. Turnbull, Dr. W.W. Kelly, and Charles Mathys, the former Packer star player of the early 1920s. The complete board of directors consisted of Joannes, Clifford, Mathys, Turnbull, Calhoun, Kelly, C.M. Berard, Ed Schuster, L.P. Ziebell, Ed Schweger, Lewis E. Peal, J.H. Golden,

Marcel Lambeau, Ralph H. Drum, and H.J. "Tubby" Bero, a member of the 1918 Green Bay squad who went on to become chief of police in the city.

What made this all the more surprising was the fact that the Green Bay Football Corporation had its head in a guillotine in the form of a legal judgment against it.

During the Packers' second game of the season against the Brooklyn Dodgers in Green Bay on September 27, 1931, Willard J. Bent was severely injured in a fall from some temporary grandstands that had been set up, inspected, and declared safe by city inspectors just the week before.

The corporation carried liability insurance against accidents like this, and no one was too concerned about it at the time. But times were not normal. The country was in the middle of the Great Depression, and although Green Bay wasn't hurting as much as most of the rest of the nation, it did have its weak spots. One of those was the Southern Surety Company. When the corporation turned in a claim for Bent's injuries, Joannes was informed by the receiver that the insurance company was in bankruptcy and not only couldn't pay the claim but refused to do so. When Bent filed his claim, Southern Surety's receiver declined to assume the defense, which was his legal right. To make matters worse, Southern Surety was a *mutual* insurance company of which the Green Bay Football Corporation was a part, and when Southern Surety went down, the court assessed the football corporation $2,500 to help pay the insurer's debts.

After seemingly dozens of delays, Bent subsequently sued the Green Bay Football Corporation, and although the corporation's attorney, Gerald Clifford, argued that Bent had been drinking and his fall was caused by his inebriated condition, Bent won a judgment of $5,200. The corporation appealed the outcome to the Wisconsin Supreme Court because Wisconsin had no appellate court system at this time. This was the correct legal procedure, but the corporation couldn't post the customary bond with the appeal. The appeal alone couldn't prevent further action by Bent. The Packers were left vulnerable to a supplemental examination at which Bent's attorney would have the right to question the corporation's officers and examine all the corporation's records. The Packers would also be subject to collection action, where the creditor could execute and levy upon the corporation's assets and their income — ticket sales, gate receipts, guarantees, etc. In short, Bent could take the team and keep it for himself.

Joannes and the corporation's other leaders didn't need any interference like this. They had a football organization to run and keep afloat during these troublesome times. There was no room for court battles, especially during the playing season. Something had to be done to preserve the assets of the corporation, apparently meaning the franchise, and to preserve the integrity of the corporation, meaning the tendency toward secrecy that was growing within the closing ranks of the corporation's official family.

Therefore, Joannes did the only prudent thing available to him in order to keep Bent from disrupting and possibly destroying the Green Bay Football Corporation. On August 15, 1933, the Packers' corporate president petitioned the circuit court to appoint a receiver for the corporation "in behalf of all creditors," meaning everyone including Bent. When Bent's attorney couldn't come up with a suitable argument to sway the court to deny the petition, Judge Henry Graass appointed Frank J. Jonet as the corporation's receiver.

Frank Jonet was a certified public accountant who had audited the corporation's books on previous occasions, and he was a stockholder in the corporation. His association with the Packers went back to the days when the team belonged to the Acme Packing Company, and he was the company bookkeeper.

Oddly, *The Green Bay Press-Gazette* stated, "Selection of Mr. Jonet as receiver was made *by the court without suggestion from either party*." (Author's italics.) Why did the newspaper make this pointed statement when it was a well known fact in Green Bay social circles that Judge Graass and Lee Joannes were good friends? Also, why didn't the newspaper explain why Joannes petitioned the court "in behalf of all creditors"? Quite simply, Joannes wanted to conceal something of great importance from the general public, the people who actually supported the Packers by buying tickets; and at the same time, he wanted to reassure those folks that everything would be all right with the Packers that fall.

As mentioned before, the Packers had "lost $6,000" the previous season and had lost money the year before that. It wasn't public knowledge at the time, but the corporation used up all of its cash reserves in 1931-32 intentionally. The trip to Hawaii and California was seemingly meant to bail out the corporation, but all it did was add to the problem because the organizers of the contests failed to make good on the guarantees they had promised the players and the corporation for sending the team on the trip. With public confidence very low because of the Great Depression and money in short supply, Joannes and the other members of the "Hungry Five" couldn't very well start up another stock drive. So Joannes did a very clever thing; he loaned the corporation the $6,000 in cash that it needed to pay off its bills. This made him a creditor of the corporation, but more importantly, it made him a bigger creditor than Willard Bent. And because he was the largest creditor of the corporation, he could effectively call the shots on behalf of *all* the creditors.

Some of the boys at the corner bar snickered that Judge Graass and Joannes were in cahoots over the entire affair. Even if they had been, it was all perfectly legal and for the most part above board. Quite often, the largest creditor of a bankrupt is appointed receiver for the bankrupt. In this case, Joannes couldn't be appointed receiver because he was also the bankrupt's top officer, and this constituted a conflict of interest. Appointing Jonet was only natural because he was a CPA, had been a receiver before, and was a friendly if not subjective leader.

Bent's attorney could have pressed the conflict of interest angle against Jonet's appointment, but he realized that it was in his client's best interests for the Packers to survive. So he let it go without argument.

The only secretive part of the episode was the loan by Joannes. At the time he made the deal, he was essentially given the corporation's main asset as collateral, meaning he had the franchise in the palm of his hand and it was his to do with as he pleased, even sell it if he had a mind to. Fortunately for Packer fans, he chose not to dispose of it.

The *Press-Gazette* had reported in July that the Packers had lost $6,000 the year before, but it didn't tell its readers that *the corporation owed that amount to Joannes.* Why?

It could be argued that Andy Turnbull, George Calhoun, and others at *The Green Bay Press-Gazette* who had a direct interest in the fortunes of the Green Bay Football Corporation fostered a cover-up when the newspaper not only didn't print all the facts of the episode but failed to point out certain details that would have made their readers aware that not everything was exactly right with the whole affair. In much simpler terms, the *Press-Gazette* was guilty of deception by omission. But was that necessarily wrong?

If the theory that the end justified the means were to be employed, then the *Press-Gazette* — meaning Turnbull, Calhoun, and others with a direct interest in the Packers — was an active partner in the cover-up. The newspaper had acted as the Green Bay Football Corporation's mouthpiece in the past, so there was no reason why it shouldn't again. After all, the Packers were good copy almost anytime of the year, and the team was an excellent indirect source of advertising revenue every fall. But better than that, the Packers were good for area business and the community as a whole. They not only brought in visiting football teams who rented hotel rooms and bought meals, but they also attracted thousands of folks from surrounding towns to Green Bay six or seven Sundays a year. These people spent anywhere from $1.00 to $5.00 per person in Green Bay at businesses other than the concession stands at City Stadium. In short, the Packers meant jobs, and with a depression on, Green Bay needed all the jobs it could get for its working people. It wasn't only in the newspaper's best interests to assure Packer fans that everything would be business as usual with the Packers in 1933; it was also the *Press-Gazette*'s duty to the community as a whole. For further assurance that everything was and would be right with the Packers, Jonet's attorney, John McHale, was paraphrased in the *Press-Gazette* the day after Jonet's appointment as saying, "The receiver's duties ... will be to preserve all assets of the football corporation, receive all monies due it, and make all disbursements. *He will not interfere with the playing schedule, nor with the hiring of players and the management of the team, which will continue in the same hands as heretofore ...*"

(Author's italics) In other words, Curly Lambeau would still be running the team.

Joannes followed up by making a plea for public support by issuing a rather remarkable statement that was printed in the same article:

"The Green Bay Football Corporation is solvent and, if given a chance, will work out of its present situation. Unfortunately, the insurance company which has been carrying our public liability insurance for the last twelve years and which has always been rated as a high grade concern, like many other concerns during the last few years, got into serious difficulties, leaving us without any protection in defending the law suit which resulted in a judgment being obtained against us. The amount of this judgment was such that we will be unable to pay it at the present time, because of two very unprofitable years of operation, due not only to business conditions, but unfavorable weather, which is a big factor in this game.

"The Packer team, an institution in Green Bay, has brought more advertising to this city, and for that matter to Wisconsin, than any other medium. In these dayes *(sic)* of stress and uncertainty, the club and the management needs more than ever the support of all of the loyal fans of this community. In a few days, the season ticket selling campaign will be under way, and while we realize that many will have to stretch a point to buy tickets this year, we are hopeful that the sale will surpass that of last season. It seems certain that the club will be a strong contender for national championship honors, and there will be plenty of thrills and excitement for the fans this fall. Let us all get behind this marvelous club and assure the continuance of professional football in Green Bay."

Lee Joannes was doing a sales job on the paying public, but he did this one from the heart as well as from his pocketbook; the Packers staying alive and in Green Bay meant that much to him.

§ § §

4

The First Losing Season

The beauty of professional sports is their constant change. Every innovation, whether sound or half-cracked, is good because it keeps the fans' attention, and attentive fans are paying customers at the gate. With this thought in their collective mind, the magnates of the National Football League leaped enthusiastically into the 1933 season.

Art Bystrom, sports editor for *The Green Bay Press-Gazette*, predicted the future of the NFL in the editor's column, *Looking Up in the Realm of Sports*, in the July 20, 1933 issue of the newspaper. Bystrom praised the league moguls for creating the new passing rule. "This will make pro football an offensive game, and a free-scoring, see-saw battle that ought to keep the customers on their toes throughout. The pass rule also is an invitation to trickery and surprise. Coaches throughout the league already have doped out scores of strange shifts, based on the deception this legislation allows."

At the top of the list of coaches mapping out new strategies to fit the new rule was Curly Lambeau. He was already an innovator of the passing game. Allowing the passer to throw from anywhere behind the line of scrimmage instead of a minimum five yards back opened up all sorts of possibilities, especially for the Packers because they had so many versatile backs on their roster already.

Returning to Green Bay for the 1933 campaign were ends Milt Gantenbein, Al Rose, Les Peterson, and Lavvie Dilweg; tackles Cal Hubbard and Claude Perry; guards Clyde Van Sickle, Rudy Comstock, Whitey Woodin, and Mike Michalske; center Red Bultman; quarterbacks Verne Lewellen and Roger Grove; halfbacks Johnny Blood, Wuert Englemann, Hank

Bruder, and Arnie Herber; and fullbacks Clarke Hinkle and Hurdis McCrary. The newcomers were end Ben Smith, Alabama; tackles Joe Kurth, Notre Dame, and Jess Quatse, Pittsburgh; guards Norm Greeney, Notre Dame, and Lon Evans, TCU; centers Al Sarafiny, St. Edwards (Texas), and Paul Young, Oklahoma; halfbacks Bob Monnett, Michigan State, Buckets Goldenberg, Wisconsin, and Buster Mott, Georgia. Lewellen and Woodin retired before the season began.

Lambeau opened training camp on September 5, and 23 players reported for workouts. Among the missing were Hubbard, Hinkle, Michalske, Comstock, and, of course, Johnny Blood, who was delayed in California. Three days into the practice season the *Press-Gazette* reported: "A fast airplane carried Johnny Blood, missing Green Bay Packer halfback, eastward today. The football player, who has been sought by Green Bay club officials for the past week to report for practice, has been spending the past few months on the Pacific coast. Early today he boarded a trans-American airplane. He will go either to Kansas City or Chicago by plane and then go direct to Green Bay by railroad, arriving Saturday or Sunday." In a previous year, Blood arrived in camp a little differently.

"... I had no money to get across the state from my home in New Richmond," Blood told Myron Cope during an interview. "I had only a dollar or two in my pocket.

"So I decided to ride free on the train. They called it the Soo Line, but its real name was the Minneapolis, St. Paul & Sault Sainte Marie Railroad, and in order to get to Green Bay you would have to change trains at Amherst Junction to the Green Bay & Western. I got on the Soo Line and rode the blinds down to a place called Stevens Point, where there was a stop. I got off and inquired about connections at Amherst Junction and was told that the Green Bay & Western would get into Amherst Junction a couple of minutes before the Soo Line but if you wired ahead they would hold the train. They did this for passengers. So I wired ahead and then got back on the blinds again and rode to Amherst Junction. There I got off the Soo and ran down a cut and grabbed on to the blinds of the Green Bay & Western. After the trainmen waited around for a few minutes for the passenger who had wired ahead, they gave up and started the train.

"Well, about ten miles from Green Bay, the door of a freight car opened and one of the crew looked out and saw me and said, 'John, what are you doing out there?' Everybody on the Green Bay & Western knew the Packer football players. The guy said, 'Come on in and wash up.' So I got me a bowl of water, and while I was washing up, he looked at me and said, 'Say, where did you get on?' I said, 'Amherst Junction.' And he started laughing. He said, 'Oh, so you're the guy who wired ahead! Well, you're the first hobo I ever heard of holding a train for.' "

So went the story according to Cope and several other writers. Their information was correct until they reached the point where Blood changed trains at Amherst Junction. Blood waited around for the Green Bay & Western passenger train from Winona, Minnesota to pull out. When it did, he jumped onto the last car, the baggage car. Not too far out of Amherst Junction, the baggageman, Leo O'Connor, saw Blood on the platform and invited him inside. O'Connor shared his lunch with Blood, figuring he was just a young fellow down on his luck. When they neared Green Bay, O'Connor advised Blood to jump off the train in order to avoid the yard detectives whose job it was to catch illegal riders. Blood took his advice.

Cope and others stated that Blood rode the rails to Green Bay in '32. Wrong year. According to retired GB&W executive, Lee Rondou, who confirmed these facts, the year was 1929. Although the railroad men around Green Bay knew most of the Packer players on sight in those days, not "everybody on the Green Bay & Western knew the Packer football players." This was quite true of O'Connor and the men on his train; they were from Winona, Minnesota and knew practically no one in Green Bay, especially "Packer football players."

When Blood arrived in camp in 1933, Lambeau immediately put him in the lineup at the quarterback spot. The coach also moved Herber to that position with the thought of taking advantage of Herber's passing ability.

Instead of playing an exhibition game against an independent pro team as the Packers had the year before against Grand Rapids, Lambeau thought to save money, meaning the guarantee that another team would have to be paid, by playing an intrasquad game pitting the veterans against the rookies. A crowd of 2,500 loyal fans paying 50 cents for the good seats and 25 cents for the not-so-good seats watched the older players beat up on the yearlings, 25-6, in spite of the fact that Michalske, Hinkle, and Grove played for the newcomers.

The Boston Redskins were the Packers' first regular season opponent on September 17. William "Lone Star" Dietz coached the Beantown eleven. Dietz's credentials went back to Carlisle Institute and the days of Jim Thorpe, first playing for Glenn "Pop" Warner then coaching with him. In 1915, Dietz took the head coach's job at Washington State and directed his team to a conference title. After two more successful years at Washington State, he became a vagabond coach, directing the Mare Island Marines, 1918-20; Purdue, 1921; Louisiana Tech, 1922-23; Wyoming, 1924-27; a Los Angeles pro team, 1929; and Haskell Institute, 1930-32. In 1928, he assisted Warner at Stanford.

Dietz was one of the more colorful coaches in the history of the National Football League. Being a Sioux Indian, he took advantage of his heritage by playing Indians in the movies. For football, he helped publicize the Redskins by posing for photographs in full Indian headdress. Among his top players for the Redskins were Cliff Battles, Ernie Pinckert, and former Packer Marger Apsit. For their opening game in Green Bay, Dietz put war paint on his players and paraded them around the field for the amusement of the fans before the game.

The Packers' management had lowered ticket prices for the season, and a crowd of 7,500 fans was expected for the Boston game. Less than 5,000 folks turned out to see the Redskins rally in the final quarter to tie the Packers, 7-7. Herber tossed a 6-yard TD pass to Rose in the third period, and Grove kicked the PAT to give Green Bay a 7-0 lead. Boston came back to score on one of only two pass completions midway through the final stanza. The Packers had two chances to win it in the closing minutes. One drive ended on downs, and the second came to a halt on Boston's 10 when a pass into the end zone went incomplete, which in those days was a touchback giving the defense the ball out on the 20. The tie extended Green Bay's unbeaten streak at home to 32 consecutive games.

Already in 1933, the newspapers were making a big deal out of how the Packers and Bears had the longest playing tradition in the NFL. Over those years, they had played 26 contests with the Packers winning 12, the Bears winning 10, and there were four ties. The previous season saw each team win one with the third game ending in a scoreless tie.

Ralph Jones had quit coaching the Bears after the '32 campaign, and Heartley "Hunk" Anderson, the man George Halas wanted to run his squad in '33, already had a job coaching at Notre Dame. This left Halas no choice but to take up the reins himself.

Fresh from winning the title in '32, the Bears were loaded with talent again in '33. Bill Hewitt and Luke Johnsos were a pair of ends that matched any in the history of two-way football, and Bronko Nagurski and Red Grange were once again in the backfield. Joining them were Gene Ronzani, Jack Manders, and Carl Brumbaugh.

After having a training camp in South Bend, Indiana, Chicago played an exhibition game against an aggregation of former Notre Dame players and defeated them handily. The trip to Green Bay was the first game of the season for the Bears, and they looked a little rusty for more than three quarters of the game. Then suddenly, the crowd of approximately 10,000 roaring Packer backers fell quiet. The Packers were leading, 7-0, on a Buckets Goldenberg TD and Bob Monnett PAT. With five minutes to go, the Bears blocked a field goal try by Hank Bruder and took over on their own 25. Chicago gained 31 yards in the next four plays, then Hewitt took a hand off on an end around and raced for the end zone. At the five, he lateralled to Johnsos who danced in for the touchdown. Manders booted the PAT, and the score was tied. The Packers took the ensuing kickoff out to their own 20 and set up for a final charge to get into field goal range. Two incomplete passes, a short gain, and a penalty later Herber dropped back to punt. Hewitt broke through the line, blocked the kick, recovered it at the five, and raced into the end zone with the game-winning score. Manders added the final point to give Chicago a 14-7 upset win that snapped Green Bay's home unbeaten streak of 32 straight wins and ties.

For three years, Oliver E. "Ollie" Kuechle, the legendary sportswriter for *The Milwaukee Journal*, had been agitating for a professional football game in the Cream City, but Green Bay Football Corporation officials were cool to the idea in '30, '31, and '32, mostly because of an article written by R.G. Lynch in the *Journal* on November 18, 1928 that described the city of Green Bay as some sort of hell–hole filled with all sorts of vice and corruption. Of course, Green Bay had a few speakeasies and one or two houses of ill–repute, but so did many towns in those days. No, Green Bayers weren't upset about the words of the article as much as they were about the tone of the story.

Lynch, whether intentional or not, made the people of Green Bay appear to be a gang of criminals who were resisting the Prohibition Act with all the tenacity of a group of traitors who were plotting to overthrow the American government, incarcerate everybody's sweet old mother, and do away with apple pie and everything else American. Lynch gave the impression that Milwaukee was a clean city that had thoroughly obeyed the law ever since the Socialists allegedly cleaned up the town in 1912. Lynch's article was a case of "the pot calling the kettle black."

To make matters worse, Lynch implicated the Packers and the team's supporters in all the so–called corruption in Green Bay. The article insinuated that they were part of the gang that controlled liquor and all the vices that went with it in northeastern Wisconsin. He named names and places where a thirsty fellow could wet his whistle and not be bothered by the local authorities who considered the enforcement of the anti–alcohol law to be a federal matter and not under their jurisdiction. The article even told about certain roadhouses west of the city that were allegedly owned by some very prominent citizens. Lynch even went so far as to imply that Verne Lewellen, the recently elected Brown County District Attorney, was put in office by the support of all the elbow–benders in the county just to protect their interests.

Rumors circulated — but not in print — that beer and booze money from the "speaks" went to support other enterprises, such as certain trucking firms that were doing a booming business hauling Canadian whiskey from any of a hundred clandestine ports-of-entry along the shores of Michigan's Upper Peninsula and Green Bay to points all over the Midwest. Some of this alleged ill-gotten gain was supposed to have wound up in the coffers of the Green Bay Football Corporation.

Lynch was guilty of character assassination by use of innuendo and hearsay. But how does a city sue for libel? It doesn't. It only fights back in the best way it can; in this case, by denying the offender something it wanted.

Ollie Kuechle felt this was a ridiculous situation and often said so in his column. There was no reason why the Packers couldn't play just one game in Milwaukee. Maybe just an exhibition game for charity. A rumor to that effect ran the circuit in August, but Packers President Lee Joannes denied it to the newspapers, saying that no backers for a charity game between the Packers and New York Giants had come forward at that time. Joannes didn't say that *he wasn't talking* to someone about moving the Packers-Giants game to Milwaukee; he just said there would be no game played for charity.

On September 9, Joannes made the announcement that the Packers would play the Giants at Borchert Field on October 1 in Milwaukee instead of in Green Bay. Within minutes, the howling could be heard from Sturgeon Bay to Manitowoc to Oshkosh to Clintonville to Marinette. Season ticket holders were outraged. How dare the Packers play a game in Milwaukee!

The *Press-Gazette* subheadline read: *Comply With Public Demand By Shifting Oct. 1 Grid Game*. To what public was the newspaper referring? Certainly not the loyal fans in the Green Bay area who had supported the Packers for the past decade. Joannes stated:

"For the past three years we have been beseeched by Milwaukeeans to stage a regular league game in that city. After careful consideration of all details, we have decided to play the New York-Packer game there as we believe it will be one of the best contests on our schedule and will be well supported by the public of southern Wisconsin. We always have had wonderful support from fans, newspapers and the Milwaukee Journal radio station of Milwaukee, and as they long have been urging a game in their city, we believe the request should be recognized."

Immediately, rumors started flying that the Packers were going to move to Milwaukee permanently if attendance was good for the Giant game. Art Bystrom correctly wrote in his column: "Most of them are rather ridiculous." Without elaborating too much, Bystrom pointed out that the Packers needed the money that a big crowd in Milwaukee would bring, then pooh-poohed the doomsayers by stating: "If the game was played here and three or four thousand dollars lost on it, the deficit wouldn't be disastrous to the Packer club by any stretch of the imagination, but there is a natural desire to avoid this loss if possible. The loss might be made up in other games, but if it was not, *business interests and the public would make up the difference in a hurry before letting football slip out*." (Author's italics.)

Bystrom made a good argument for playing the game in Milwaukee, but he could have done a better job of calming suspicious readers who were worried about the team moving to Milwaukee for good by making the point that John Torinus made in his book, *The Packer Legend*, when he wrote: "Wisconsin statutes provide that a corporation cannot sell or dispose of its major assets without the approval of the stockholders. Can you conceive of the stockholders of the Green Bay Packers, most of whom live in the Green Bay area, approving a sale or transfer of the franchise when they would not only receive no profit from such a sale but would not even recoup their original investment?"

Of course, Torinus wrote his book nearly 50 years later, but the argument would have been valid in 1933. The rebuttal to all the rumors was made by the man who authored the Green Bay Football Corporation's constitution, that legal giant, Attorney Gerald F. Clifford. He was the one person who conceived of the idea that once enough people in the Green Bay area owned stock in the corporation that owned the team then the team's life in Green Bay should never be in jeopardy.

In spite of the controversy, the Packers were set to play Steve Owen's New York Giants at Borchert Field in Milwaukee on October 1.

The Giants featured such great players as Ray Flaherty, Mel Hein, Tiny Feather, Ken Strong, and former Packer Bo

Molenda. Adding to this array of talent was a shifty rookie quarterback from Michigan, Harry Newman, who was making New York fans forget that Benny Friedman was tossing the pigskin for the Brooklyn Dodgers.

The Packers had a career record of 6-3 with Tim Mara's hirelings since the two teams had begun playing each other in 1928. New York had only managed to win one of four games in Green Bay and two of five in the Big Apple. Their contest in Milwaukee would start a whole new tradition between the two great franchises.

"A crowd of 13,000 turned out for what they expected was to be a great football game," wrote Art Bystrom the day after the game in the *Press-Gazette*. "They didn't see it. What they saw was the Packers playing one of their worst games, offensively, in many years. They probably retired to their homes, convinced that there is a cog or two missing in the great machine that so many years was the Packers.

"Somewhere between Green Bay and Milwaukee, the Packers lost the punch they showed against the Bears in Green Bay only a week ago. You can call it lack of spirit, punch, drive or any other word that means the same thing, but in the parlance of 'Jugger' Earpe, who for so many years was the sparkplug in the Green Bay line, the Packer squad didn't 'fog.' "

Strong booted a first quarter field goal for New York, and Newman completed a 19–yard scoring toss to left halfback Dale Burnett very late in the first half to give the Giants a 10-0 lead against the hapless Packers. Both teams mounted scoring threats in the third period. The Packers took it down to the New York eight before Buckets Goldenberg fumbled the ball away, and the Giants got as close as Green Bay's 15 before Strong missed a 28–yard field goal attempt just before the end of the stanza. Clarke Hinkle put the Giants deep in their own territory early in the fourth quarter with a 75–yard punt. On the ensuing New York series, Strong shanked a kick that was downed on the Giants' 32. Two plays later Johnny Blood hauled in a pass from Bob Monnett and raced 30 yards for the score. Monnett booted the PAT, and the Packers were making a game of it, trailing, 10-7 with about a third of the period to go. Unfortunately, two final charges at the Giants availed them nothing, and the game wound up in the win column for New York.

After three weeks of play, the NFL standings were beginning to take shape, and it didn't look good for the Packers. The Portsmouth Spartans (3-0-0) had beaten Cincinnati, New York, and the Chicago Cardinals in Portsmouth on successive Sundays. The Chicago Bears (2-0-0) had beaten the Packers and Boston. Cincinnati (0-1-0) and the Cardinals (0-2-0) had yet to win. The Packers (0-2-1) found themselves in a very unaccustomed position, at the bottom of the Western Division pile. The Giants (2-1-0) led the Eastern Division, followed by Pittsburgh (1-1-0) and Boston (0-1-1). Philadelphia and Brooklyn were still waiting to begin their seasons.

Curly Lambeau was definitely not happy with his team when they returned to the practice field on Monday. He put the players through hell, which was unusual in that they normally didn't practice the day after a game. Portsmouth was coming to town, and if the Packers were going to make anything of the '33 season, they had to beat the Spartans.

Potsy Clark was once again the Portsmouth coach, but Dutch Clark, the All–Pro backfielder, was missing from the Spartans' lineup. Dutch had quit the game and gone back to his native Colorado to coach football, basketball, and baseball at the Colorado School of Mines because he lacked confidence in the financial condition of the Portsmouth organization.

Just as in Green Bay, the businesspeople of Portsmouth supported their franchise because they knew it was a good thing for their community. The situations weren't exactly the same, however. Whereas Green Bay was one of the larger towns in a state that could boast of only one real city, that being Milwaukee, Portsmouth was a just another town in a state with six fairly large cities: Akron, Cincinnati, Cleveland, Columbus, Dayton, and Toledo. A lack of population wasn't the only problem in the Ohio River town. While Green Bay had several towns of similar size within an hour and a half travel time from which to draw support, Portsmouth, although larger than Green Bay itself, was rather isolated in that respect. Therefore, with times being what they were, the Portsmouth management had a more difficult task of meeting its monetary obligations. Compared to the Packers who had won three straight titles and who had had the same basic leadership for more than a dozen years, the last 10 under their corporate structure, the Spartans, in spite of a rich tradition as an independent professional team that dated back as far as many other clubs in the Ohio Valley, were relative newcomers as a community-owned organization. The Green Bay Football Corporation had given its players reason to believe it was a stable concern, but according to Dutch Clark in his interview with Myron Cope, the Portsmouth group had yet to achieve this level of confidence with the men who took the playing field for it.

In spite of the money problems, the Spartans were a good team on the field. Potsy Clark didn't have a whole lot of potential hall-of-famers, but he melded the talent he did have into a cohesive unit that had the respect of every team in the NFL. Portsmouth was out to erase the 2-1-1 series lead the Packers held over the Ohio eleven.

On the day the Spartans visited Green Bay, it rained — all day. Even so, the words of Andy Turnbull, advising Lambeau and Calhoun to play the game no matter what the weather was, echoed out of the past, and the game was on. A brave crowd — and it was just that, *a brave crowd* — of 4,000 sat through a sometimes driving downpour to witness a better game than they had seen in previous weeks.

After missing a 17-yard field goal attempt on their first possession and punting on their second, the Packers jumped out in front, 7-0, on a one-yard plunge by Hank Bruder and a PAT by Roger Grove. Portsmouth made one decent stab at scoring in the second quarter but lost the ball on downs at the Packers' 11. Clarke Hinkle ran back the second half kickoff 63 yards to the Portsmouth 32. The Packers failed to make a first down, so Hinkle attempted another field goal, making this one from 30 yards out and giving Green Bay a 10-0 lead. Buckets Goldenberg intercepted a desperation pass late in the fourth quarter and returned it to the Portsmouth 14. Three plays later he plunged over from three yards out, then Arnie Herber completed the only Packers' pass of the day to Johnny Blood for the PAT to make the final score, 17-0.

The weather made the game a throwback to the days when defense and punting were everything and offense was just a second thought. Hinkle punted 11 times, 10 in the first half, having one blocked. Herber booted the soggy ball eight times in the second half, and Hank Bruder kicked it once in the fourth quarter. This gave the Packers an astounding 20 punts, while Portsmouth had two men punt a total of 15 times. The Green Bay total (20), the total between both teams (35), and Hinkle's number of punts (11) were all records for the Packers that were still standing at the time of the writing of this volume.

Green Bay's victory moved the Packers (1-2-1) up a notch in the standings of the Western Division to fourth and dropped Portsmouth (3-1-0) out of the top slot. The Bears (3-0-0) knocked off Brooklyn to take over first. The Chicago Cardinals (1-2-0) slipped past Cincinnati to move into third. Cincinnati (0-2-0) brought up the rear. Boston (2-1-1) took over first in the Eastern Division by beating Pittsburgh (1-2-0) on Wednesday night, then nipping New York (2-2-0) at home on Sunday. Brooklyn (0-1-0) was off to a bad start, and Philadelphia was still waiting to play its first game.

As stated in Chapter 3, the NFL gained some new teams and some new owners in 1933. One of these was the Pittsburgh Pirates, and the man with money was Art Rooney, a political ward chairman in the predominantly Irish First Ward of Pittsburgh and the son of a saloonkeeper. Rooney paid $2,500 for his NFL franchise because he figured it would be good for his independent pro team to have a league schedule and that eventually the NFL would be a moneymaker. He chose that particular year to join the circuit because Pennsylvania was planning to repeal its "blue law" banning football on Sundays.

Rooney told a great story to Myron Cope concerning his team's *first* home game:

"But a couple of days before our opening game, the mayor phoned me and said, 'I got a complaint here from a preacher that this game should not be allowed because it's against the blue laws. The repeal hasn't been ratified yet by City Council, and won't be till Tuesday.'

" 'Well,' I said, 'I never heard of this thing, ratification.'

"Nobody else had heard anything about it either, until this preacher brought it up. The mayor told me he didn't know what I could do about it but that I should go see a fellow named

Harmer Denny, who was director of public safety and was over the police department.

"So I went to Denny and I said, 'We're in the big leagues now. We can't have a thing like this happen to our opening game.' But this Denny was pretty much of a straightlaced guy. All he would say was that he was going away for the weekend. 'Good,' I told him. 'You go away.' Then I went to see the superintendent of police, a man named McQuade, and told *him* my problem.

" 'Oh, that there's ridiculous,' he said. 'Give me a couple of tickets and I'll go to the game Sunday. That'll be the last place they'll look for me if they want me to stop the game.'

"So McQuade hid out at the game, and on the following Tuesday the council met and ratified everything."

As previously stated, it was a great story, but the facts don't back up Rooney's tale. The Pittsburgh Pirates opened the 1933 campaign on Wednesday night September 20 at home against the New York Giants and were beaten. Pittsburgh's next game was the following Wednesday night at home against the Chicago Cardinals, which the Pirates won. They lost their third game a week later to Boston, then defeated Cincinnati seven days after that. Their first road game was scheduled for October 15 in Green Bay.

That first Pittsburgh team was no match for the Packers. In an off-and-on drizzle, a crowd of about 4,000 watched their home town favorites maul the Pirates, 47-0. Bob Monnett and Buckets Goldenberg scored a pair of touchdowns each, and Clarke Hinkle, Wuert Englemann, and Hank Bruder crossed the goal line once apiece. Monnett also gained 93 yards on 15 carries to lead the rushers.

Although the win pushed the Packers back to the .500 mark, Green Bay could gain no ground in the Western Division standings. Portsmouth (4-1-1) shut out Boston (2-2-1), and the Bears (4-0-0) nipped the Cardinals (1-3-0). The Giants (3-2-0) regained the top spot in the East by demolishing the fledgling Philadelphia Eagles (0-1-0) in their first ever NFL game, 56-0. Brooklyn (1-1-0) won its first game of the year, defeating the hapless Cincinnati Reds (0-4-0).

October 22 was rematch day with the Bears in Chicago. With two solid wins under their collective belt, the Packers felt that they were ready to face Halas's Monsters of the Midway on equal terms again. The team was in fairly good shape. Hank Bruder had a case of intestinal flu but was expected to play. Johnny Blood was reported as having spent a night in St. Mary's Hospital with an infected hand but was released in time to take part in Tuesday's practice. The truth was Lambeau had fired him the week before for being drunk during the week — Blood missed the Pittsburgh game — but took him back because Arnie Herber was hurting and Buster Mott would miss the Chicago game with a broken bone in his lower leg.

The second Packers–Bears game was a severe case of *deja vu*. Once again Green Bay controlled the field for better than 90% of the time only to lose in the closing moments. The Packers tried to make a second quarter TD by Johnny Blood stand up, but the Bears fought back in the closing minutes to eke out a 10-7 win on a Jack Manders field goal after a Luke Johnsos touchdown. Green Bay had three golden opportunities to score, marching down to Chicago's four–, eight–, and 11–yard lines on different occasions only to come away empty-handed.

With three losses already, Green Bay's chances for a division title appeared to be doomed, especially with the Bears being undefeated and Portsmouth having only one loss. Gloomy though their prospects may have been, the Packers were determined to give it their best the remainder of the season.

Bert Bell came from roots firmly established in high society. George Halas described Bell as "a heller" who married a Ziegfeld Follies girl named Frances Upton. Frances told him straight from the shoulder that he had to choose between alcohol and her; to which Bell repsonded by finishing his drink, turning over his glass, and only drinking coffee from that day forward.

Although the owners continued to insist that their team was from Frankford, the Yellowjackets more or less represented Philadelphia in the NFL. For a time, Frankford was one of the league's powerhouses, having won the 1926 title and finishing close to the top spot on other occasions. The Great Depression swatted the Yellowjackets and put the franchise in limbo until Bell came along and bought it with his wife's money. He talked four former college friends into putting up some operating capital for the '33 season, and he nicknamed his club the Eagles after President Franklin D. Roosevelt's National Relief Act emblem.

The *Press-Gazette* was touting the Eagles as the same franchise as the Frankford Yellowjackets, and they were correct, although some football historians don't consider them to have been the same because of the '32 hiatus when Philadelphia wasn't represented in the NFL. Bert Bell was wise enough not to field a team that one year without the proper capital to run it.

One of Bell's partners was the team's head coach, Lud Wray. The Eagles had yet to score a single point in the NFL when they arrived in Green Bay for their October 29 encounter with the Packers. The Giants had mauled them unmercifully, and Portsmouth had spoiled Philadelphia's first home game by whipping the Eagles, 25-0, on a Wednesday night. This fooled the Packers into thinking their opponent would be a pushover. Not so as the Eagles tacked nine points on the board through the first three quarters and trailed by less than a touchdown, 14-9. The Packers scored early on a plunge by Buckets Goldenberg and an intercepted pass by Wuert Englemann that he returned for a 55yard TD to take a 14-0 lead in the first period. Philadelphia made its comeback, and it was a real game until the fourth quarter when Green Bay came to life again. Cal Hubbard intercepted a pass late in the third stanza, returning it to the Green Bay 43. From there, the Packers mounted a drive that culminated with Bob Monnett throwing a seven–yard scoring strike to Goldenberg early in the final period. On Green Bay's next possession, Monnett threw 20 yards to Johnny Blood for another six–pointer to put the Packers up, 28-9. Goldenberg scored his third TD of the game when he ran back a partially blocked punt 30 yards to paydirt, making the final score, 35-9.

The win kept the Packers (3-3-1) in the race as the Bears (6-0-0) beat the Giants (4-3-0) and Portsmouth (5-1-0) played a nonleague contest that week. The Chicago Cardinals (1-5-0) and Cincinnati (0-4-1) were practically eliminated in the West by this time, while Brooklyn (2-2-0), Boston (3-3-1), and Pittsburgh (3-3-1) were beginning to breathe down New York's neck. The Eagles (0-3-0) were still winless but not hopeless yet.

The Chicago Cardinals were next up for the Pack. The two teams had played each other on 18 previous occasions with the Packers winning 10 games to the Cards' six and two ties, but this would be their first encounter since yachtsman Charlie Bidwill had become the new owner of the Chicago franchise.

The Packers entered the game a little short-handed. Half of their backs were on the shelf with injuries, but the linemen were healthy for the most part. Bob Monnett, Roger Grove, and Clarke Hinkle played the entire game for Green Bay, and Blood and Arnie Herber switched off at one halfback slot. After a scoreless first half, the Packers got on the board first on a 21-yard run and PAT by Monnett. Chicago stormed back late in the period to cut the margin to one point, then Green Bay iced the victory midway through the final quarter on a Hinkle plunge to win, 14-6.

Art Bystrom had a weekly *Pick'em* section to his regular column in the *Press-Gazette*, and this particular week his forecast called for a few upsets. He went so far as to predict the final score of the Packers-Cards game. Bystrom should have set up shop as a great swami because he was perfect with his picks and he hit the Packers-Cards score right on the nose. The Packers (4-3-1) gained ground on the Bears (6-1-0) and Portsmouth (5-2-0) as Chicago was upset by Boston (4-3-1) and the Spartans were taken into camp by the Giants (5-3-0). Brooklyn (2-2-1) and Pittsburgh (3-3-2) fought to a tie, and Philadelphia (1-3-0) won its first game over Cincinnati (0-5-1).

The Packers still had a good shot at the division title in spite of their three losses and a tie. Green Bay was scheduled to play Portsmouth, Boston, New York, Philadelphia, and the Bears on the road. A clean sweep of those five games and a little help from the other teams playing Chicago and Portsmouth would put the Pack on top in the West. It wasn't to be, however.

Of course, George Whitney Calhoun accompanied the team on this eastern trip, and he reported back to the folks in Green Bay in his inimitable style through the *Press-Gazette*. He started off the Portsmouth game story by writing how a fighting Packer squad had been "handicapped at several crucial stages by dumb signal calling," and that was why the Packers lost, 7-0.

From reading the play–by–play of the game, Cal was right. The Pack had the ball on the Portsmouth 22 on their first possession with fourth and two to go. Instead of attempting a field goal, Lambeau opted for a dive play that barely made a yard. Late in the game, Green Bay had the ball on the Portsmouth 13 with a first down and plenty of time left. Instead of continuing the intense rushing attack that had gotten them there, the Packers chose to pass — into the end zone. This was extremely risky because if the pass was incomplete the ball went over to Portsmouth. Monnett's toss didn't reach its mark, and the Spartans got the ball and the game.

The loss hurt the Packers (4-4-1) a lot because the Bears (6-1-1) were tied by Philadelphia (1-3-1). By winning, Portsmouth (6-2-0) was only a half game behind Chicago and had an excellent chance of winning the division because the Spartans had two games left to play against the Monsters of the Midway. New York (6-3-0) won again in the East, knocking off second-place Boston (4-4-1), while Brooklyn (3-2-1) moved ahead of the Redskins by beating Pittsburgh (3-4-2). Cincinnati (1-5-1) won its first game ever and mathematically eliminated the Chicago Cardinals (1-7-0) from the race.

Cal made no excuses for the Packers when Lone Star Dietz's Boston Redskins handed Green Bay its second straight loss, 20-7, but he did praise the work of Jim Musick, Boston's crushing backfielder. Bob Monnett gave a similar performance for the Pack, but he was unfortunate in that his supporting cast didn't hold up as well as Musick's teammates.

Green Bay (4-5-1) blew another golden opportunity to gain on the Bears (6-2-1) and Portsmouth (6-3-0) as the Giants (7-3-0) slipped by Chicago and Cincinnati (2-5-1) downed the Spartans. Philadelphia (2-3-1) climbed out of last place in the East by swamping Pittsburgh (3-5-2), and Brooklyn (4-2-1) kept pace with the Giants by nipping the hard luck Cardinals (1-8-0).

The Giants were on a roll, having won three straight and five of their last six, when the Packers invaded the Polo Grounds on the last Sunday in November. Dale Burnett ran back an interception 85 yards for New York's first score, and New York added 10 more points to take a 17-6 lead into the fourth quarter.

Green Bay finally got untracked in the late going, but Gantenbein's TD reception of an Arnie Herber pass was a case of too–little–too–late.

The loss to New York (8-3-0) put Green Bay (4-6-1) down for the count because the Bears (7-2-1) dumped Portsmouth (6-4-0) to take a commanding lead in the Western Division race. Although they had two more league contests to go, the Packers were really only spectators the rest of the way as the Giants won their last three to take the Eastern Division title and the Bears did likewise in the West.

It had been a long autumn for Curly Lambeau and the Packers, but it would be a longer winter.

§ § §

5

Excuses, Excuses

"If — the biggest word in the dictionary."
"Hindsight is always 20-20."

Such lovely axioms! Curly Lambeau found them to be quite handy at the conclusion of his first losing season as head mentor of the Green Bay Packers.

With nothing left to play for except pride, the Packers completed their 1933 season by beating the Staten Island Stapletons, 21-0, in a non–league game on Thanksgiving Day and by whipping the Eagles again, 10-0, in Philadelphia before losing to the Bears, 7-6, in Chicago to close out the campaign. Green Bay finished the playing season by thrashing the independent St. Louis Gunners, 21-0.

Art Bystrom, sports editor of *The Green Bay Press-Gazette*, lamented how things could have been much different if the Pack had been able to hold on to the lead in their first two encounters with the Bears and if the Packers had been able to score from close in against the Bears in the last game. Reverse those three losses, and Green Bay would have been 8-4-1 to Chicago's 7-5-1. Then it would have been the Packers facing the Giants in the first ever playoff game for the NFL championship.

Bystrom could have pinned the final loss on the fact that Arnie Herber missed the game because he had been injured in a traffic accident four days before the game. Herber suffered severe injuries to his right forearm, right hip, and face when he crashed his car into a truck belonging to the Remick Trucking Company of Menasha and driven by Cecil Smith, also of Menasha. Another motorist, Louis Lassaro, a salesman from Brookfield, Illinois, picked up Herber and drove him to the hospital. Herber lost a lot of blood through the four-inch gash that ran from his cheek into his scalp between his left eye and ear, and this concerned the doctors more than Herber's arm injury or dislocated hip. Fortunately, the prognosis was good for Herber. He would play football again.

Lambeau had his share of excuses for the lack of wins in '33. He was quoted extensively in the *Press-Gazette* that December:

" 'It has been a tough season in more ways than one,' Coach Lambeau commented today in discussing the year and prospects for next season. 'One bright spot has been our ability to go through the year without financial loss. It has taken a lot of economy that has hurt us, but it will be proven that it was worthwhile.

" 'We have made mistakes. I've made them and am willing to admit it, but don't think they'll occur again. And don't forget we've had more than our share of breaks that have made a world of difference. To begin with, I called the team together too late. Blood, Hubbard, Mike (Michalske), and Hinkle reported even later than the others. Then we missed getting a quarterback that we should have had and Barrager didn't report for center at the last minute. Hinkle's tonsils had to come out and he wasn't ready for the early games. All those things make a lot of difference. Bruder was injured and out a good share of the season. Some of our men didn't live up to expectations. Just a few little things like that, all helped to make enough difference to cost us victories.

" 'Then before the Portsmouth game we got another break. Cal Hubbard, following his dispute at Chicago in the Cardinal game, received a letter from Joseph Carr, president of the National league. It was decidedly untactful of Carr, to say the least. In it, Carr warned Cal, not in so many words, but in inferences, that if he got into any more disputes such as that which happened in Chicago his baseball umpiring career would be jeopardized.

" 'Cal has his heart set on an umpire's position in the big leagues. The letter from Carr, who is one of the 'big guns' of organized baseball, took all the starch out of him. He wasn't as good a man after that. We were a different ball club.' "

Lambeau had a valid complaint against Carr. The league's

top man mishandled the entire episode concerning Hubbard and the Cardinal–game incident. He reacted strongly to a letter of complaint submitted to his office by the Cardinals management, sending a letter of reprimand directly to Hubbard "warning him that 'further ungentlemanly conduct' on the field of play would result in his fine and suspension." George Whitney Calhoun argued in Hubbard's behalf that "Carr penned the letter to Hubbard without even giving the Green Bay management a chance to present his side of the affair. Coach Lambeau claims that Mr. Carr should have communicated with Hubbard through the club and not direct to the player."

The incident in question occurred during the third period of the Packers–Cardinals game in Chicago:

"Dick Nesbitt got off a great kick, sending the ball over the head of Roger Grove, Green Bay quarterback. Grove let it roll, never getting within five feet of the ball. Three Cardinals followed it, Chuck Kassel touching it on the six-yard line, Milan Creighton falling on it on the three-yard mark. Umpire Morris ran to the six-yard line, marking the spot. 'A Packer touched it here,' he said. Referee (George) Lawrie shouted, 'Cardinal ball,' marking the three-yard spot.

"That started the fire-works. Cal Hubbard rushed at Referee Lawrie. He grabbed the official by the shoulders. Other Packer players stormed around. Lawrie wouldn't listen to Hubbard. *Someone* (Author's italics) started to swing, a pair of players grabbed *him* (Author's italics). The Cardinal and Packer benches were deserted as everyone rushed to the field. Fans joined the crowd, pushing, shoving and trying to swing. No one was hit, however, the crowd was too dense.

"Finally, Morris, who had been shouting to be heard, was able to get over what he was attempting to say. 'I called that wrong,' he shouted. 'I meant to say a Cardinal touched the ball on the six-yard line. No Packer touched it.' "

Lawrie reversed his decision but penalized the Packers by putting the ball on the one instead of the six or three which would have been half the distance to the goal. Lambeau and the Packers let it go at that, feeling they had been given justice.

For his part, Hubbard was wrong to grab Lawrie. He made it

worse by taking a swing at the referee. Fortunately, the big lineman failed to connect.

From all indications, Lawrie reacted to the situation appropriately. He had every right to penalize the Packers for Hubbard's conduct, even though the incident had been caused by a mistake by one of his own officials.

Carr was wrong because he should have gone through channels to Hubbard, meaning he should have sent the letter to Lee Joannes who should have forwarded it to Lambeau to give to Hubbard. Carr was also wrong to threaten Hubbard's budding umpiring career by making "inferences" to that end. The NFL president's third mistake was his failure to contact the Green Bay management and ask them for Hubbard's side of the incident. Carr should have controlled his own temper and handled the affair as calmly as an unbiased judge should rule in any legal case.

The oddest part of the whole matter was the complaint came from the Cardinals' management and not George Lawrie, the referee who had the legitimate beef. Dr. David Jones, who was still functioning as the Cardinals' president although he had sold the team to Charlie Bidwill, wrote Carr about the Hubbard–Lawrie affair. His complaint sounded more like sour grapes over losing the game than over any concern for Lawrie and playing the game in a gentlemanly manner.

Lambeau practically blamed the losing streak on Hubbard's uninspired play, while he admitted making some mistakes himself. Of course, he didn't elaborate on what his miscues were, evidently because he felt there was no need to point the finger of blame at himself, especially when there were so many bad "breaks" that had gone against the Packers.

The victory over the Chicago Cardinals had kept the Packers in the race for the Western Division title. At that point, they were only two games behind the Bears and one behind Portsmouth. With five games remaining, including one each against the leaders, the Packers needed only to win to gain the top spot. A loss anywhere along the line might spell their doom.

As George Whitney Calhoun called it, play selection hurt the Packers against Portsmouth. They could have attempted a field goal on their first possession when they drove down inside the

Spartans' five-yard line then lost the ball on downs. More than likely, one of Green Bay's placekickers would have made the three points, and the Pack would have had the lead early on. Green Bay could have tied the game in the fourth quarter if not for an ill-advised pass into the end zone that fell incomplete, turning the ball over to Portsmouth. The Packers had run the ball effectively all day, and almost every drive had been killed by incomplete passes or interceptions. If they had stayed on the ground on that late drive, they might have scored the tying points.

Of course, it was easy to second-guess after the fact, but both of those missed opportunities to score were Lambeau's responsibility as head coach, making him as much at fault for the loss as were the players who failed to execute.

The loss to Boston was a case of simply being outplayed on that particular day. The Redskins had their act together, and they stuck it to the Packers. It was that simple. Okay, maybe Cal Hubbard didn't play with his usual zeal, but that might have been caused by the fact that he had a broken thumb and not because of some implied threat by Joe Carr as Lambeau indicated.

The New York game was another matter. Lambeau didn't tell the fans back home that he released Jesse Quatse *the day before the game*, weakening his already injury-riddled bench and forcing Hubbard to play the whole 60 minutes with his fractured paw. Calhoun covered for Lambeau by reporting that Quatse had been released *the day after the game*. He also reported that Johnny Blood had been "suspended for breaking training rules." Blood told Myron Cope what brought about the suspension and subsequent events:

"Curly Lambeau used to say that I trained harder than anybody on the club. That is, I spent more energy on the training field than the average guy, and I believe that to be true or I would not repeat it. But in 1933 Lambeau fired me. We were in New York that year to play the Giants, and we were having a medium season, with about three or four games to go. It was a Friday night, about eight o'clock, and I got a call at the hotel from some millionaire's wife — the wife of some millionaire from the Fox Valley around Green Bay. She wanted me to meet her at the Stork Club.

"I said, 'Oh, no. I couldn't do that. The game's only (the) day after tomorrow.' So I got ready for bed, and here two god–damned nurses rapped on the door. So my roommate and I ordered up a few drinks. Well, we got pretty loaded. Next morning, I went out for practice in not the best of condition. Alcohol, you see, hangs on me. I don't sober up real fast. It's a family characteristic — I have plenty of recuperative power, but alcohol doesn't fall out of me. It hangs on to me.

"So I went out to practice and got ready to punt, and the first ball I kicked, I fell flat on my ass. Lambeau sent me back to the hotel. He came up afterward and said, 'I've got to let you go.' I didn't argue with him. I never argued. Well, the team played New York without me and lost the game, but the fact was I was fired. I went over to Paterson, New Jersey, and played a couple of games with a Paterson semi–pro team, and finally the Packers were playing Chicago in their last game of the season, and Lambeau got in touch with me to come back. He got to thinking about next year, I suppose, and that I'd be a free agent if I was still fired. About June the next year, 1934, he sold me to Pitts–burgh."

If Lambeau "suspended" Blood, why didn't he discipline Blood's unmentioned roommate, too? Was Lambeau jealous of Blood as Johnny claimed in later years? Yes, he was. Curly Lambeau liked being center stage — alone. He had that much ego. He didn't like sharing the spotlight with anyone; and the older he got, the more attention he demanded. Lambeau sing–led out Blood because the Vagabond Halfback was more pop–ular than he was that season. Besides that, Blood made the perfect scapegoat for the Packers' losing season — if Lambeau needed one. It would have been quite easy to blame Blood for his off–the–field shenanigans as being a bad influence on the younger players and for undermining Lambeau's authority.

Throughout the year, Lambeau released several players beginning in the early stages of pre–season practice when he asked Verne Lewellen to retire. Lewellen was the Brown county district attorney and didn't need the football money any longer. When he hung up his football cleats, he was the leading scorer in Packer history with 301 points.

By the beginning of the playing season, Lambeau had reduced the roster to 25 players, then cut it to 22 before the third game as league rules dictated. By the end of the year, the Packers had only 14 men under contract.

Lambeau had second thoughts about Blood and brought him back to the club because he was shorthanded for the Chicago game. With Herber in the hospital with injuries from his auto accident, the Packers had only five backs left on the roster, and one of those, Hank Bruder, had been nursing injuries all year long and wasn't really ready to play. Lambeau called Blood and told him he was only "suspended" and not fired — as Blood understood it — and was still a part of the team. Blood went to Chicago and sat on the bench for the whole game.

The Packers' head mentor did speak a bit of truth when he said, "It has taken a lot of economy that has hurt us." That was the real reason behind almost all of Lambeau's personnel moves. The Green Bay Football Corporation needed to economize, and the best way to do that was to keep the payroll down. But not having a full bench all the time cost the Packers dearly in the win and loss columns.

Like the Curly of old who thought of others first and himself last, Lambeau sacrificed the 1933 season to save the future for the Green Bay Packers.

§ § §

6

Back on Track

Just about the time the farmer thinks the rain is going to let up, hail begins to fall from the sky and there go the crops for another year.

That must have been how Curly Lambeau felt in early 1934 when two of his star linemen decided that they'd had enough of pro football and joined the coaching ranks on the college level. Cal Hubbard tossed in the towel and announced that he was off to coach the line for Texas A&M, and Rudy Comstock called it a career by joining the Oklahoma A&M coaching staff. The loss of Hubbard was especially painful because the big tackle had once again made the National Football League's All–Pro team. To replace them, Lambeau hired Adolph Schwammel, an All–American tackle from Oregon State, and Bob Jones, an All–American guard from Indiana. Also known as "Ade" and "Tar", Schwammel played for the College All–Stars against the Bears in the summer charity game.

Lambeau missed signing Harry Newman, the quarterback he wanted in '33, but not the one he sought in '34. He went to work right after the regular season ended in '33 and attended the East–West Shrine game in San Francisco where he made contact with Joe Laws, the fine lefthanded passer and kicker from Iowa. In early February, Laws agreed to terms and signed a contract with the Packers. Laws was the starting right halfback in the College All–Star game.

After Laws signed, Lambeau recruited Champ Seibold, a strapping 6'4", 235–pound tackle who hailed from Oshkosh. Seibold had played a freshman year at Ripon College, then transferred to Wisconsin, playing another freshman season before being ruled ineligible by the Big Ten for a financial transaction in which he had been involved before leaving Ripon. With his college days seemingly at an end, Seibold sought out Lambeau and received a pro contract to play with the Packers.

Chester "Swede" Johnston, back, Marquette, had received a tryout with the Packers in '31 but had failed to make the team. After a couple of seasons playing for an independent pro team, the St. Louis Gunners, the Appleton product appeared to be ready for the big time.

Another signee that Lambeau garnered out of the East–West game was Carl Jorgensen, a 200–pound tackle from St. Mary's College in California. Also to come aboard Lambeau's ship in '34 were Frank Butler, a center from Michigan State; Charley Casper, back, TCU; Al Norgard, end, Stanford; Earl Witte, back, Gustavus Adolphus; and Harry Wunsch, guard, Notre Dame.

Although Lambeau lost two veteran linemen, he regained one when Nate Barragar decided playing was more fun than coaching and returned to the Packers for '34. Returning from the '33 squad were ends Lavvie Dilweg, Milt Gantenbein, Les Peterson, and Al Rose; interior linemen Art Bultman, Lon Evans, Joe Kurth, Mike Michalske, and Claude Perry; and backs Buckets Goldenberg, Roger Grove, Arnie Herber, Clarke Hinkle, Bob Monnett, and Hank Bruder. Dilweg and Perry were entering their eighth season with the Packers; Michalske his sixth; Herber his fifth; Gantenbein, Bruder, and Grove their fourth; Barragar, Bultman, Hinkle, Peterson, and Rose their third; Evans, Goldenberg, Kurth, and Monnett their second.

The NFL moguls met in New York on June 30 and July 1 to make a few rule changes and set up a schedule for the coming season. Joe Carr and Carl Storck were re–elected to their respective posts of president and treasurer, and a new executive committee consisting of George Halas, Dr. Henry March, and Bert Bell was elected. The gathering approved the transfer of the Portsmouth franchise which had been sold in March to a Detroit syndicate headed up by George A. Richards who re–named the team the Lions using the same logic that Halas had used in 1922: "If baseball players are Tigers, then football players must Lions."

Once more the league magnates moved to put more excitement into the pro brand of football. They started by eliminating some penalties; specifically the five-yarder for two consecutive incomplete passes and the turnover for an incomplete pass thrown into the end zone on first down. A change in the fumble rule was discussed but tabled until the following year. The biggest innovation of all was the implementation of game clocks in the stadiums so everybody would be able to see how much time was remaining in a quarter.

The NFL leaders took no notice of two new pro leagues that had started up earlier in the year. One circuit was made up of franchises located primarily in the South, while the other originated in California. Neither posed a threat to the NFL in '34 and were actually encouraged by Joe Carr because he felt they were inferior organizations that could possibly act as feeder leagues to the major loop.

Carr and the owners also patted themselves on the back for the success of the first ever championship game between the league's two division winners, the New York Giants and Chicago Bears. The crowd was announced as being 30,000, but receipts said only 18,000 or so paid to get into Wrigley Field to see the Bears nip the Giants, 23-21.

Coach Lambeau called the troops together to begin practice on September 1. For a tuneup game, he managed to arrange a contest with S.O. "Sod" Donkle's Fort Atkinson Blackhawks, a semi-pro team that was considered the best in the Midwest that year. The Hawks were easy marks for the Packers, 28-7, but a good warm up for the coming league campaign.

Lud Wray's Philadelphia Eagles were the first NFL opponent for the Packers. Joe Kresky, who hailed from nearby Marinette, had graduated from Wisconsin, and had played for the Packers in 1930 before seeking greener pastures, led the Quaker City eleven into Green Bay for the September 16 encounter. Other featured Philly stars were George Kenneally and Swede Hanson. The Packers held a 6-4-1 edge over the Philadelphia franchise since the two teams began playing each other in 1925, including victories in the last four straight contests.

A good opening day crowd of 5,500 turned out to watch their favorites down the Eagles, 19-6. Bob Monnett was a one-man show in the first half, scoring all 16 of Green Bay's points. After Arnie Herber passed the Packers into scoring territory late in the first period, Monnett booted a 20-yard field goal. He set up his first touchdown with a 36-yard pass to Roger Grove, then danced over the goal line from four yards out and booted the PAT to give Green Bay a 10-0 lead after one possession in the second stanza. He added another six-pointer in the second quarter, this one from 28 yards out. Ade Schwammel kicked a third period field goal to give the Pack a 19-0 lead from which they coasted home.

The '34 Chicago Bears roster read like a "Who's Who" of NFL stars with Bronko Nagurski, Keith Molesworth, Gene Ronzani, Carl Brumbaugh, Jack Manders, George Musso, Beattie Feathers, Luke Johnsos, Walt Kiesling, Bill Hewitt, and Red Grange when the Monsters of the Midway invaded Green Bay for the 30th meeting of the two rivals. The 12,582 spectators who jammed City Stadium watched the Bears and Packers play even for three periods before Chicago put together a pair of fourth quarter TDs to down Green Bay, 24-10.

The Packers' next *home* game was scheduled to be played in Milwaukee at State Fair Park. This was the second straight year the Green Bay management had opted for a contest in the Cream City, and their opponent would once again be the New York Giants. State Fair Park had about the same seating capacity as Borchert Field, but it was much more suited for football than the baseball stadium was. The Giants, losers to Detroit the week before, came into the fray as heavy favorites. Like the Bears, New York's lineup was filled with veterans of high caliber, but the Gothamites didn't have a Nagurski or a Feathers on their squad, while Green Bay had Hinkle and Monnett. Hinkle ground out the yardage with punishing power plays through the line, and Monnett booted a pair of field goals and two PATs as the Packers won going away, 20-6, in front of 11,000 avid fans.

Every team had seen action in league play by the end of the third week of the schedule; Brooklyn being the last eleven to join the race. The Bears (2-0-0) and Lions (2-0-0) were atop the

Western Division standings with the Packers (2-1-0) in hot pursuit. The Cardinals (1-1-0) were a better club than they had been the year before, but Cincinnati (0-3-0) had actually gotten worse. The loss to Green Bay put the Giants (0-2-0) in an unaccustomed place for New York: last in the East. Brooklyn (1-0-0) had beaten Boston (1-1-0) which had handed Pittsburgh (1-2-0) its first defeat the week before. The Eagles (1-1-0) picked up their first win over the Pirates that week.

Potsy Clark's Lions were next up for the Packers. As the Portsmouth Spartans, the Detroit eleven had been a tough opponent in '33, but Dutch Clark wasn't on the roster that year. He was back for the '34 campaign. Dutch had led the league in scoring in '32, then teammate Glenn Presnell took that title in '33. This tandem was expected to wreak havoc on the Packers, but only Presnell's toe presented a problem for Green Bay as the Detroit placekicker booted a 54–yard field goal in the second quarter that stood up until the final gun to give the Motor City crew a 3-0 win.

The win kept Detroit (3-0-0) apace with the Bears (3-0-0) who beat Brooklyn (1-1-0) handily. The Packers (2-2-0) slipped to fourth behind the Cardinals (2-1-0) who had beaten Cincinnati (0-4-0) for the second time. New York (2-2-0) won a pair of contests that week, beating Pittsburgh (2-3-0) and Boston (1-2-0). With the Pirates avenging an earlier loss to Philadelphia (1-2-0), the Eastern Division race was still up for grabs.

Cincinnati's hapless Redlegs came to Green Bay the following week, and the *Press-Gazette* was hard put to print something exciting about the Ohio eleven. Even with Buckets Goldenberg sidelined with a gash in his left knee that he had sustained against Detroit, the Packers were grossly favored to win, and they did, 41-0. Hank Bruder had a field day with the Ohioans, scoring three TDs and four PATs, catching three passes for 57 yards, and rushing for 32 yards.

In the Western Division standings, Green Bay (3-2-0) stepped over the Cardinals (2-2-0) who lost to the first–place Bears (5-0-0) who had also beaten Pittsburgh (2-5-0) in the middle of the week. Detroit (4-0-0) remained undefeated, too, slipping by Philadelphia (1-3-0). New York (3-2-0) and Boston (2-2-0) began to separate themselves from the rest of the East by downing

Brooklyn (1-2-0) and the Pirates respectively.

Times still weren't great for the NFL, especially for the Green Bay Football Corporation, which was still trying to get out of receivership. To help them, just as the Packers' president, Lee Joannes, had helped him two years earlier, George Halas agreed to play a "non–league" game with the Packers in Milwaukee. The contest was set for Wednesday night, October 17. Just as they had in most of the recent games played against the Packers, the Bears did their scoring in the fourth quarter, tacking up 10 points in the late going to beat Green Bay, 10-6. A crowd of nearly 7,000 turned out to help the Packers reach for financial stability once again.

The Chicago Cardinals had never been much of a draw in Green Bay, and they still weren't in '34, although the contest was the last home game for the Packers that year. Chicago owner Charlie Bidwill had rebuilt the club significantly but not enough for the Cardinals to seriously threaten the supremacy of the Bears, Lions, and Packers in the Western Division. The Cardinals entered the game as favorites, but 4,000 loyal Packer fans rooted their boys to a 15-0 victory. Arnie Herber showed some of his great passing ability by connecting on six of eight attempts, including one to Joe Laws for 61 yards, a TD toss to Hinkle for 69 yards, and another six–pointer to Roger Grove from three yards out.

The win solidified the Packers' (4-2-0) hold on third place, a game and a half ahead of the Cardinals (2-3-0), but still two games behind the undefeated Bears (6-0-0) and a game and a half behind the Lions (5-0-0). Cincinnati (0-6-0) had yet to win a game. The Giants (4-2-0) won their fourth in a row, and Boston (3-3-0) held on to second ahead of Brooklyn (1-2-0), Pittsburgh (2-6-0), and Philadelphia (1-4-0).

Lambeau's plans for the season had suffered a setback early on when the St. Louis Gunners were able to reclaim Swede Johnston from the Packers after he had played just one NFL game because he was still under contract to the American League team. Green Bay felt another heavy blow when Champ Seibold was ruled ineligible for the rest of the season because his college class had yet to graduate. Under NFL rules, no man could play for a league team until that time. This rule was a direct result of George Halas signing Red Grange in 1925.*

Green Bay's next encounter was a make-or-break game with the Bears in Chicago. The Packers needed a win to stay in the race for the division title and a shot at the league championship. A loss would surely put them out of the hunt, even though they would still be in it mathematically.

Hard as they tried, the Packers just couldn't master the Bears for the seventh straight time, including the exhibition in Milwaukee 11 days earlier. Nagurski was his usual punishing self, crunching the Green Bay line for 79 yards on 13 carries and tackling Packer runners so hard that he put them on the sidelines for several plays at a time. But the real star for the Bruins was Feathers who amassed 150 yards on just 16 rushing attempts and scored two touchdowns. Although the Pack put up a real fight, the Bears were too much for them, winning 27-14.

Detroit (7-0-0) kept pace with the Bears (7-0-0) by beating Brooklyn (2-3-0) and Cincinnati (0-7-0), while the Packers (4-3-0) were effectively dropped from the chase for division honors. New York (5-3-0) dumped Philadelphia (1-5-0) to continue its winning streak, and Boston (4-3-0) nailed the Cardinals (2-4-0).

The '34 season now had little left for the Packers except the roll of spoilers. They had games remaining with contenders New York, Boston, and Detroit and could make a difference in the outcome of both division races.

Just a sidelight, the Packers completed what had to have been the longest "for-a-player-to-be-named-later" trade in the history of sports when they secured Tiny Engebretsen from the Brooklyn Dodgers in a deal begun at the tail end of the '32 season. At that time, Tom Nash was sent to Brooklyn "on loan" but was still the property of the Packers. Engebretsen, from Northwestern, had played one year with the Bears before coaching a year, then joined the Dodgers in '34. He was just the man Lambeau needed to replace Cal Hubbard, and Joe Kurth was released to make room for Tiny on the roster.

First up on the eastern swing for the Packers were the Boston

---

*See Chapter 10, pages 130-133 of the first volume of *The History of the Green Bay Packers: The Lambeau Years — Part One.*

Redskins. Lone Star Dietz had his gridiron warriors playing some excellent football, but their best wasn't good enough to hold the Packers. A Herber pass to Lavvie Dilweg for a six-pointer and a field goal and PAT by Clarke Hinkle gave Green Bay a 10-0 win.

The Green Bay (5-3-0) victory didn't hurt Boston (4-4-0) all that much because the Bears (8-0-0) swamped the Giants (5-3-0). Detroit (8-0-0) stayed right with Chicago by mauling Pittsburgh (2-8-0) that week.

Lambeau's charges had taken the measure of the Giants in Milwaukee earlier in the year, but when the Packers met the Gothamites in New York, it was a different story. Harry Newman ran through and around the invaders from Wisconsin, and when he couldn't run, he passed, leading the Giants to victory, 17-3.

The Bears (9-0-0) and Lions (9-0-0) each won again as they headed for their Thanksgiving Day showdown game. Boston (4-5-0), Detroit's victim, fell two games behind New York (6-3-0), while Brooklyn (3-4-0) held close with a win over the improving Eagles (2-6-0).

In an unprecedented move that week, the Cincinnati franchise was sold to Ed Butler of the St. Louis Gunners in the middle of the season. Butler added some of the Redlegs' players to the St. Louis roster, and the Gunners also took Cincinnati's record of 0-8-0. The Gunners (1-8-0) downed Pittsburgh (2-9-0), embarrassing the Pirates and the league.

Milwaukee hosted the Packers for the third time in '34 as the Chicago Cardinals provided the opposition. Rain had turned the state fairgrounds into a muddy bog, so only 3,000 fans came out to see the Cardinals break the Packers' four-game win streak over them, 9-0. Art Bystrom reported in the *Press-Gazette* that the Packers were totally without spirit during the game.

The loss to the Cardinals (4-5-0) put Green Bay (5-5-0) in jeopardy of falling a notch in the standings. As far as the division title race was going, the Bears (10-0-0) and Lions (10-0-0) were still tied for first. In the East, Boston (5-5-0) and Brooklyn (4-4-0) both gained on New York (6-4-0).

For several weeks, the Lions had been demolishing all opposition by enormous scores, such as 38-0 over Cincinnati,

40-7 over Pittsburgh, and 40-7 over St. Louis. The Cardinals had given them a hard time of it, losing only 17-13 the week before they beat the Packers, and that was Detroit's only close game since nipping Green Bay, 3-0, earlier. With the Bears due to invade Detroit the following Thursday for their first annual Thanksgiving Day game, the Lions were ripe for an upset and the Packers were just the team to give it to them. Green Bay caught the Lions looking ahead on the schedule, turning the tables on them as Detroit suffered its first defeat of the year, 3-0. Clarke Hinkle provided the only score of the game with a 47-yard field goal in the fourth quarter.

The win practically guaranteed the Packers (6-5-0) third place in the Western Division standings because the Bears (11-0-0) beat the Cardinals (4-6-0). New York (7-4-0) remained atop the East, downing Boston (5-6-0), while Brooklyn (4-5-0) was losing to Philadelphia (3-7-0).

The Packers also had a date for Thanksgiving Day, but theirs was with the Cardinals in Chicago. The two elevens were playing for the third time that year, and this was the rubber match for them. Lon Evans and Milt Gantenbein were too hurt to play, and Mike Michalske and Hank Bruder were walking wounded for the tilt. Injuries and a muddy Wrigley Field proved to be the Packers' undoing again as Green Bay lost, 6-0. The lone tally of the contest came on Homer Griffith's 96-yard return of the opening kickoff.

Again, the Cardinals (5-6-0) threatened to pass the Packers (6-6-0) in the standings with just one week remaining in the regular season. The Bears (12-0-0) wrapped up the Western Division title by nipping the Lions (10-2-0), and the Giants (8-4-0) did the same in the East by beating Brooklyn (4-6-0).

Green Bay (7-6-0) closed out the season with a win over the Gunners (1-10-0), 21-14, in St. Louis and finished third. The Bears (13-0-0) completed their undefeated season by nipping Detroit (10-3-0) once more and got set to meet the Giants (8-5-0) for the third time that year.

The Bears entered the NFL title game with an unbeaten streak of 34 consecutive games. Of course, this included several games against non-league opponents on a barnstorming tour of the West the year before. The last NFL team to beat Chicago was the Giants when the two foes met near the end of the regular season in '33. Since that time, the Bears had reeled off 18 straight wins against league opposition, not including their exhibition victory over the Packers in Milwaukee.

The 1934 National Football League Championship game turned out to be one of the greatest sports stories of the 20th Century. The Chicago Bears entered the contest as heavy favorites to win their third straight NFL title, and for three quarters, it looked like they would do just that as they mounted a 13-3 lead going into the final stanza. Then a miracle happened.

At halftime, end Ray Flaherty of the Giants suggested to Coach Steve Owen that the New York eleven switch their footwear from their regular cleats to rubber-soled shoes. The Giants weren't getting anywhere with the Bears on the frozen Polo Grounds turf, so Owen had his ends and backs don the more pliable basketball shoes. With the beginning of the last period of play, the Giants suddenly came to life and began running the Bears ragged as the New York team scored four unanswered touchdowns to claim the NFL title, 30-13.

The game was momentous to the Green Bay Packers in only one way. They were still the only team in the history of the National Football League to win three straight championships.

§ § §

7

The Green Bay Packers Incorporated

Unlike many other sports, success in football depends a great deal on emotion. Get a half-pint player all churned up inside, and he can move a man twice his size, who isn't keyed up, all over the field. A whole team of properly motivated players can perform miracles. Leland Joannes, Gerald Clifford, Dr. W.W. Kelly, and Andrew B. Turnbull knew this coaching principle, but better yet, they knew how to apply it to the people of Green Bay.

The Green Bay Football Corporation had been in receivership since August 15, 1933, and it didn't seem to be getting anywhere toward regaining solvency, in spite of all the efforts made by Curly Lambeau to curb spending. After two fairly successful seasons at the box office — successful considering the times — the corporation was still in the hole financially. In fact, little gain on the debt situation had been made in the two full seasons; the Packers were still over $19,000 in debt with less than $6,000 in cash to pay it off. At the time the corporation went into receivership, its debts amounted to more than $20,000. That total had been shaved to $12,332. Bills totaling $7,100 had been accumulated for the 1934 season. This situation couldn't go on and the Packers survive. Something had to be done.

Lee Joannes called together the members of the executive committee — Jerry Clifford, Dr. Kelly, Andy Turnbull, and Charlie Mathys — who were appointed by receiver Frank Jonet, and with Jonet, they worked out a plan to save the Packers once more. It was very simple: they needed at least $10,000 in cash to prevent the Packers from either folding up or selling out.

As soon as the Christmas season was over, the executive committee met with a group of Green Bay businessmen and told them point blank that they had two choices: dig deep into their cash registers or lose the Packers to Milwaukee. Joannes made the threat. He argued that the receivership couldn't go on forever. Sooner or later, the court would demand that something be done to remedy the debt situation, which would mean the assets of the corporation would have to be sold. The only real tangible asset the corporation owned was its National Football League franchise. It was probably worth more than the amount owed, but it wasn't likely to sell for that much because of the debts. That was the bad news.

For the good news, Joannes asked this body of business leaders, of which he was one, to help him organize a fundraising drive to rescue the Packers from becoming a footnote in the history of professional football. There was general agreement that something had to be done, but a drive like this would require dozens of volunteers, hundreds of man-hours, and some official sanctioning within the business community. How did the executive committee plan to go about accomplishing this feat?

Joannes and Turnbull took the next step when they met with the Green Bay Association of Commerce's retail advertising committee on January 8, 1935. Joannes outlined a proposal to reorganize the football corporation and explained what had already been done toward that end. The Association of Commerce men — L.C. Atkinson, Jack Stiefel, Ceil C. Baum, Charles A. Raasch, W.F. Tyson, Oscar Bielefeldt, A.G. Carson, and J.M. Busch — voted to support the Packers by forming subcommittees that would solicit funds from retail businesses in the city of Green Bay and help reach the goal of $10,000 by the end of January.

Two days later it was announced in *The Green Bay Press-Gazette* that the Association of Commerce committee was on the job already:

"Working in teams of two, the business men started making calls this morning, taking pledges under the reorganization plan. The city was parcelled into districts and each team assigned an area. The action follows a decision at a recent meeting of the retail advertising committee to get behind the Packer reorganization plan. Whole-hearted support has been offered by everyone asked to do the solicitation, the committee reported.

"Teams working Washington, Walnut, Main, Cherry, and Pine streets are composed of John Busch and George Bertrand, C.L. Atkinson and W.J. Tyson, Charles Raasch and Jack Stiefel, King Weeman and Franklin W. Krueger, Frank Moore and W.E. Haefs, S.M. Kersten and J.A. Holtermann, Sam Cohen and Norman Danz, A.G. Carson and Henry Bruder, Ceil Baum and Ed Wochenske, Pat Maloney, Abe Miller and Art Slater, Walter Dettmen and Samuel Alk. Northside business men will be solicited by Al De Groot and Norman Clusman. James Stathas and Frank Buth will contact automobile dealers. The southside will be handled by Oscar Bielefeldt and Earl Gigler, and the central west side by Frank Walker. J.H. Quinn and Hubert Shaughnessy are soliciting the northwest side."

These men had only one solid argument in favor of supporting the Packers: the Green Bay Packers were the *Green Bay Packers* and they were good advertising for the city. In economic terms, they explained that every dollar brought into the city as a direct result of the Packers was spent four times before it left the city. These were terms that all businessmen, not just those who liked professional football, understood.

The drive went well right from the start because the business community had the money and the spirit. In fact, just about every Green Bayer had the spirit as witnessed by W.H. Grunert who heard about the fund drive while he was wintering in Valparaiso, Florida and wrote Joannes to instruct him to put him down for $25.

Finally, on January 29, 1935, the reorganization meeting was held at the Brown County Courthouse. Joannes detailed the plan:

(1) The Green Bay Football Corporation would be dissolved but would be succeeded by the Green Bay Packers, Inc., a new corporation designed along the same lines of the first concern.

(2) The Green Bay Packers, Inc., would be a non-profit sharing

corporation just as its predecessor had been.

(3) Any profits made by the Green Bay Packers, Inc., would be *donated* (Author's italics.) to the Sullivan Post of the American Legion.

(4) The Green Bay Packers, Inc., would issue 600 shares of no par common stock at a price of $25 a share.

(5) The stock sale had the potential of raising $15,000 and the fund-raisers were already close to that figure, having received $11,900 in pledges.

(6) A deal had already been made with the creditors of the old corporation to accept approximately 50 cents on the dollar on those debts that were outstanding at the time of the bankruptcy. This would use up $6,700. Another $1,500 and the $5,600 the old corporation had would go to pay off the bills from the 1934 season. This would leave the new corporation about $3,700 to begin operations in 1935. Joannes said he would like to see this increased to $5,000 in order to give Coach Lambeau a little more leverage with which to hire players coming out of college that year.

(7) An annual meeting of the stockholders would be held on the first Monday after July 4 each year. At this gathering, the stockholders would elect a board of directors numbering 20, and the board would meet once during each of the months of August, September, October, November, and December. The board would also elect an executive committee of seven that would operate the corporation, to be composed of the president, vice-president, treasurer, and four directors.

(8) None of the directors or officers would receive salaries.

Jerry Clifford pointed out to the gathering that the old corporation had donated $4,000 in profits to the Sullivan Post over the years and had contributed $39,000 toward the construction of City Stadium. Of course, this was done before the suit by Willard Bent.

The new stockholders then voted unanimously to accept the reorganization plan, and a nominating committee of Harold L. Frank, D.V. Pinkerton, Ray Leicht, James Stathas, and L.J. Kelly was named to nominate directors. This group presented a list of 20 names, and these were elected unanimously. The new directors then elected officers: Joannes, president; Fred Leicht, vice-president; George W. Calhoun, secretary; and Frank Jonet, treasurer. The first board of directors of the Green Bay Packers, Inc., consisted of:

H.J. Wintgens, L.G. Wood, A.B. Turnbull, Harvey Lhost, John Moffett, Ed Schuster, Leland Joannes, Gerald F. Clifford, Leslie J. Kelly, Charles Mathys, H.J. Bero, Frank Walker, Fred Leicht, H.J. Stoltz, Dr. W.W. Kelly, Fred L. Cobb, C.A. Raasch, E.R. Fischer, J.E. Paeps, and Arthur E. Schumacher.

In succeeding weeks, the court accepted the reorganization of the old corporation into the new Green Bay Packers, Inc., and more funds were raised. Once again, the Packers were saved from financial destruction and the future of the team was secure — for the moment.

§ § §

8

Lightning Comes to Green Bay

Clarke Hinkle once said of Curly Lambeau, "He was one of those rare coaches like Paul Brown or Vince Lombardi — he could see things in a ballplayer that other coaches couldn't." It was this rare ability to recognize talent that made Lambeau a great coach, and he demonstrated this trait very well in the mid1930s.

Mike Michalske, Johnny Blood, Cal Hubbard, and Hinkle — to mention only a few — often remarked that Lambeau wasn't much of a field strategist, but he made up for it in other ways, mostly with hard work. Every year Lambeau scouted the East-West Shrine All-Star game in San Francisco, then took in the Rose Bowl if he could. Unlike other National Football League coaches, Lambeau personally went looking for players all over the country instead of just reading about them in the newspapers. He wanted to meet them, to see them play. A kid on the West Coast might have great press releases, but maybe he didn't have the temperament to play in a place like Green Bay. There was a lot you couldn't tell about a player without seeing him in the flesh.

Lambeau's trip to California in late 1934 was the single most important journey of his coaching career since the time he traveled to Ohio to save an NFL franchise for Green Bay in 1922. On this particular scouting trek, he made the acquaintance of the one man who was more responsible for putting excitement into the game of football than probably any other in its history.

On New Year's Day 1935, the Crimson Tide of Alabama met

the Stanford Indians in the Rose Bowl. Playing end for Alabama was Donald Hutson, a modest fellow from Pine Bluff, Arkansas. Standing six feet tall and weighing somewhere in the neighborhood of 185 pounds, he hardly looked like one of the better pass receivers in college football. Even so, he caught six passes that first day of January and two of them went for touchdowns as the Crimson Tide dumped Stanford, 29-13. While most coaches in the NFL said Hutson was too light to play in the pro circuit, Curly Lambeau and John "Shipwreck" Kelly, owner of the Brooklyn Dodgers, saw a rising star.

"I had offers from all the pro teams to come and try out," said Hutson in an interview with Myron Cope, "but it narrowed down to Brooklyn and Green Bay. Those were the teams that were bidding — if you can call it bidding — for my services. The strange thing is that until I started receiving letters from Curly Lambeau, I had given no thought at all to playing pro football. None at all. I'd never heard of the Green Bay Packers. Down in Alabama there was nothing in the papers about pro football. They didn't even have the results in the papers. It was a whole different country down there. For example, the first tavern I ever saw was when I got to Green Bay.

"Anyhow, Shipwreck Kelly, who owned the Brooklyn team, came to see me at Alabama and said, would I agree that I wouldn't sign with anybody else without giving him a chance to bid? I said yes, I would agree to that. So the bidding started — at around eighty dollars per game, or somewhere around that figure. And it rose in five-dollar jumps. Every time Curly would call me and raise his price five dollars a game, I would call Shipwreck collect in Brooklyn, and he would say, 'That's all right, I'll meet that offer.'

"Finally, Curly's offer got up to $175, which was far above anything that anybody was making or ever had been making in Green Bay. I tried to phone Shipwreck, but his office said he wasn't there and they didn't know where he was. So I sent him a wire, thinking they might forward it to him, you know, but I didn't hear from him. I sent him two or three more wires within the next couple of days, but still I didn't hear from him. So when Curly called me to see where things stood, I said, 'All right, fine. I'll sign.' The next day, I received the contract air mail. I signed it and put it in the mail. About an hour later, Shipwreck showed up.

"He said, 'What's been happening?' He explained that he had been down in Florida and had left word with his office that he didn't want to be disturbed, but finally the office, as I recall, had sent him my telegram or told him about it and he hurried right up to Tuscaloosa. Shipwreck said, 'I think the least you can do under the circumstances is to sign the same contract with me that you signed with Lambeau.'

" 'That's probably right,' I told him. I said, 'I *did* promise you a chance to meet his offer, so I'll sign with you, too, and let somebody else decide where I'm going to play.'

"That's what I did, and I called Curly to tell him about it. I didn't want to be underhanded about this thing. I told him what had happened and what I had done, and he said, 'That's perfectly all right. You just leave it to me.'

"Joe Carr was president of the league at the time, with headquarters in Columbus, Ohio. And as far as I know, a case like this had never come up, so there was no way of knowing how Carr would settle it. Anyhow, as soon as Curly got my contract he mailed it to Carr. It was delivered to Carr's office the same day that my contract with Shipwreck arrived there, but the Green Bay contract got there just ahead of the other. So on that basis, Carr's ruling was that I would go to Green Bay. And that was a very fortunate thing for me, because in Arnie Herber, Green Bay had by far the best passer in the league and one of the greatest long passers that ever played."

On George Washington's birthday 1935, *The Green Bay Press-Gazette* announced the signing of Hutson with a 90-point type headline double-stacked over three columns. Most Packer fans didn't know it at the time, but the fortunes of their favorite team were on the verge of greatness once again.

Don Hutson wasn't the only player Lambeau signed up in 1935. He had a whole shopping list of 60 some players he wanted to see and possibly sign up for the '35 campaign.

The coach started by resigning Frank Butler, the big center from Michigan State who had quit the team after four games in '34 because of an argument with Lambeau and had taken a job with the federal government doing harbor survey and research work. Butler was able to arrange a leave of absence for the '35 season.

Lambeau went to the West Coast looking specifically for a pair of tackles, feeling the team was weak in that area, meaning he needed potential replacements for Claude Perry and Mike Michalske, who were getting up there in football age. In this day of two-way football, the guards and ends on offense were often pulled out on defense and substituted by bigger tackles; thus, another reason for Lambeau desiring a pair of hefty linemen. He found them in George Maddox and Ernie Smith. Maddox was an All-American with Kansas State in '34 and had played in the East-West Shrine game. Smith had spent his college days at Southern California, graduating from there in '33. Also an All-American his senior year and also having played in the charity all-star game in San Francisco in '32, he joined the Los Angeles club in the California pro league for '33 and '34.

Lambeau was able to find some backfield help when he signed George Sauer and Herm Schneidman. Sauer was an All-American from Nebraska who came with a suitcase full of press clippings touting his talents. Schneidman played college ball at Iowa but didn't gain the reputation Sauer had because he was a blocking back, not a ball carrier.

Rounding out the list of newcomers were Bob Tenner, end, Minnesota; Dominic Vairo, end, Notre Dame; Bob O'Connor, tackle, Stanford; and George Svendsen, center, Minnesota.

The Packers hit it big when Cal Hubbard decided to return for one more season. Also, Swede Johnston rejoined the Pack because the St. Louis Gunners were defunct. Finally, Lambeau was able to pick up future Hall-of-Famer Walt Kiesling.

Returning veterans from the '34 squad were Arnie Herber, Roger Grove, Hank Bruder, Milt Gantenbein, Clarke Hinkle, Al Rose, Lon Evans, Buckets Goldenberg, Bob Monnett, Nate Barragar, Tiny Engebretsen, Joe Laws, Ade Schwammel, and Champ Seibold. Arnie Herber was the senior man on the roster in August, joining the Packers in 1930. Grove, Bruder and Gantenbein had seen continuous service since '31, and Hinkle and Rose had been in Green Bay since '32. Evans, Monnett, and Goldenberg were beginning their third year as members of the

Pack, while Seibold, Engebretsen, Laws, and Schwammel were starting their second. Johnston and Butler were considered second-year men as well, while Hubbard was beginning his sixth campaign in a Packer uniform and Barragar his fourth.

With most of this list of players under contract already, it was no wonder that Lambeau was extra excited when the stockholders of the Green Bay Packers, Inc., met for their first annual meeting in July. The board of directors elected the executive committee, which consisted of Lee Joannes, Fred Leicht, Andy Turnbull, Tubby Bero, Emil Fischer, Frank Jonet, and Jerry Clifford. Plans for the season ticket sale were made, and Joannes called for Spike Spachmann's crew to set themselves a goal of 3,000 tickets.

To support the annual season ticket sales, the new sports editor of the *Press-Gazette*, John Walter, wrote in the editor's column, *Looking Up in the Realm of Sports*, three reasons for buying tickets to Packer games:

"(1) Your purchase will help keep the Packers in Green Bay. Facing year by year a great financial outlay, and competing with bank rolls as impressive as the fourth period temperament of the Chicago Bears, the team absolutely cannot do without the 100 per cent support of every one of its fans. It would be a dull Sunday afternoon in the autumn without a Packer team in Green Bay.

"(2) Your purchase will assure you the same seat for every one of the six home games, which bring to Green Bay the cream of the professional football league. By a new arrangement at the Packer ticket office, you may obtain special accommodations for special guests — thus, if your party is increased by one or two on the eve of a game, your seats will be changed so that the entire group may sit together.

"(3) Your purchase will enable you to see the Packer-Bear game, probably the outstanding annual clash in midwestern professional football, at no advance in price."

Walter's reference to the Packer-Bear game ticket prices pointed to the fact that the management had raised the price of all but the cheapest seats for that single contest. The annual invasion of the Chicago team always brought in the largest crowd of the year, so they thought they should capitalize on it.

The Lambeau Years — Part Two

Times being what they were, who could blame them?

Unlike other teams with more money, the Packers had never had a real training *camp*. Lambeau simply told the boys to report on a certain date, and that's when they began practicing for the first game of the season. That had to change because the game of football was changing — and very rapidly, too. With all the new rules in football, especially those that opened up the passing game, play was becoming more complex and players were having to study a little harder. The Bears and Giants, the two participants in the first two NFL championship games, were good examples of what a training camp could mean to a team.

With that in mind, Lambeau searched for a suitable site for a training camp for his Packers. He found one at Pine Wood Lodge on Lake Thompson only four and a half miles from Rhinelander in Wisconsin's Northwoods country. Camp would open on August 24, and all the players were ordered to meet the team bus in Green Bay on the 23rd. All the recreation the Packers would be permitted during the camp would be golf and fishing. No swimming, no drinking, no carousing at some of the local establishments, a few of which had unsavory reputations, especially since they catered to a large portion of Chicago's mobsters who often vacationed in the area. The team would bus into Rhinelander twice each day for a week for workouts at the Rhinelander High School field.

After breaking camp, the Packers were scheduled to play a series of exhibition games against four *semi-pro* teams.

The *Press-Gazette* reported that most of the 1,500 fans who turned out to watch the Pack demolish the Merrill Fromm Foxes, 34-0, were hostile to the Green Bay eleven. Two nights later, an estimated crowd of 6,000 showed up in Chippewa Falls to see Johnny Blood and the Chippewa Falls Marines give the Packers a decent game only to lose, 22-0. Another 1,500 devotees of football came out to watch Green Bay annihilate a Stevens Point College All-Star squad, 40-0. The final game was against Johnny Blood and the La Crosse Old Style Lagers, and once again the Packers came out on top, 49-0.

Actually, the Merrill and Stevens Point teams were made up of nearly the same players — the Stevens Point College squad. The college team was severely disciplined by collegiate authorities for their participation in the games.

Blood had a reason to play for both the Marines and the Lagers. Art Rooney, owner of the Pittsburgh Pirates, had released Blood — on his request — so he could have the opportunity to impress Lambeau and possibly land a job with the Packers. It worked because Lambeau signed him the following week and put him in the first regular game of the season against the Chicago Cardinals.

The NFL had made a few changes during the off-season of 1935. The moguls started by adopting a waiver rule at a special meeting held in May, then they dropped the St. Louis Gunners from the league for not meeting its financial obligations. At the regular summer conference, Detroit owner George Richards suggested the league get a new head man, someone who could promote the circuit a little better. The other owners ignored the thought and re-elected Joe Carr for five years.

Instead of seeking a replacement for St. Louis at such a late date, the owners voted to play the 1935 season with only nine teams. The Eastern Division would remain the same with New York, Brooklyn, Boston, Pittsburgh, and Philadelphia, but the Western Division would only have Detroit, Green Bay, the Chicago Bears, and the Chicago Cardinals.

Prognosticators were predicting another title for the Chicago Bears in spite of the fact that Green Bay, the Cardinals, and the Detroit Lions were all improved teams. The New York Giants were once again the best bet in the East. Boston and Brooklyn were both better on paper, but neither had proven its worth on the field.

When the Cardinals arrived in Green Bay, they were greeted by a Packer team sporting new uniforms. For the first time in the club's history, the players wore green and gold as their colors. The jerseys were Kelly green with old gold sleeves and numbers, and the pants were also old gold. For contrast, the leggings were Kelly green.

New uniforms or not, the Packers lost their first game to Chicago, 7-6, because of a shortage backs. Clarke Hinkle and George Sauer missed the game entirely, and Arnie Herber,

Buckets Goldenberg, and Hank Bruder were limited to the amount of duty they could see because of some minor injuries. The Cardinals should have won by more, but a valiant Packer defense held the invaders at bay on all but one series of plays.

During the following week, Lambeau signed Mike Michalske to a new contract, and Iron Mike began practice immediately for the next game, which was the *legendary 1935 home game* against the Chicago Bears. But again, that's getting ahead of the story.

The Packers were in better shape for the Bears than they had been for the Cardinals. Michalske was back on the line, and Herber, Hinkle, and Sauer were healthy again. The important man was Herber. All week long the Packers practiced a special play, one that would set the football world on fire — if it succeeded.

As Hutson told Myron Cope, Arnie Herber was one of the greatest long passers in the history of the game. He was once asked to throw a football through a glass window for a Hollywood stunt. The window was put in place about 50 yards away, and Herber was told to have a go at it, a practice toss. The camera wasn't running when he broke the glass on the first try. The glass was replaced, and Herber was told to take another shot at it — this time with the camera running. He broke the glass again on the first try.

The Bears kicked off, and Hank Bruder returned it to the Packer 17. Frank Butler led the Packers out of the huddle. The special play was on. The team lined up. Buckets Goldenberg barked out the signals. The ball was snapped to Herber. He faded back to the four. At the same time, Don Hutson slipped past the defensive end and ran straight at Beattie Feathers of the Bears. Herber let fly the ball. Feathers relaxed; it was out of his reach and he assumed Hutson couldn't get to it either. He was wrong. Hutson turned on his deceptive speed and caught the ball over his shoulder near the midfield stripe. Feathers and Gene Ronzani raced after him, but neither man came close as Hutson sped across the goal line with the game's only touchdown. It was Hutson's only reception of the day. Bob Monnett kicked the PAT, and the Packers led, 7-0, with less than a minute gone in the contest. The shocked Bears never recovered, and their regular season winning streak of 17 straight came to a sudden halt.

Several writers have stated that Hutson played his *first NFL game* against the Bears in Green Bay. John Torinus, Sr., wrote that Hutson's *first play* was in this game, meaning it wasn't his first game but the first time Hutson was involved in a pass play. Neither was the case. Hutson entered the Cardinal game *the week before* at the beginning of the second period, and Bob Monnett threw him a pass on Hutson's very first play from scrimmage. The aerial attempt was incomplete. This wasn't exactly the kind of thing legends are made of.

In years to come, Packer fans everywhere would say, "I was there when Hutson caught his first touchdown pass." All but 13,000 or so of them would be stretching the truth.

The legend about Hutson's first TD reception had its printed beginnings in an article penned by Art Daley in the *Press-Gazette* on December 10, 1942. Daley had only been with the newspaper for a year, having come to Green Bay from the *Fond du Lac Reporter*. Not having been at either game and looking for a good angle on Hutson, Daley looked at newspaper clippings of the Bears-Packers game but not at the Cardinals-Packers game. From an interview with Hutson himself and from talks with sports editor Ray Pagel, Daley got the impression that Hutson's first game in the NFL was against the Bears as neither man gave any indication that Hutson had played against the Cardinals the week before. This minor oversight on their part misled the 25-year-old Daley into believing Hutson's NFL career had gotten off to one spectacular start. He then compounded their faux pas by writing it up in the newspaper. Quite marvelously, Daley added to the growing Hutson mystique and the many legends that pepper the history of the Green Bay Packers.

Lambeau made a bold move the following week when he appointed Michalske and Hubbard as the Packers' line coaches. Until this time, Lambeau had no official helpers. Later he added Blood and Gantenbein as assistants.

For the first time since '32, the New York Giants came calling on the Packers in Green Bay instead of Milwaukee as they had the previous two years. The Packers had a four-game winning streak over New York when they played in the bay city. As John

Walter wrote in the *Press-Gazette*, it was veterans' day — Packer veterans, that is. Hank Bruder ran 65 yards for a third quarter score. Bob Monnett kicked a 17-yard field goal to give Green Bay the lead, 9-6, in the fourth quarter. And Cal Hubbard batted a pass into the air, then caught it for a touchdown that sealed the victory, 16-7, in the late going.

The Packers (2-1-0) were in third place in the Western Division standings behind Detroit (1-0-1) and the Cardinals (1-0-1) who had played the league's first tie since '33. The Bears (1-1-0) found themselves in a strange place — last. Boston (1-0-0) won its first game, downing Brooklyn (0-1-0). Pittsburgh (1-2-0), a loser to the Bears, trailed the Giants (1-1-0). The Eagles (0-2-0) brought up the rear in the East.

Curly Lambeau thought to save his veterans for more important duty against the Cardinals when he started almost every rookie and second year player on his team against the Pirates. Blood and Herber were the only real veterans to start. The ploy paid off that week as the Packers blew out Pittsburgh, 27-0. Hutson gave the fans a look at the future when he caught four passes for 104 yards and two TDs.

The Packers (3-1-0) moved up a notch in the standings as Detroit (1-1-1) lost to Brooklyn (1-1-0). New York (2-1-0) beat Boston (1-1-0) to take over first in the East.

Just as they had in '34, the Packers and Cardinals scheduled three games against each other, playing one in each home city and one in Milwaukee. The Cards had won the first '35 encounter — played in Green Bay — and now it was time to play the Milwaukee affair.

The Packers had a chance to take control of first place, if they could beat the Cardinals. They couldn't do it. Lambeau chose not to attempt field goals on three occasions, and when the game was over, he rued the decisions because Chicago didn't pass up their single opportunity to score. The Cards went back to the Windy City as 3-0 winners.

Although the date of the game was October 14, it was hot in the Cream City that Sunday, and the heat took its toll in weariness that led to several injuries. Johnny Blood suffered a severe concussion in the game and had to be hospitalized. Al Rose, Cal Hubbard, Frank Butler, Herm Schneidman, and Hank Bruder were also hurt. Buckets Goldenberg and Mike Michalske played valiantly, but both had to be removed from the game due to the warm temperature.

Many people who followed the NFL thought the Cardinals (2-0-1) were the luckiest team around. They had two wins over Green Bay (3-2-0) and a tie with Detroit (2-1-1). Both victories could very easily have been ties. The Bears (2-1-0) swamped the Eagles (1-3-0) to move out of the division cellar that week. New York (3-1-0) dumped Brooklyn (1-2-0), and Boston (1-2-0) lost.

The Packers and Lions had split their two games in '34 by identical 3-0 scores. Both teams had essentially the same stars as the year before, so their first tilt of '35 promised to be a low–scoring, hard–fought defensive battle as the Lions made their invasion of State Fair Park in Milwaukee. The 8,500 fans who turned out for the contest saw the Packers rally to win, 13-9, on two field goals by Ade Schwammel and a 25–yard TD run of a punt blocked and recovered by Hutson.

Green Bay (4-2-0) jumped two places in the standings, one over Detroit (2-2-1) and another over the Cardinals (2-1-1), losers to the upstart Pirates (2-4-0). The Bears (3-1-0) beat Brooklyn (1-3-0) to take over first place. New York (4-1-0) whipped Boston (1-3-0) to put more room between themselves and the rest of the Eastern Division.

Sometimes the schedule makers knew what they're doing, especially when the Packers were slated to travel to Wrigley Field to take on the Bears the next week. Green Bay had a chance to be masters of their own fate. Another win over the Monsters of the Midway, coupled with a Cardinals loss or tie, and the Pack could take sole possession of first place.

In recent years, the Bears had stolen victory from the Packers in the late going and won a couple of division titles and one NFL crown, and they almost did it again in their first game of the '35 season. The second encounter would be different.

Ade Schwammel booted a second quarter field goal to give the Pack a 3-0 halftime lead. Then the Bears bounced back in the second half, scoring a TD in each quarter and building a 14-3 lead with only two and a half minutes to play. With the game almost decided, many of the 20,426 paid customers began filing out of the park, but before they could reach their cars or the el-train platform, lightning struck Chicago in the form of Arnie Herber and Don Hutson.

The Bears had just scored to seemingly ice the victory. Manders kicked off, and Hinkle returned it to the Packer 30. Three plays later Herber faded back and fired a pass to Hutson inside the Bear 45 where the fleet-footed end hauled it down, then eluded tackle after tackle as he raced into the end zone. Schwammel added the PAT, and the Packers were in business, trailing by only four points now.

Schwammel kicked off over the goal line, and the Bears took possession on their own 20. On the first play from scrimmage, Chicago fumbled and Ernie Smith recovered for Green Bay on the Bear 13. After a run of one yard and a pass interference penalty on the Bears, the Packers had the ball on the 11 with a new set of downs. George Sauer plowed his way to the three. Hinkle failed to gain on the next play. A field goal wouldn't do. The Pack needed a six-pointer to win. Herber dropped back, saw Hutson racing for the end zone, fired the ball to him, and the "Alabama Antelope", as sports reporter John Torinus called him in the *Press-Gazette* the next day, crashed over the goal line to give Green Bay a 17-14 win in a Hollywood finish.

The Packers (5-2-0) didn't take over first place that week because the Cardinals (3-1-1) pulled off another close win, this one over the Giants (4-2-0) by a 14-13 margin. Pittsburgh (3-4-0) upset Boston (1-4-0) to put pressure on New York, and Brooklyn (2-3-0) downed Philadelphia (1-4-0).

The schedule makers gave the Packers a bonus in '35, an extra home game. As they had in the past, the Green Bay management turned the last home game into a variation of the collegiate homecoming. All week long the merchants put ads in the paper wishing the team luck, and many even decked out their stores in green and gold. There were dinners, and former Green Bay players were paraded for the public to review and to remember. And like college homecomings, the home team responded with lots of good old rah-rah spirit.

The Detroit Lions were the guests of the Packers that first Sunday in November. The Motor City eleven was a tough outfit, and Lambeau figured his boys were in for a real fight. So he prepared his team that week as if they would be playing for the

NFL title. The extra duty paid off because the Packers canned Lion meat that Sunday, 31-7, behind two TDs by Blood and one each by Sauer and Hutson.

By beating Detroit (4-3-1), Green Bay (6-2-0) kept pace with the Cardinals (4-1-1) who were victorious over Philadelphia (2-6-0). The Giants (4-3-0) remained on top in the East, a half game ahead of Brooklyn (4-4-0) and a game in front of Pittsburgh (4-5-0). The Bears (4-2-0) held on to third in the West with a big win over dismal Boston (1-7-0).

Another quirk in the schedule faced the Packers the second week in November. They had played the Lions twice already in Wisconsin, but now it was their turn to visit Michigan. Lambeau was worried all week because Sauer, Bruder, Hinkle, Michalske, Gantenbein, and Butler were all banged up, and their status was day-to-day. This made it hard to practice for the coming game, and when it did come, it showed. Detroit turned the tables on Green Bay, 20-10, behind the brilliant play of Bill Shepherd and Dutch Clark.

Although they lost, the Packers (6-3-0) moved into a tie for first with the Cardinals (4-2-1) who lost to the Bears (5-3-0) that week. The Bruins also lost to New York (5-3-0), the only eastern team to play because the others postponed their games due to rain. The Lions (5-3-1) were suddenly back in the hunt for the division title.

When the Packers headed east for their annual road trip, they traveled not just in first class but also in first place because the Redskins nipped the Cardinals when their postponed contest was played that Tuesday. Filled with confidence, the Pack added Pittsburgh to their list of victims, crushing the improved Pirates, 34-14, as Blood and Sauer each scored a pair of touchdowns and Hinkle added another. Bob Monnett was the rushing and passing star with 92 yards on 12 carries and 106 yards on five completions in nine attempts. Blood also caught four passes good for 78 yards. Amazingly, Green Bay mounted all this offense without Hutson who was in the hospital with appendicitis.

Already in the top spot in the Western Division, Green Bay (7-3-0) gained very little ground. Detroit (5-3-2) and the Bears (5-3-1) fought to a tie, while the Cardinals (5-3-1) beat Boston

(1-8-0). The Giants (6-3-0) moved up to a full game ahead of idle Brooklyn (5-4-0) by beating Philadelphia (2-7-0).

Some United Press International wire service writer wrote that Green Bay had a chance to clinch their division's crown by defeating the Cardinals in their next game because the Lions and Bears were playing each other in Detroit and one of them had to lose or they could tie again, which would be even better for Green Bay. The man was obviously a journalist because he wasn't any good at math. If the Packers won, they would be 8-3-0, and at the very worst, the Bears would be 6-3-1 or the Lions would be 6-3-2. The Packers still wouldn't have a lock on the title because the Bears had two games remaining and the Lions had one. In order to clinch the title, the Packers had to win both of their remaining games, while Detroit and both Chicago teams lost at least once each.

On Thanksgiving Day, the Packers were hoping to make turkeys out of the Cardinals because the Chicago eleven had dumped them twice already that season by the narrowest of margins. They just couldn't do it — not without Hutson who was still ill — as the Cards took another squeaker from them, 9-7, in Chicago.

At the same time, the Lions (6-3-2) beat the Bears (5-4-1) to move ahead of the Packers (7-4-0) into a tie with the Cardinals (6-3-1). The Giants (7-3-0) beat Brooklyn (5-5-0) to clinch a tie for the Eastern Division championship.

On the following Sunday, Detroit (7-3-2) clinched at least a tie for the Western crown by whipping the Dodgers (5-6-0), while the Cards (6-3-2) and Bears (5-4-2) fought to a 7-7 tie. The Lions' victory eliminated the Bears and the Packers from contention, and the Giants (8-3-0) sewed up the East.

While most pro football fans waited for the outcome of the Bears-Cardinals game in Chicago, the Packers played their last game of the season, coming from behind to beat the Eagles, 13-6, in Philadelphia. Hinkle was the game star by scoring a touchdown, kicking a field goal and a PAT, and rushing for 81 yards on just 12 attempts.

When the Bears (6-4-2) dumped the Cards (6-4-2) on the last Sunday of the regular schedule, the Packers (8-4-0) moved back into second place and the Lions became division champs for the first time ever. Detroit went on to defeat the Giants for the NFL title the following week, bringing the league crown back to the West.

Looking back over the season, Lambeau saw several bright spots ahead for 1936 and he was reminded of an earlier campaign. The Pack had played well in 1928 only to finish just a shade out of the money. Lambeau had known then that all he needed to get the Packers to the top of the NFL was a few key people. For '36, he knew he needed just a few more good men — and a healthy Don Hutson for the whole season.

§ § §

9

A New System, A New Title

Nothing will ruin fan interest in a professional sports league quicker than the continued inequity among the competing franchises. This was witnessed in the early days of Major League Baseball when the Chicago White Stockings dominated the National League's early going by winning six titles in 11 years. Only one other franchise that began that era survived it, and only two other franchises that came into existence then lived into the 20th Century.

Comparably, pro football had the same sort of attrition during the 1920s. The Chicago Bears, Chicago Cardinals, and Green Bay Packers were the only three franchises that began their lives in the National Football League before 1925 to survive into the 1930s and beyond in the same cities and with the same basic organizations. The New York Giants joined the NFL in 1925 and became one of the elite in a short time. During the 11 years from 1925 thru 1935, the Packers won three titles, the Bears won two, and the Giants two. The Cardinals also won a championship (1925), but they weren't the force that the other three teams were during this period. As if this weren't enough to show their domination, the Giants won their division the first three years after the NFL moguls divided the teams into east and west, and the Bears won the Western Division twice. As further evidence of their mastery of the NFL, the Bears, Giants, and Packers had only one sub–.500 season each during this time.

This trio of franchises also dominated at the box office. Green Bay's best drawing cards were the Bears and the Giants, while the Packers and Bears were New York's best and the Packers and Giants were Chicago's best. In fact, those three teams were the best draws all over the league. There was nothing wrong with that, but the rest of the teams couldn't just play those three.

Because the Bears, Giants, and Packers had the best attendance figures in the NFL, both at home and on the road, they could afford to pay the highest salaries and thus hire the best players and coaches. This perpetuated the status quo of each of them being on top, or near it, year after year, which perpetuated their continued success at the box office at the expense of the other franchises. The National Football League could never be taken seriously outside of New York, Chicago, and Green Bay as long other teams kept coming into the league, playing two or three seasons, then folding and fading away into history.

Also, the league was faced with another problem that could prove ruinous to it. With improving attendance and revenues, players were demanding and getting higher salaries, and college prospects, as free agents, were selling their services to the highest bidder. For example, several teams tried to sign Stanley Kostka, the 1934 Minnesota star, and in the process, the price for signing him was run totally out of proportion for an untried rookie. Don Hutson had also been a player up for auction between the Packers and the Dodgers. If not for a failure in communications, the bidding for his services might have escalated far beyond the $175 a game he was paid.

Something had to be done.

The NFL magnates met in Philadelphia on February 8-9, 1936 to prepare the coming year's schedule and conduct any other pertinent business. Bert Bell, owner of the Philadelphia Eagles, made a solid proposal that the league do something about balancing the talent among the teams. A discussion was held and a plan that was primarily Bell's was adopted. As *The Green Bay Press-Gazette* reported it:

"In its new plan for selection of college prospects, the league ruled that hereafter, at the end of the regulation season, each club owner will submit the names of eight college prospects. The 72 names will be listed, and the tail-end club of the league will have first call on any one of the candidates.

"Under this system, the last place club will have first chance to establish negotiations with up-coming players without interference from other teams. This selection will be followed by each club having a choice in the reverse order of the standing of the clubs at the close of the season."

It didn't exactly work out that way. Each team providing the names of eight players as top prospects was a system that couldn't possibly have worked because more than one team could and probably would list some of the same players. For example, everyone's top player of the 1935 collegiate season was Jay Berwanger, the University of Chicago's one-man team and the recipient of the first Heisman Trophy. Berwanger was bound to top everyone's list.

To prevent this sort of confusion, Tim Mara, owner of the Giants, brought a lengthy list of the nation's top graduating players from the 1935 season to a later meeting. It was from this roster of prospects that the very first NFL draft was made. Bert Bell, by virtue of his Eagles finishing last in the Eastern Division with the worst record of any team in the entire league, was given first selection, and naturally, he took Berwanger. Boston had second choice, and George Marshall chose Riley Smith, quarterback, Alabama.

The Packers had the eighth pick, and Lambeau chose Russ Letlow, guard, San Francisco. In eight subsequent rounds, Lambeau picked, in turn, Bob Wheeler, tackle, Oklahoma; Bernard Scherer, end, Nebraska; Theron Ward, back, Idaho; Darrell Lester, center, TCU; Bob Reynolds, tackle, Stanford; Wally Fromhart, quarterback, Notre Dame; Wally Cruice, halfback, Northwestern; and J.C. "Iron Man" Wetzel, SMU.

Picking was one thing; signing quite another. Some of these players had never even heard of Green Bay, Wisconsin, not to mention the Packers. Lambeau had his work cut out for him.

The Packer mentor was able to sign Letlow immediately after the draft. The Chicago Cardinals had signed the San Francisco guard to a contract prior to the draft, but the agreement was voided when Charlie Bidwill didn't name Letlow as his first choice and Lambeau did.

Bert Bell, who originated the draft, thought he would have a clear road to land the services of Jay Berwanger, but when Berwanger demanded $1,000 a game to play for the Eagles, Bell told him what he could do with that idea. Halas tried to get the rights to Berwanger, but it did him no good as Berwanger continued to demand the exorbitant salary. The NFL magnates refused to give in to such outrageous demands, so Berwanger went unsigned.

As was becoming his usual mode of operation, Curly Lambeau headed west after the '35 season to take in the East-West Shrine all-star game in San Francisco and get a good look at the latest crop of college stars. This year would be a little different because the Packers would be joining him in January for a few exhibition games against the Detroit Lions and assorted all-star aggregations from the California area.

Lambeau used this time for scouting and as a sort of spring practice where he could have a better look at the younger men on his squad who hadn't played much during the regular season. It was also a time for the Packers to work on a new passing attack built around the team's leading scorer, fleet-footed end Don Hutson who had snared seven TD passes during the regular season and had tallied 43 points. The coach didn't need to see Hutson in action to know that the Alabama Flash would be around for a long time, but he did want to take another look at George Sauer, Herm Schneidman, Ernie Smith, George Svendsen, Bob Tener, and a few others and see if they still fit into his plans for '36.

The Packers played a local pro team called the Hollywood Light Horsemen, sponsored by that great character actor, Victor McLaglen, in San Diego for their first contest of the tour. Except for the opening kickoff which Cotton Warburton ran back 93 yards for a TD, the Light Horsemen weren't much competition as the Packers won in a cake walk, 61-7. The Pacific Coast All-Stars were much better than the Hollywood eleven as the Packers only beat them, 24-14. Then the Pack played the NFL champion Detroit Lions for charity and lost, 10-3. Lambeau had seen enough, and instead of taking the team to Hawaii for another contest or two, he sent the players home for the off season.

Off the field that year, the Green Bay Packers, Inc., put up with a minor annoyance but nothing that a clever lawyer like Jerry Clifford couldn't handle.

Larry Bettencourt, who had played several games with the

Packers in '33, attached $1,000 of the gate of one game played by the Packers in California, alleging that $800 was due to him for back pay. Bettencourt's claim was made against the former corporation but could be passed on to the new concern. Clifford informed the California court where the case was instigated that the Packer players were playing the games with the corporation's permission but not with its sponsorship, that all profits from the games were to go to the players and not to the Green Bay Packers, Inc. Bettencourt's claim was subsequently denied, and the funds that were tied up in court were released.

Before the first draft, Lambeau traded Roger Grove to Brooklyn for end Wayland Becker and guard Bill Croft*. Becker hailed from Green Bay and had graduated from East High. He then went to Marquette where he was a standout performer. George Halas signed him, then loaned him to the Dodgers for cash, then sold him later to Brooklyn. Croft had played his college ball at Utah and had one year of experience in the NFL.

After signing Letlow, Lambeau went after his other draft choices and some free agents. The first man to ink a contract was Tony Paulekas, a center from Washington & Jefferson. Paulekas was recommended to Lambeau by his coach, NFL Hall of Famer Fats Henry, which was good enough for the Packer mentor.

Next to sign was third round draft choice Bernie Scherer, the tough end who had been George Sauer's teammate at Nebraska. Then free agent Paul Miller, a speedy back from South Dakota State, mailed in his contract. As training camp approached, Cal Clemmens from USC and Harry Mattos from St. Mary's, both backs, joined the Packers. The last newcomer to the '36 squad was another free agent, Lou Gordon, a tackle out of Illinois.

The biggest addition of all to the organization was the hiring of a full-time assistant coach for Lambeau. The man he chose for the job was Richard "Red" Smith, the former Packer

---

* Bill Croft is not to be confused with Milburn Croft who played for the Packers in the '40s.

player from Kaukauna.

A host of veterans returned to Green Bay that year. Al Rose, Champ Seibold, Frank Butler, Hank Bruder, Bob Monnett, Joe Laws, Clarke Hinkle, Don Hutson, Milt Gantenbein, Ernie Smith, Tar Schwammel, Tiny Engebretsen, Walt Kiesling, Lon Evans, George Svendsen, Herm Schneidman, Swede Johnston, George Sauer, Buckets Goldenberg, and Arnie Herber.

Among the missing when camp opened were Cal Hubbard, Mike Michalske, Johnny Blood, Claude Perry, and Nate Barragar. Back in April, an announcement was made by Henry W. Clark, director of athletics at Lafayette College in Pennsylvania, that Michalske had been appointed varsity basketball coach and assistant football coach. Hubbard finally got his appointment as an umpire for the American League, and Perry had jumped to the new American Football League Pittsburgh Americans being coached by former Packer Rudy Comstock. Barragar retired, and Blood was a holdout, although Lambeau wasn't saying so.

The Packers routed the semi-pro Madison Cardinals, 62-0, in their only tune-up game of the summer.

With roster limits raised to 25 for the season, Lambeau felt he could depend a little more on his bench in '36 and could maneuver his troops a little better. It certainly paid off in the opening contest of the campaign when the Packers came back from a 7-0 halftime deficit to defeat the Chicago Cards, 10-7, in Green Bay, on a fourth quarter field goal by Ernie Smith.

The Bears were the next opponent due into City Stadium, and the Monsters of the Midway came in roaring. Chicago scored in every quarter to slam the Packers, 30-3, before a crowd of over 14,000 disappointed Packer fans.

Lambeau made a few roster moves during the following week. First, he released five-year veteran Al Rose and two rookies. Then came the big surprise. The coach met Johnny Blood's salary demands and signed the holdout halfback to a contract. As an added bonus, the Packers had the week off from the NFL wars.

Blood didn't play in the next scheduled game, but just having him around put new life into the team. The Cardinals met the Pack in Milwaukee on the first Sunday in October, and the result was the same as the opening game of the season. Green Bay downed Chicago, 24-0, as Johnston, Hinkle, and Laws scored touchdowns.

The standings after four weeks of play had the Bears (3-0-0) in first, Detroit (1-0-0) in second, the Packers (2-1-0) in third, and the winless Cardinals (0-3-0) in last in the Western Division. In the East, the surprising Pittsburgh Pirates (3-1-0) were on top with the Redskins (2-2-0) in second, Brooklyn (1-2-0) and New York (1-2-0) tied for third, and Philadelphia (1-3-0) bringing up the rear.

Buckets Goldenberg was healthy again and Johnny Blood was ready to play when the Redskins came into Green Bay looking for Packer scalps. The Packers were well prepared for Boston. The two teams threw a total of 60 passes, and 24 were completed. The difference came when three Green Bay aerials ended up as touchdowns in the hands of Don Hutson, Blood, and Paul Miller, tossed respectively by Arnie Herber, Bob Monnett, and Joe Laws. Green Bay's fourth TD was scored by Bernie Scherer when he returned an interception 60 yards. Ernie Smith added a field goal and two PATs as the Packers stuffed the Redskins, 31-2, to remain a game behind the Bears.

Cal Hubbard visited Green Bay the following week. Although the *Press-Gazette* didn't say so, Hubbard came to join the team, but Lambeau told him he wasn't needed and released him. Hubbard went to Pittsburgh and signed on with the Pirates.

In another strategy move, Lambeau moved Goldenberg from the backfield to the line. Buckets had been a blocking back and a short yardage ball carrier throughout his career, so when Lambeau needed help at guard, it was only natural that Goldenberg should be the man to move.

The NFL champion Detroit Lions were next into City Stadium to face the Packers. The Lions were just as powerful as ever, and Lambeau had good reason to fear the champs. The *Press-Gazette*'s John Walter promised it would be a great game, and he proved to be quite a prognosticator. The Packers built up a 10-0 lead at the half on a Tiny Engebretsen field goal and a TD pass from Herber to Gantenbein. Detroit closed the gap to

10-9 in the third period, then took the lead, 15-10, early in the fourth. Herber hit Blood with another scoring toss minutes later, and the Pack led, 17-15. Dutch Clark dropkicked a field goal to put the Lions on top again, but Engebretsen booted the game winning field goal from 18 yards out to give Green Bay a dramatic 20-18 victory.

The win moved Green Bay (4-1-0) ahead of Detroit (3-1-0) in the standings but left the Packers a game behind the Bears (5-0-0). Pittsburgh (4-2-0) continued to lead the East, but Boston (3-3-0) and New York (2-2-1) were closing in on the Pirates.

Since coming into the league in '33, the Pittsburgh Pirates had faced the Packers three times. They failed to score in the first two tilts and managed 14 points in the third. They were supposed to be a much improved team in '36. They weren't improved enough as the Packers demolished them again, 42-10, behind two touchdowns each by Miller and Hutson and one each by Blood and Laws.

The Green Bay (5-1-0) win knocked the Pirates (4-3-0) out of first in the East and set up a showdown with the undefeated Bears (6-0-0) for first in the West.

The NFL's brand of professional football was becoming very popular in Chicago, especially when the Bears played the Packers at Wrigley Field. The best house yet to attend a Packers–Bears game turned out on the first of November and saw another bruising affair. Most of the 31,364 spectators on hand roared their approval as the Bears ran up 10 first quarter points on a Bill Hewitt touchdown and a PAT and field goal by Jack Manders. Then the cadre of loyal Packer fans in the stadium got their chance to do some yelling in the second period when Hutson and Hinkle crossed the goal line and Tiny Engebretsen and Ernie Smith added the extra points to give the Pack a 14-10 halftime lead. In the second half, the Green Bay defense turned back the Bears on every possession and finally forced a turnover late in the game. Milt Gantenbein picked up a loose ball on the Chicago 40 and ran it down to the two before being stopped. Then George Sauer banged around the Bears' left end for a TD to ice the win, 21-10.

The story of this game wouldn't be complete without re–

peating a column by Lloyd Lewis of *The Chicago Daily News*:

"While the blanketed Bears on their bench watched the enemy players out on the field during the 21 to 10 defeat at the hands of the Green Bay Packers, a little nest of their assistant coaches spent most of the time peering under their palms at a large, fattish man in a brown hat, yellow sweater and dark overcoat who was giving imitations on the north end of the Packers' bench.

"Tarzan Taylor, Marquette's line coach, who was Manager George Halas' guest on the Bears' bench, started the group watching the man in the brown hat.

" 'He's Red Smith, assistant coach up there,' he said decisively.

"At that moment Mr. Richard Smith, as he is more formally known, was looking out into the field where his men were making one of their marches. He was taking off Napoleon Bonaparte, anyone could tell that. Not Napoleon standing up, looking on the sad and solemn sea from the cliffs of St. Helena, but the one of Napoleon sitting down, one hand on his bosom, a scowl upon his face, making up his mind to divorce Josephine.

"Mr. Red Smith wasn't able to get his hand in his vest, because he had a sweater on, but he laid it across his stomach and achieved what I thought was a pretty good imitation, everything considered.

"Out on the field, muddy Mr. Bruder, the Green Bay quarterback, was admiring Mr. Smith's mimicry, too, and with it in mind, ducked into a huddle and came out calling a play which was quite a surprise to the Bears. A special kind of reverse play it was, one that sucked in even so astute an end as Mr. William Hewitt of the Chicago team.

"As the scattered players picked themselves up and followed the ball down some nineteen yards, where the Packers' Mr. Miller had at last been downed, Mr. Red Smith shifted himself on the Green Bay bench and went into another impersonation. He took his right knee in both arms, rocked it tenderly and looked wistful.

" 'This one is harder,' mumbled Halas as he leaned forward, squinting painfully.

" 'It's Lillian Gish, ain't it?' said Tarzan Taylor, his fists white with gripping. 'He's doing Lillian Gish from 'Intolerance' or something.'

"Quarterback Bruder turned his eyes from Smith and called signals which prompted his halfback, Herber, to throw a pass to his end, Hutson. The ball was now very close to the Bears' goal, and the substitutes were howling for their fellows to hold that line. But the board of strategy, still as death, bent its eyes again on Red Smith to see what he would do next.

"That artist leaned forward, almost rose from the bench, placed a hand on each knee, lifted up his chin and smiled. It was quite a large smile, and he held it a long time, long enough for Quarterback Bruder to admire it thoroughly before Green Bay went into the huddle again.

" 'I know,' said one of Halas' scouts, whispering to Taylor. 'I know. Don't tell me.'

" 'Tell you, hell,' said Taylor. 'That's Shirley Temple — '

" 'And a reverse around right end,' gritted Halas as he ran out onto the field roaring into the officials' ears a demand that they make the Packers quit their illegal coaching from the bench. The shocked officials went over and laid down the law to Head Coach Lambeau, while Red Smith looked innocently and patiently into the distance.

" 'I get it,' said one of Halas' helpers. 'Now he's Bruno Hauptmann.'

"In the latter part of the game, Mr. Smith stood up, took a lapel in each hand and looked very full of forgiveness. It must have been something in the nobility of that pose that fired the Packers, for they responded by sending three backs into the Chicago line, while the fourth back, Mr. Sauer, stole stealthily out to the right and ran in where Mr. Hewitt had lately been, and so traveled on to a touchdown — the enemy's third of the afternoon.

"While the screams of some 30,000 people came up, Mr. Taylor still stared across the field at the statuesque Mr. Smith.

" 'I know,' he concluded triumphantly, 'it's Lincoln.'

" 'It's the ball game,' sighed the tragic Mr. Halas, pointing at the clock."

Coaching from the sidelines was still illegal. The men on the field had to call the plays, and a new man into the game couldn't talk in the huddle until the second play he was in. Lewis was trying to point out that the Packers had cheated and that everyone in the stadium knew it except the officials who would have had a tough time proving it anyway.

Lambeau, Smith, and the Packers put a new wrinkle in the game of football with their signals from the sidelines. It soon became quite evident that the officials wouldn't be able to properly enforce the rule banning such sideline coaching, but it was a long time before the rules committee legalized the system.

By defeating the previously unbeaten Bears (6-1-0), the Packers (6-1-0) moved into a tie for first. Detroit (3-3-0) slid out of the title of picture a bit by losing to New York (4-2-1), the Eastern Division's leaders over Pittsburgh (5-3-0) and Boston (4-3-0).

Now it was time to head east, and the Packers made their first stop in Boston where they faced the revitalized Redskins. The Redskins held the Packers scoreless in the first half and took a 3-0 lead into the locker room. Then Herber hit Hutson with a short pass for a touchdown in the early going of the third period before the rain started. That was all the scoring as the Packers won, 7-3, in front of a sparse crowd.

While Green Bay (7-1-0) was beating Boston (4-4-0), the Bears (7-1-0) were slamming the Giants (4-3-1) and Detroit (4-3-0) was whipping Eastern Division leading Pittsburgh (6-4-0), winners over Philadelphia earlier in the week.

Lambeau had made several trips into New York by 1936, and many of them proved unsuccessful. He claimed the lure of the city lights fouled his players' minds and prevented them from concentrating on their purpose for being there. To save them from being vamped by the Big Apple, Lambeau quartered them at the Blue Hills Country Club in Orangeburg, New York, 40 miles from Broadway, where he drilled them for the coming game against the Dodgers at Ebbetts Field. The stay at the country club didn't last because the players grumbled about there being nothing to do when they weren't practicing. Lambeau gave in and moved them back to New York.

Brooklyn had never had a team of championship caliber, and the '36 version of the Dodgers was less than spectacular as well. With a crowd of 22,000 looking on, the Packers thoroughly demolished the Flatbushers, 38-7. Don Hutson caught two TD passes, and Clarke Hinkle, Joe Laws, and Wayland Becker also tacked up six–pointers.

The Bears (8-1-0) won again, swamping the Redskins (4-5-0), remaining tied with the Packers (8-1-0) for first in the West. In the East, Pittsburgh (6-5-0) remained on top in spite of losing to the Cardinals (2-7-0) because the Giants (4-4-1) were shut out by Detroit (5-3-0).

With the Packers due to play the Giants next, the New York scribes inundated the Green Bay contingent with questions for their papers. Lambeau warned his crew to guard against having their heads turned by all the attention they were getting from the press and told them the Giants would be gunning for them, especially since the Lions had thoroughly thrashed them, 38-0, in Detroit. The Packers had won eight of their 14 previous meetings with the Giants, but the Green Bay coach said the past meant nothing. If the Packers had any hopes of a title, they had to beat the Giants, and that meant checking Tuffy Leemans' ground gaining and keeping Mel Hein and Cal Hubbard — oh, yes, the same Cal Hubbard who had spent several seasons with the Pack was now with the Giants — out of the Green Bay backfield. Also, they would have to get the ball to Hutson who was on the verge of breaking New York's Tod Goodwin's pass–catching record of 26 receptions in a season.

When game Sunday arrived, inclement weather kept the crowd down to 20,000, which was just as well for the Giants. Ernie Smith booted a field goal in the first quarter to give the Packers the early lead, 3-0, and that was all the scoring in the half. On their first possession of the second half, Hinkle went over from two yards out and Smith converted to put Green Bay up, 10-0. After an exchange of punts, Herber hit Schneidman with a 60–yard scoring toss and Smith kicked another PAT to pad the Packers' lead, 17-0. The Giants were hardly dead as they scored before the stanza ended to cut the score to 17-7. Then New York closed the gap to 17-14 early in the final period. The Green Bay defense rose to the occasion at this point and blocked a punt into the end zone which the Giants recovered for a safety, making the score 19-14. With the clock winding down, Hank Bruder intercepted a New York pass and returned it to the Giants' 20. Three plays later George Sauer put the lid on the victory by racing in from 16 yards out. Smith converted to make the final score, 26-14.

While the Packers (9-1-0) were fighting it out in New York (4-5-1), the Bears (9-1-0) had a cakewalk in Philadelphia (1-10-0). Boston (5-5-0) picked up a half game on idle Pittsburgh (6-5-0) in the East by eliminating Brooklyn (2-6-1) from contention. Detroit (6-3-0) kept its slim title hopes alive by downing the Cardinals (2-8-0).

The Packers spent Thanksgiving Day in Detroit, but instead of playing football, they watched the Bears (9-2-0) take it on the chin from the Lions (7-3-0). At the same time, the Giants (5-5-1) were putting themselves back in the running in the East by downing Brooklyn (2-7-1).

With just two days of rest, the Lions then played hosts to the Packers on Sunday. A large crowd of 22,000 turned out at Titan Stadium to watch the Western Division rivals fight it out. And fight they did. The Packers drew first blood on a Don Hutson TD, but the Lions came back to tie it, 7-7, on a Dutch Clark slice through the line. Then Hinkle put up six on a three-yard plunge, but Detroit tied it again, 14-14, early in the second quarter on a Bill Shepherd pass interception. Green Bay made the halftime score, 20-14, when Ernie Smith forced a fumble that Hutson picked up and ran back 28 yards for a touchdown. Smith missed the extra point, his first miscue of the season. The second half was almost anticlimactic as Tiny Engebretsen kicked one field goal in the third period to move the Pack ahead, 23-14, only to have Clark bring Detroit back to 23-17 with a dropkick. Smith put the final points on the board with a late three-pointer to make the end result, 26-17.

The win over Detroit (7-4-0) eliminated the Lions and gave the Packers (10-1-0) at least a share of the Western Division crown. If that wasn't enough to excite the Green Bay boys, then news that the Cardinals (3-8-0) had upset their crosstown rivals was. Many of the Packers were in their hotel rooms cleaning up after the game when word came that the Bears (9-3-0) had lost their final game of the season, making Green Bay the city of champions once again.

Green Bay had one more regular season game to play, but the tilt with the Cardinals was of little significance. Lambeau used it as a practice for his substitutes, while resting his first line players most of the game. Bitter cold had settled over Chicago after a few days of rain, making the playing conditions at Wrigley Field less than ideal. Both teams slopped through 60 minutes of football, each attempting just one field goal and missing it, as they played to a scoreless tie.

Lambeau and his players had their sights set on what was happening in the East that weekend. The Sunday before Boston (6-5-0) took over first place by eliminating Pittsburgh (6-6-0), while the Giants (5-5-1) had the week off. The schedule makers must have had a crystal ball when they made up the '36 slate of games because the Redskins' victory set up a showdown for the division title on the final day of the campaign between Boston and New York at the Polo Grounds. In the rain and mud, the Redskins took the Eastern Division crown, 14-0, and earned the right to play the Packers for the NFL championship.

With sub-freezing temperatures a daily occurence in Wisconsin at that time of year, Lambeau took his team east to train for the title tilt that was being held at the Polo Grounds in New York because George Marshall was angered by the lack of support for his Redskins from the fans and newspapers in Boston. The players were put up at the Victoria Hotel in Manhattan, and they were given use of the Polo Grounds as a practice field as long as they stayed in the area beyond the goal posts. Since this proved inadequate, Lambeau moved the team drills to Central Park.

When game Sunday arrived, the sun shone through on a field that had suffered from three straight days of rain. It was not an easy track, but the runners made the most of it all the same. The official attendance was 29,543, and gate receipts were reported as being $33,471, which meant a lot of folks got in free.

The Packers scored first in typical Green Bay fashion. Boston fumbled a lateral pass, and the Packers recovered it on their own 46. After Sauer gained three yards and Hinkle one, Herber hit Hutson with the bomb for six points, and Smith converted the PAT to give Green Bay an early 7-0 lead. Boston closed the gap to 7-6 at halftime, but the Packers took command in the third period. Green Bay took the opening kickoff and marched 74 yards up the field to score, the drive culminating with a five-yard TD pass from Herber to Gantenbein. Engebretsen made the PAT, and the Packers were ahead, 14-6. The score stayed this way until early in the final period when the Pack blocked a Boston punt and Hinkle recovered it on the Redskins' three. Two plays later Bob Monnett swept around right end for the score. Smith put Green Bay's final point through the uprights, and the lead was now 21-6. For the remainder of the contest, Boston coach Ray Flaherty pulled every play out of his bag of tricks, but nothing worked to any degree of success as the Packers held on to win the game and their fourth NFL title in eight years.

After winning it all, the Packer players were as proud as peacocks and just as haughty. Lon Evans got hold of the game ball and began running all over New York getting autographs signed on it. He barged into the studios of the National Broadcasting Company and came away with such signatures as those of comedian Parkyakarkas, Eddie Cantor, Kate Smith, and Walter Winchell. Evans kept up an autograph–a–minute pace until he collared one "radio star" coming out of a broadcasting room.

"What program do you sing on?" demanded Evans.

"Give me that football," replied the other, reaching for a fountain pen.

And he signed: "J. Edgar Hoover."

After returning to Green Bay and being showered with accolades and presents at the victory banquet, Lambeau summed up the '36 season in two simple paragraphs:

"Every man was working all the time. Can you imagine an extended professional football trip during which every man was in bed at 11:30 and no player broke training so far as to take a glass of beer?

"We had it. These Packers, the new champions, are as fine a squad of men as ever represented any city. They have been marvelous — not only on the football field, when they came back after a crushing defeat to win the national title, but in their everyday relations toward their work, their coaches and the city they repesent."

§ § §

10

To Repeat Or Not To Repeat

Repeating as champion is the hardest thing for any team or individual athlete in any sport to do the season following a championship year. This didn't seem so difficult to the '29 Packers or the '30 Packers, but by 1936 times were changing in the National Football League.

Curly Lambeau started his quest for a second straight NFL title the day before the Packers won the '36 crown. That was the day the second draft of college players was held in New York. Ed Jankowski, a fullback in the cut of Buckets Goldenberg and from the same college, Wisconsin, was Lambeau's first choice. In succession, the Packer mentor picked Averell Daniell, tackle, Pittsburgh; Bud Wilkinson, quarterback, Minnesota; Earl Svendsen, center, Minnesota; Irish Gavan, tackle, Holy Cross; Merle Wendt, end, Ohio State; Dick Dahlgren, guard, Michigan State; Dick Chapman, tackle, Tulsa; Baldy Baldwin, guard, Louisiana State; and De Witt Gibson, tackle, Northwestern. Of these 10, Lambeau was only able to sign three — Jankowski, Daniell, and Svendsen — which was one better than the year before when he contracted just two of his draft choices. Jankowski already had a Wisconsin connection and was a Packer fan. Svendsen was the younger brother of Packer center George Svendsen. And Daniell just liked to play football and was willing to accept money to play.

The most famous of the men on the '36 draft list turned out to be Bud Wilkinson, the same Bud Wilkinson who became one of the greatest coaches in the history of college football when he was the mastermind of the Oklahoma Sooners in the 1940s and 1950s. Wilkinson opted to take an assistant coaching job at Syracuse instead of playing for the Packers.

As the year 1936 wound down, the honors for the champion

Packers came pouring in. To start with, Don Hutson received his due for setting a new pass reception record when he hauled in 34 aerials during the season good for 526 yards. Hutson, Lon Evans, Ernie Smith, and Clarke Hinkle were selected to the NFL All-Star team. Hutson led the league in TDs with nine. In only two years, the Alabama Flash had become the fifth all-time scorer in Packer history behind Verne Lewellen, Johnny Blood, Clarke Hinkle, and his coach, Curly Lambeau. Hinkle had only advanced to third that same season.

With the championship trophy all locked up in Green Bay, Curly Lambeau headed west on his annual scouting trip to California, while Red Smith took the team to Denver for an exhibition game against the Brooklyn Dodgers. The Packers beat the Dodgers, 21-13, on January 2, then headed to California to join Lambeau and play a few more charity games. The first of these was against the Salinas Iceberg (Lettuce) Packers, which the Green Bay Packers demolished, 42-7. Then with Victor McLaglen and famed jazz singer Al Jolson sitting on their bench, the Packers faced the Los Angeles Bulldogs, a prospective member of the NFL. The Bulldogs had beaten NFL elevens from Pittsburgh, Philadelphia, and Chicago — the Cardinals; had tied Brooklyn, and had lost a narrow 7-0 decision to the Bears. The Packers held up the NFL's honor and mauled the Dogs, 49-0. An exhibition with the Bears was staged next in Los Angeles, and it ended in a tie, 20-20. In a rematch a week later, the Packers nipped the Bruins, 17-14.

The first tussle with the Bears was no mere exhibition of football. Arnie Herber was forced to leave the game with a broken nose that he said was the result of a punch from a Bear lineman. Which Bear, he didn't say. Clarke Hinkle went *Bear hunting* along the Chicago sideline in defense of his teammate, but none of the Monsters of the Midway wanted anything to do with Hinkle. Later in the game, Green Bay tackle Lou Gordon and Chicago back Beattie Feathers squared off in a mismatch of fisticuffs. Gordon had 60 pounds and a few inches on Feathers. To even things up a bit, Chicago lineman Joe Stydahar left the Bears' bench and took a poke at Gordon. Fortunately, he missed. That night, several Packers went hunting for Luke Johnsos, believing he was the culprit who had broken Herber's nose. There was blood in their eyes as they checked out every night club in town looking for the Bear end who was in his hotel room reading a book as he told Jim Ford some years later. The real villain had been Joe Stydahar.

Lambeau really liked Hollywood, and Hollywood liked him. He *rented* the Packers to MGM Studios to make a Pete Smith short about professional football in general and the Packers and Green Bay in particular. Of course, the players were paid for appearing in the film, which was an added bonus to the $650 each of them earned from the barnstorming tour.

At the league meeting in February, the formal approval of the shift of the Redskins from Boston to Washington by owner George Marshall was approved, then the moguls discussed the subject of expansion. The Cleveland Rams, recently of the American Football League and owned by Homer Marshman, applied for admittance to the NFL, and petitions were also received from representatives of clubs in Boston, Buffalo, and Minneapolis. President Joe Carr expected to receive an application from a Los Angeles group, but none was presented. The owners were looking for a team in the West, so Boston and Buffalo were set aside for that reason alone. Minneapolis was also tabled because it was felt Cleveland had a larger population base from which to draw fans and the Rams were an established team, albeit an AFL squad. The Rams were accepted into the NFL and placed in the Western Division.

The schedule was then made up. To begin with, the season was shortened by one game from 12 to 11. This was done in hopes that the title game in December could be played in better weather. Then a regular formula for devising the schedule each year was agreed upon. For '37, each team would play the other teams in its own division twice and would play three teams from the other division once. This would make divisional games more meaningful.

Lambeau felt an urgency about signing his regulars as well as the college stars he had drafted and any free agent college players that might be available throughout the spring and summer of '37. In the first place, the Packers were NFL champs, and this meant they had the privilege of playing the College All-Stars in Arch Ward's benefit game in Chicago in late August. Secondly, an earlier than ever start to summer practice was called for, which would be a hardship on some of his players because their off-season jobs would be cut short, making Lambeau's task all the more difficult.

The coach signed his first free agent Ray Peterson, a back out of San Francisco, in January. After losing Bud Wilkinson to the college coaching ranks, Lambeau signed Carl Mulleneaux, a big end from Utah and the brother of Lee Mulleneaux who had been playing in the NFL for the past five seasons with the Giants, Cincinnati, St. Louis, and Pittsburgh. Lyle Sturgeon, a tackle from North Dakota State, came to terms with Lambeau in early spring. Lambeau had been unable to sign his fifth round choice of the year before, but Darrell Lester, the center from TCU, inked a Green Bay contract for '37 in early May. In June, the coach dug into the ranks of the smallest colleges and came up with Herbert C. Banet, a quarterback from Manchester College in Indiana. Francis "Zud" Schammel graduated from Iowa in '34 and had spurned pro football to be an assistant coach at his alma mater, but Lambeau convinced him that playing guard for the '37 Packers wasn't a bad thing.

Returning from the '36 team were Wayland Becker, Milt Gantenbein, Don Hutson, Bernie Scherer, Lou Gordon, Champ Seibold, Ernie Smith, Paul Engebretsen, Lon Evans, Buckets Goldenberg, Russ Letlow, Frank Butler, George Svendsen, Hank Bruder, Arnie Herber, Clarke Hinkle, Joe Laws, Swede Johnston, Paul Miller, Bob Monnett, and Herm Schneidman. Also returning to the Packer fold was one August "Iron Mike" Michalske. But gone was the Vagabond Halfback, Johnny Blood, who had signed to play and coach for the Pittsburgh Pirates. For an assistant, Blood took along Walt Kiesling, the big tackle who had played the last two years with the Packers.

Since the whole football world would be watching the College All-Star Game, Lambeau really wanted to showcase his Packers. In the spring, he ordered new uniforms for the team that would outfit them in a "style becoming to national champions." The jerseys featured a myrtle green body and 10-inch gold letters fore and aft. The helmets and pants were gold, and the socks were to be myrtle green. The colors were fine, it was felt all around, because it was about time someone put some green in the uniforms of the *Green* Bay Packers. It was the material that was the problem. The jerseys and pants were made of jockey satin. The fabric didn't "breathe" well; that is, it didn't allow air to pass through it.

Curly Lambeau never took an opponent lightly, no matter who that team might be. The College All-Stars were no exception. He prepared the Packers for their game in Chicago as if they were playing for the national title. He worked them into shape with two-a-day drills that became one-a-day and one-a-night the week before the contest was scheduled to be played. When the night of the game arrived, Lambeau had his players in fine physical condition, but he wasn't positive about their mental attitude. As John Walter put it in the *Press-Gazette*, the Packers "looked like a beaten team" from the onset. Walter didn't blame anything or anyone for the lack of spirited play, but he could have pointed the finger at Green Bay's new uniforms. The temperature and humidity at Soldier Field were both in the 80s at the kickoff. Although they looked very pretty when they took the field for their pre-game exercises, all the Packers were already suffering from the heat when the game began. A crowd of 84,560 watched the NFL champs wither as the evening wore on, then go down to defeat, 6-0.

Back in Green Bay, other matters were afoot. With prosperity now everywhere, including the NFL, the officers and executive committee of the Green Bay Packers, Inc., showed their enthusiasm for the economy by adding 5,000 seats to City Stadium and by building a new practice field for the team at the east end of East High School. The older part of the stadium was given a fresh coat of paint, too. The only changes made in the corporation were on the board of directors. Milan Boex and A.A. Reimer replaced L.G. Wood and C.A. Raasch.

Besides the loss of Blood and Kiesling to Pittsburgh, Lambeau had to start the '37 campaign without the services of Ade Schwammel and Tony Paulekas, two big linemen who had contributed heavily to the title team of '36. Also among the missing on opening day against the Chicago Cardinals in Green Bay were Arnie Herber and Frank Butler. Herber had suffered a shoulder separation and was out indefinitely. Butler left the team because of a dispute with Lambeau. The coach wanted the big center to play tackle, and Butler didn't like the idea. Herber was especially missed because of his passing ability. In the opener, the Packers attempted 19 passes, completed just four, and had five intercepted. Green Bay did gain more yards on the ground than Chicago, 246 to 119; but the Cardinals won the game, 14-7, by exploiting those turnovers.

To help the passing attack, Lambeau signed Ed Smith, a back out of New York University who had played with the Boston Redskins the year before. Smith wasn't enough to stop the Bears from beating the Pack the following Sunday, 14-2, in front of a record crowd of 16,658 at City Stadium. Again, Green Bay's aerial assault failed as 23 passes were thrown but only eight completed and four were intercepted, effectively thwarting the Packer offense.

The Packers (0-2-0) hadn't gotten off to this bad of a start since '33 when they began with a tie and two losses. With a week off, they found themselves at the bottom of the Western Division behind Detroit (2-0-0), the Bears (1-0-0), the Cardinals (1-1-1), and Cleveland (1-2-0). In the East, Johnny Blood got his Pirates (2-1-0) off to a good start with a pair of wins before losing a close one to the Giants (1-1-0), and Pittsburgh was tied with Brooklyn (2-1-0) for the top spot.

"You can hold down the Green Bay Packers just so long," wrote John Walter in the *Press-Gazette*. "You can lick them in tough, low-scoring games, as has been done three times this season, and you can keep them bottled up now and then, but every so often, just as sure as little green apples grow on trees, they are going to break out like an epidemic of chicken pox and swarm all over someone."

That "someone" turned out to be Dutch Clark's Detroit Lions. Dutch had replaced Potsy Clark as head coach. A new attendance record of 17,553 crammed into City Stadium to see the Packers maul the Lions, 26-6, as Hinkle, Paul Miller, Gantenbein, and Bob Monnett scored TDs. The attendance mark was all the more remarkable because it was set against a team other than the Chicago Bears, traditionally the Packers' best drawing card.

The win pulled the Packers (1-2-0) out of the cellar ahead of Cleveland (1-3-0), but they were still behind the Bears (2-0-0), the Cards (3-1-1), and Detroit (2-1-0). Pittsburgh (2-2-0) slipped from the top in the East by losing a tough one to the Bears. Brooklyn (2-2-0) also lost, while Washington (2-1-0) and New York (2-1-0) won to take over first.

Lambeau was forced to reduce the roster to 25 men after three games as league rules dictated, so he released Ed Smith, who didn't pan out as the passer needed to replace the injured Herber, and Ray Peterson. Herber's injured shoulder was healing fast, and Dr. Kelly declared him fit to play in the Packers' next game against the Cardinals in Milwaukee.

Although the contest was played in the Cream City, the second Cardinal game was considered a *road game* for the Packers and a *home game* for Chicago. The Cards were off to their best start in a long time, and their fans helped create a new attendance record for Milwaukee of 17,187 paid admissions. Gate receipts were also aided by the hundreds of friends and relatives of Eddie Jankowski who came out to see their home town boy make good. The extra cheering didn't help the Redbirds as much as it did Green Bay. The Packers mixed a revitalized pass attack with their already formidable ground game to crush Chicago, 34-13. Jankowski didn't let down the home folks as he rushed for 92 yards on 11 carries and scored a third quarter touchdown on a 46–yard gallop.

The win didn't get the Packers (2-2-0) out of fourth place, but it did keep them apace the Bears (3-0-0) and Detroit (3-1-0). The Cardinals (3-2-1) continued to cling to third, and the Rams (1-4-0) brought up the rear. The Redskins (2-2-0) were upset by the Eagles (1-4-1), so the idle Giants (2-1-0) took over first in the East by default.

Cleveland had been in the NFL four times before the Rams were accepted into the league. The Cleveland Indians were an original member of the circuit but dropped out for the 1922 season. They rejoined the loop in '23, then became the Bulldogs and won the NFL title in '24 when the Cleveland management purchased the roster of the Canton Bulldogs. The Bulldogs sat out the '26 season, then came back for the '27 campaign. Once again as the Indians, the city placed one more team in the league in '31. As an entrant into the second American Football League in '36, the Rams finished in second place with a 5-2-2 record behind the Boston Shamrocks at 8-3-0.

Unlike expansion teams in the NFL in later decades, the Rams weren't permitted to draft players off the established elevens. Cleveland was practically a whole new organization for '37 with only four players being carried over from the '36 squad. One of these was former Packer Harry Mattos. Among the newcomers on the Cleveland squad was Dick Zoll, former Green Bay West High standout. Zoll was the son of Frank Zoll and the younger brother of two of the original Packers, Martin and Carl Zoll. Mattos, Zoll, and their teammates couldn't do much to stop the rampaging Packers in Cleveland as Green Bay slammed the Rams, 35-10, in front of 12,000 fans. Don Hutson pulled down six passes for 101 yards and three TDs; two thrown to him by Herber and one by Monnett. Hinkle also had a big day, rushing for 80 yards and scoring a TD. Joe Laws tacked up the final touchdown, and Ernie Smith booted four PATs.

Green Bay (3-2-0) finally moved ahead of the Cardinals (3-3-1) who lost to the undefeated Bears (4-0-0), but the Pack still remained behind the Lions (4-1-0). New York (3-1-0) won in the East to stay a half game ahead of Washington (3-2-0).

An oddity in the schedule had the Rams visiting Green Bay the following week. The result was practically the same as in Cleveland as the Packers poured it on again, 35-7. Hinkle had another big day, gaining 84 yards on 17 attempts and scoring one touchdown and kicking five extra points, a Packer record. Hank Bruder, Herm Schneidman, Laws, and Zud Schammel also scored TDs. Laws and Schammel crossed the goal line after receiving laterals from Packer captain Milt Gantenbein.

Finally, the Packers (4-2-0) moved into a tie with Detroit (4-2-0), losers to the Bears (5-0-0). Although the Cardinals (4-3-1) didn't have much chance of overtaking all three teams ahead of them in the standings, the Western Division was still a four–team race. In the East, New York (4-1-0) and Washington

(4-2-0) both won to put some distance between them and the remaining clubs.

Lambeau traded Schammel to Brooklyn the following week for tackle Bill Lee, an Alabama product who had played alongside Don Hutson. Schammel nixed the trade by saying he wasn't going to play for Brooklyn and that he would return to coaching first. So Lambeau sent promising tackle Averell Daniell to the Dodgers.

With the trade behind him at last, Lambeau was able to concentrate on the next game against Detroit. In Green Bay, the Lions hadn't been much more than pussycats, but in Detroit, they were an entirely different animal. After a scoreless first half, Dutch Clark scored twice for his Motor City fans but converted only one of the two PAT attempts to give Detroit a 13-0 lead. Jankowski raced 34 yards for a TD later in the period, and Ernie Smith split the uprights for the PAT to close the gap to 13-7. Very late in the game, the Packers mounted a 14-play drive that began on their own 48. They drove down to the Detroit nine and had a fourth down and a yard to go when Schneidman bucked the center of the line for the needed distance. On the next series, Green Bay had a fourth and goal on the two. A field goal wasn't enough; the Packers had to cross the goal or lose the game. Hinkle, with Schneidman leading him, swept around left end and bulled his way into the end zone to tie the score. Smith calmly booted the extra point to give the Pack the lead, 14-13. Then Green Bay held on as Detroit fought back and drove down to the Packers' 21. With time nearly run out, Clark dropped back to attempt a dropkick from the 31, but the ball sailed left of the posts to give Green Bay a breathtaking victory.

While the Packers (5-2-0) were taking second place from Detroit (4-3-0), the Bears (5-0-1) played the Giants (4-1-1) to a tie, and the Cardinals (5-3-1) hung another loss on Cleveland (1-7-0). Washington (5-2-0) won again to move to a half game behind New York in the East.

The Packers were given a golden opportunity to gain some important ground on the Bears the following week when they traveled to Chicago. A record crowd was expected at Wrigley Field, and the Bruins were favored by a narrow margin. Prospects for victory seemed dim for Green Bay as Michalske was definitely out of the lineup and Russ Letlow and Paul Miller were doubtful. Letlow healed quickly and was able to start the contest, while Miller was able to fill a substitute's role.

A throng of 44,977 turned out on a near-perfect afternoon weatherwise to witness the fray. Neither team could mount much of an attack in the first period, but the Packers poured it on in the second. The scoring started with Arnie Herber throwing a 78-yard bomb to Don Hutson. Near the end of the half, Ernie Smith placekicked a field goal from the 29 to give the Pack a 10-0 lead. Then Eddie Jankowski intercepted an errant Chicago pass three plays later and returned it 27 yards for a TD. Green Bay led, 17-0, going into the locker room.

The Bears were not to be denied, however. Chicago came roaring back with 14 points in the third quarter and threatened to take the lead early in the fourth when the mighty Green Bay defense rose up to stomp out the challenge. The Packers' offense got going once again, and Bob Monnett hit Clarke Hinkle for a four-yard scoring toss in the late going to seal a 24-14 win.

The Packers (6-2-0) were now only percentage points behind the Bears (5-1-1) in the Western Division standings. The idle Cardinals (5-3-1) and the Lions (5-3-0), victorious over the Rams (1-8-0), also moved a little closer to the top, while the Giants (5-1-1) picked up a little breathing room on Washington (5-2-0) in the East.

Victory over the Bears was not without its drawbacks. As always when the two rivals met, bodies were carried from the field of battle. Miller and Hank Bruder were both banged up so badly that neither was able to report for practice the next week, forcing Lambeau into some personnel shuffling. Herb Banet was shifted from right half to left, and Buckets Goldenberg was taken off the line and returned to the backfield as the blocking back in Lambeau's offensive scheme as Michalske's condition improved enough to allow him to resume play.

Lambeau was grateful for such depth in his roster and for the schedule that had his Packers slated to meet the still hapless Eagles in Milwaukee the following week. A brilliant passing attack crushed Philadelphia, 37-7, as Jankowski, Bernie Scherer, and Goldenberg each scored one TD and Hutson tacked on a pair of six-pointers.

The Bears (6-1-1) also won to maintain their slim lead over the Pack (7-2-0), and the Lions (6-3-0) won, too, to stay in the race. The Cardinals (5-3-1) were again idle. Over in the East, both New York (5-2-1) and Washington (5-3-0) lost.

Only two games remained on Green Bay's schedule, and both were in the East against the other division's top two clubs. New York was the first stop for the Packers, and although the Giants weren't exactly the powerhouse they had been in past years, they were not a team to be taken lightly, even after Detroit had manhandled them, 17-0, the week before. The beating by the Lions must have stirred something in the Gothamites because they came out of the Polo Grounds clubhouse as angry as a swarm of bees to stop the Packers at every turn, defeating Green Bay, 10-0.

The loss didn't eliminate the Packers (7-3-0) from the race because the Bears (6-1-1) were idle. It did allow Detroit (7-3-0) to move into a second-place tie with them as the Lions dumped the Cardinals (5-4-1) and put the other Chicago eleven out of the title chase. Washington (6-3-0) won to keep pace with the Giants (6-2-1) for the eastern crown.

The Packers' final game of the '37 season turned out to be practically meaningless from the start. The Bears (7-1-1), who had whipped Detroit (7-4-0) on Thanksgiving Day to eliminate the Lions, were scheduled to host the expansion Rams on the same Sunday, and the Monsters of the Midway were hardly expected to lose. They didn't, of course, but the Packers (7-4-0) did. The Redskins (7-3-0) scored two second-half TDs to down Green Bay, 14-6, and set up a showdown with the Giants (6-2-2) for the top spot in the Eastern Division the following week.

Lambeau and the Packers could only sit on the sidelines and watch as Washington crushed New York, 49-14, for the eastern title, then came from behind to beat the Bears for the NFL championship, 28-21, at Wrigley Field in the middle of December.

§ § §

11

Best Man at the Wedding

While 1937 post-season honors were being handed out to Clarke Hinkle and Lon Evans for making the NFL All-Star team and to Don Hutson for leading the league in pass receptions for the second straight year and also setting new records of 41 catches and 552 yards gained by a receiver, Green Bay Coach Curly Lambeau went to work drafting players for the following year.

The National Football League moguls were still very new at this draft business, 1937 being only their third year at it, when they met at the Sherman Hotel in Chicago the day before the title game between the Bears and Redskins at Wrigley Field. So they had some problems.

For starters, the second division clubs — Cleveland, Philadelphia, Brooklyn, Pittsburgh, and Chicago Cardinals — wanted to draw five players each before the first division teams — Washington, Chicago Bears, New York, Green Bay, and Detroit — drew one. Of course, the top five put down that notion in a hurry, but they did agree to a compromise.

Each franchise made its first choice in the reverse order of finish, beginning with Cleveland taking Corbett Davis, a back from Indiana; and followed by Philadelphia, Jim McDonald, quarterback, Ohio State; Brooklyn, Wendell Butcher, back, Gustavus Adolphus; Pittsburgh, Byron "Whizzer" White, back, Colorado; Chicago Cardinals, John Robbins, back, Arkansas; Detroit, Alex Wojciechowicz, center, Fordham; Green Bay, Cecil Isbell, back, Purdue; New York, George Karamatic, back, Gonzaga; Washington, Andy Farkas, back, Detroit; and Chicago Bears, Dick Gray, back, Oregon State. After this, each of the lower five was allowed to pick two players each before the top five could pick another man. This process was repeated once before the regular order of drafting was resumed.

After Isbell, Lambeau chose Martin Schreyer, tackle, Purdue; Chuck Sweeney, end, Notre Dame; Andy Uram, back, Minnesota; John Kovatch, end, Northwestern; Phil Ragazzo, tackle, Western Reserve; John Howell, fullback, Nebraska; Frank Barnhart, guard, Greeley State; Pete Tinsley, guard, Georgia; and Tony Falkenstein, back, St. Mary's.

With the draft behind him, the coach went about signing players for the '38 campaign, including whatever free agents — college or otherwise — he could find, starting with Dick Weisgerber, a back out of little Willamette College in Salem, Oregon. In January, he signed a quartet of linemen: Ragazzo; Leo Katalinas, a big 246-pound tackle from Catholic University in Washington, D.C.; Fred Borak, end, Creighton; and Tom "Potsy" Jones, a guard who had been a teammate of Clarke Hinkle's at Bucknell and who had seen a few years of pro experience with the New York Giants. Isbell and Schreyer inked contracts in February, and in March, Lambeau signed Leroy "Bunny" Schoemann, a center from Marquette.

In the meantime, big George Svendsen announced his retirement from the pro game to coach the high school team of Antigo, Wisconsin; and his brother Bud Svendsen did likewise, saying he would be heading for Kirksville Teachers College in Missouri to coach. Then Lambeau traded Swede Johnston and Buckets Goldenberg to the Pittsburgh Pirates for a pair of draftees, Pat McCarty, center, Notre Dame, and Ray King, end, Minnesota. In a second swap, he sent Walt Bartanen, a tackle who had split time between Green Bay and the minor league St. Louis Gunners in '37, to the Pirates for Ed Brett, an end from Washington State. Goldenberg queered the one deal by announcing his retirement from the game. Johnny Blood, Pitt's head coach, merely laughed at that notion, stating Buckets just wanted "a boost in his paycheck." Blood was wrong; Buckets simply didn't want to leave Green Bay for Pittsburgh.

In May, Lambeau signed a pair of tackles. The first was Nick Miketinac who hailed from Hermansville, Michigan and had played his college ball at St. Norbert College in De Pere, Wisconsin. The second was one of the greatest lineman to ever don a Packer uniform.

Buford "Baby" Ray hailed from Nashville, Tennessee and played football at Vanderbilt University under Ray Morrison. He stood six feet seven inches tall and weighed in at 280 pounds. *The Green Bay Press-Gazette* described him as "a behemoth," which he was for his day. Ray wasn't drafted and went unheralded during his college career because he played in front of highly touted Carl Hinkle (no relation to Clarke Hinkle of the Packers), the All-American back and linebacker. Ray would clear out the blockers of the opposing team, then Hinkle would make the tackles and get the credit. Lambeau described Ray as being all muscle and bone and an unselfish player who would fit in perfectly with the Green Bay style of football.

In July, Lambeau completed yet another trade that sent Lou Gordon to the Cleveland Rams for Charles "Ookie" Miller. The veteran center played his college ball at Purdue and had participated in the East-West Shrine Game of '32. Besides the Rams, Miller had also played for the Bears during his pro career.

In August, Carl Mulleneaux, who had signed a contract with the Packers in '37 but didn't report, signed on again, this time to play. Andy Uram signed the week after that.

A few days later Lambeau announced that Hank Bruder and Mike Michalske wouldn't be returning to the team because Bruder was retiring and Michalske wanted to join Johnny Blood's coaching staff at Pittsburgh. The truth was Bruder and Michalske wanted more money, and Lambeau wasn't about to give either the often injured Bruder or the aging Michalske a raise. This typified the problems Lambeau was having with his veteran players, many of whom were holding out for pay increases. With less than two weeks to go before the opening of training camp, 11 key men were still unsigned, including Don Hutson, Clarke Hinkle, Wayland Becker, Ernie Smith, Lon Evans, Zud Schammel, Tiny Engebretsen, Darrell Lester, Arnie Herber, Herm Schneidman, and Buckets Goldenberg who had come out of "retirement" once the deal with Pittsburgh was called off. Veterans who had signed included Joe Laws, Eddie Jankowski, Bill Lee, Russ Letlow, Champ Seibold, Bob Monnett, Milt Gantenbein, Frank Butler, Bernie Scherer, Lyle Sturgeon, Paul Miller, and Swede Johnston who remained in

1933 Packer team: Insets; Bruder, Michalske, Hinkle, Herber — Lambeau, Quatsoe, Perry, Bultman, Rose, Smith, Dilweg, Hubbard, Engelmann, Sarafiny, Blood — Evans, Kurth, Gantenbein, Van Sickle, Comstock, Grove, Monnett, Greeney, Bettencourt.

1934 Packer team: (standing) Lambeau, Butler, Bultman, Kurth, Dilweg, Jorgensen, Seibold, Peterson, Jones, Witte, Earpe. (middle) Norgard, Evans, Laws, Herber, Michalske, Goldenberg, Bruder, Schwammel, Perry. (front) Monnett, Gantenbein, Barrager, Hinkle, Grove.

1935 Packer team: (top) Lambeau, Blood, Rose, Butler, Seibold, Hubbard, Kiesling, Perry, Hutson, Smith. (middle) Goldenberg, Laws, Engebretsen, Hinkle, Herber, Grove, Bruder, Gantenbein, Schneidman, Johnston. (bottom) Michalske, Tenner, Barrager, Schwammel, Svendsen, Evans, Sauer, O'Connor, Monnett, Woodard.

1936 World Champions

1936 World Champion: (top) Laws, Herber, Schneidman, Letlow, Becker, Miller, Hinkle, Hutson, Gantenbein, Monnett. (middle) Lambeau, Scherer, Bruder, Gordon, Svendsen, Kiesling, Blood, Smith, Johnston, Smith. (bottom) Paulekas, Engebretsen, Evans, Schwammel, Seibold, Butler, Sauer, Clemens, Goldenberg.

1937 Packer team: Front row, left to right, Johnson, Monnett, Jankowski, Laws, Lester, Weisgerber, Tinsley, Mulleneaux, Miller; second row, Katalinas, Scherer, Micketinac, Hinkle, Schneidman, Clemens, Engebretsen, Balazs, Schwammel, Isbell; third row, Head Coach Lambeau, Borak, Herber, Letlow, Peterson, Becker, Goldenberg, Hutson, Banet, Line Coach Richard Smith; back row left to right, C. Mulleneaux, Kell, Lee, Butler, Daniell, Seibold, Svendsen, Hubbard, Schoenmann.

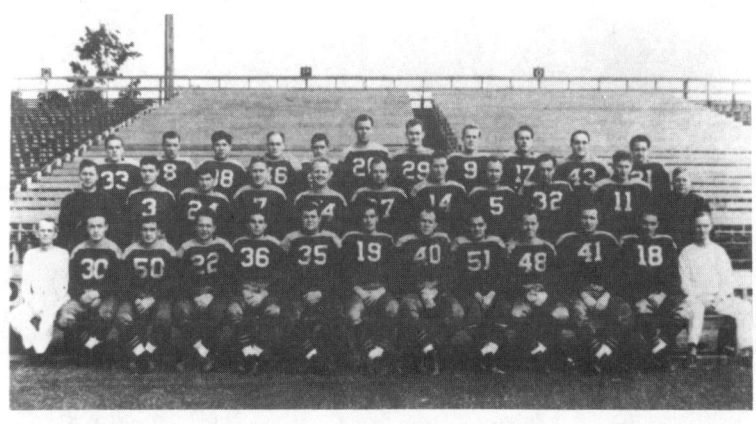

1938 Packer team: Front row left to right, Trainer Woodward, Hinkle, Monnett, Gantenbein, Scherer, Butler, C. Mulleneaux, Asst. Trainer Jorgenson,; second row, Head Coach Lambeau, P.Miller, Laws, Jankowski, Engebretsen, Jones, Hutson, Bruder, Becker, Katalinas, Line Coach Smith; back row, Weisgerber, Uram, Herber, Letlow, Howell, Ray, Lester, Borak, Isbell, Goldenberg, Tinsley.

1939 World Champions

1939 World Champions: Front row left to right, Uram, Brock, Wilson, Schneidman, Laws, Thompson, Zoll, Twedell, Johnson, Weisgerber, Tinsley, Biolo, Jankowski; second row, Head Coach Lambeau, Craig, Kell, Hinkle, Gantenbein, Herber, Svendsen, Lee, Isbell, Goldenberg, Bruder, Mulleneaux, Letlow, Engebretsen; back row, Brennan, Balazs, Jacunski, Kilbourne, Steen, Greenfield, Ray, C. Mulleneaux, Buhler, Moore, Hutson, Schultz, Popp, Coach Smith.

1940 Packer team: Front row left to right, Riddick, Zarnas, Lee, Uram, Weisgerber, Jankowski, Herber, Craig, Mulleneaux, Brock; second row, Head Coach Lambeau, Goldenberg, Laws, Feathers, Jacunski, Svendsen, Ray, Engebretsen, Berry, Coach Smith; Third row left to right, Seamann, Gantenbein, Johnson, Tinsley, Hinkle, Hutson, Adkins, Letlow, Isbell, Brock; back row, Evans, Kell, Greenfield, Midler, Schultz, Buhler, Disend, Seibold, Van Every.

1941 Packer team: Front row left to right, Rohrig, Craig, Hinkle, Uram, Jankowski, Laws, Bucchianeri, Lee, Hutson; second row, Fruitig, Canadeo, Engebretsen, Johnson, Adkins, Schultz, Isbell, Riddick, Brock, Goldenberg; third row, Paskvan, Brock, Johnson, Van Every, Greenfield, Jacunski, Urban, Buhler, Tinsley, Kuusisto; back row, Coach Lambeau, Lyman, Balazs, Mulleneaux, Svendsen, Ray, Pannell, McLaughlin

1942 Packer team: Front row left to right, Coach Lambeau, Coach Smith, Canadeo, Ohlgren, Lee, Goldenberg, Brock, Letlow, Ray, Hutson, Berezney, Trainer Jorgenson; second row left to right, Laws, Ingalls, Isbell, Carter, Hinte, Miller, Vant Hull, Mason, Craig, Uram, Tinsley, Asst. Coach Kotal; back row, Brock, Ingalls, Pannell, Flowers, Stonebreaker, Croft, Kahler, Kuusisto, Fritsch, Starrett, Sample, Finley.

1943 Packer team: Front row left to right, McPherson, Laws, Uram, Goldenberg, Tinsley, Falkenstein, Brock, Canadeo, Hutson; second row, Head Coach Lambeau, Sorenson, Kahler, Jacunski, Adams, Ray, Crofts, Fries, Mason, Kuusisto, Coach Smith; back row, Trainer Seaburg, Lankas, Flowers, Schwammel, Evans, Berezney, Comp, Craig, Starrett, Fritsch, Trainer Jorgenson.

1944 World Champions

1944 World Champions: Front row left to right, Goldenberg, Duhart, Starrett, Tinsley, McPherson, Craig, C. Brock, L. Brock, McKay, Laws; second row, Trainer Jorgenson, Kuusisto, Wheba, Sorenson, Flowers, Jacunski, Fritsch, Perkins, Tollefson, Mason, Seaburg; back row, Head Coach Lambeau, Hutson, Berezney, Schwammel, Comp, Crofts, Kercher, Kahler, Ray, Bucchianeri, Coach Trafton.

1945 Packer team: Front row left to right, Hutson, Smith, Goodnight, Bucchianeri, Mosley, Tinsley, McPherson, C. Brock, L. Brock, McKay, Craig, Goldenberg, Starrett, Laws; second row, Head Coach Lambeau, Crimmins, Flowers, Adkins, Mulleneaux, Neal, Crofts, Ray, Pannell, Perkins, Tollefson, Barnett, Mason, Coach Kiesling; back row, Trainer Jorgenson, Sorenson, Snelling, Luhn, Coach Blood, Lipscomb, Comp, Fritsch, Kuusisto, Keuper, Frankowski, Trainer Proski.

Old City Stadium At It's Peak. The stadium behind East High School had been expanded to seat 23,500 fans..

Don Hutson holding footballs which represent some of his scoring and passing records. What might he have accomplished if he played as many games as are played today.

Picture day for some of the Packers left to right Arnie Herber, Mike Michalske, Curly Lambeau, Red Smith, Milt Gantenbein, Hank Bruder.

Curly Lambeau (left) on the bench with screen actress Myrna Kennedy and Red Grange.

Don Hutson makes one of his patented great catches; this one against Detroit.

Looking for "daylight" is fullback Clarke Hinkle during a 1940 game. Notice the jockey silk pants.

The first great Packer aerial team. Arnie Herber (left) in his high school uniform and Don Hutson.

Six–seven, 280–pound Buford 'Baby' Ray (left) played his college ball at Vanderbilt.

Ted Fritsch (below) hailed from Spencer, Wisconsin and played at U.W. Stevens Point.

"Buckets" Goldenberg from Wisconsin a blocking and short yardage back early in his career was moved to guard. At that position he was named to Lambeau's all-time Packer eleven team.

Tony Canadeo was the NFL's first 1,000 yard rusher.

Fighting Over That Same Young Lady Again

One of the many cartoons drawn by Harold Elder. This one was published Wednesday December 6, 1939 in the *Green Bay Gazette*

the fold when Goldenberg nixed the Pittsburgh trade. Most of the holdouts signed before the first practice. Evans and Schammel retired to go into coaching; Smith decided to play on the West Coast; and Bruder finally put his name on the dotted line the week before the Packers played an intrasquad game at City Stadium.

In the front office, Lee Joannes, Fred C. Leicht, Frank Jonet, and George Whitney Calhoun were re-elected to their respective positions as corporate president, vice-president, treasurer, and secretary at the annual meeting of the Green Bay Packers, Inc., stockholders. The only change in the board of directors was the election of Edward A. Bedore to replace H.J. Stolz. Joannes described the new additions to the stands at City Stadium that would increase seating capacity to 22,355. The east end of the stadium would be enclosed, completing a solid horseshoe around the field from the west end. Jonet reported that the corporation would be starting the new season in the black for a change.

After playing an intrasquad game on September 2, the Packers traveled to Ironwood, Michigan for an exhibition game against the Cedar Rapids, Iowa Crushers the following Monday evening. It was hardly a test for the NFL team as Green Bay ran and passed at will to annihilate the Crushers, 75-0.

The next week Lambeau made his first cuts toward getting his roster down to the new 30-player limit set by the league that year. The only players of importance in the first reduction were Eddie Brett, the end who came over in the Bartanen trade with Pittsburgh; veteran Lyle Sturgeon; and No. 8 draft choice Frank Barnhart.

As usual, the Packers opened the season at home. A sparse crowd of only 8,247 turned out to see Dick Zoll and the much improved Cleveland Rams. The Rams took an early 3-0 lead on a Nelson Peterson field goal in the first period, then the Packers reeled off 17 straight points and never looked back again, winning decisively, 26-17. Arnie Herber and Don Hutson both had big days, Herber completing six of eight passes for 89 yards and Hutson catching 5 for 65 yards and a mere three touchdowns.

Blooded by their victory over Cleveland, the Packers were

ready to host the division champion Bears the following week. A full house was expected, but no one told Mother Nature a bright sunshiny day was needed to put fans in the stands in '38. "Rain and a slippery field — the great levelers of the gridiron," wrote John Walter in the *Press-Gazette*, "changed what was booked as a great aerial demonstration into a submarine struggle between two powerful lines as the Green Bay Packers and Chicago Bears fought it out to a 2 to 0 decision before 15,172 at City stadium yesterday afternoon. The Bears, by virtue of a safety scored on the second play of the fourth period, were the winners."

The weather was more co-operative the next week when the Packers met the Cardinals in Milwaukee for their *mutual home* game. This was the fifth straight season that the two teams were scheduled to play in the Cream City. Beginning in '34 and continuing through '36, the Packers and Cardinals played each other three times, once each in Green Bay, Chicago, and Milwaukee. In '37, they played in Milwaukee and Green Bay, and in '38, they were set to play in Milwaukee and Buffalo, New York (an item in itself detailed below). With the initiation of the Cream City series, the two clubs alternated as the home team, the Packers being the host in even numbered years and the Cardinals in the odd. The game was placed at State Fair Park because the Packers and Cardinals drew better crowds there than when they played together in either Chicago or Green Bay.

In their previous meetings in Milwaukee, the Cardinals shut out the Packers in '34 and '35, while the Packers won handily in '36 and '37. Overall, since they first met in 1921, the Packers had won 15 of the 30 contests, while there had been three ties. There was no split decision when they squared off in Milwaukee that Sunday as four different Packers — Milt Gantenbein, Clarke Hinkle, Arnie Herber, and Eddie Jankowski — each scored TDs to lead Green Bay to a 28-7 win to move the Pack a half game closer to the idle Bears and Lions.

The Packers and Cardinals boarded a train the next day and shuffled off to Buffalo to play again on Wednesday night at the New York city's brand new $2-million Civic Stadium. Promoter Charlie Murray wanted to put an NFL team in Buffalo, so he talked league President Joe Carr and his scheduling committee into slating a couple of games there. The Philadelphia Eagles and Pittsburgh Pirates played in the 40,000 seat stadium two weeks earlier and had drawn fairly well. A crowd of 20,000 was expected to show up for the Packers and Cardinals. George Whitney Calhoun, who was still traveling with the team on its eastern road trips, reported on the game for the *Press-Gazette* in his own inimitable style:

"Football drama of the 'steenth' degree was penned here Wednesday night at the Civic stadium when the Green Bay Packers came from behind in the waning minutes of the last quarter to nose out a hardfighting Chicago Cardinal team, 24 to 22, before some 20,000 fans.

"Right at the start of the final frame Coach Milan Creighton's 'huskies,' and they sure were husky last night, helped them–selves to a one–point lead over Lambeau and company and the way the Windy City footballers were cutting capers it seemed as if it was all over but the shouting for old Green Bay.

"However, a fighting team can't be beat and the Packers kept on bearing down with all their might.

"Several times promising Green Bay advances fizzled out and gloom was knee deep for the handful of Wisconsin rooters in the stands.

"The worm turned as the lighted time clock at top the big stadium was showing but minutes to go. Pangle, the Cardinal back, fumbled the oval and Baby Ray covered it like a hot potato. This was the break that steeled the Bays for a final offensive charge which was to spell victory in capital letters."

Calhoun went on to relate how "Tiny Engebretsen ambled back for a place kick with victory or defeat hinging on the result." Engebretsen then kicked the winning field goal "in a blaze of glory," and the Packers held off a last ditch effort by the Cards to win the seesaw contest.

Don Hutson hauled down a Cecil Isbell pass and raced 17 yards for an early second quarter score, and Engebretsen made good on the PAT to give the Pack a 7-0 lead. Chicago came back on their next drive to close the gap to 7-6, only to see Green Bay go up, 14-6, in the late going of the half when Hinkle crossed the goal line with a Bob Monnett pass. The Packers built their lead to 21-6 on their first possession of the second half when Isbell hit Arnie Herber with a 15–yard scoring toss. Chicago then scored 16 unanswered points to take the lead midway through the final quarter, 22-21, before Engebretsen came through in the clutch for Green Bay.

The Packers (3-1-0) had the following Sunday off, but the rest of the division played. The Bears (3-0-0) swamped the Eagles to retain first place, while Cleveland (1-3-0) nipped the Lions (1-1-0) to move ahead of the Cardinals (1-4-0) who lost their third game in eight days.

Although the season was still quite young, the game between the Packers and Detroit in Green Bay the following week was vital to both clubs. With the Bears unbeaten and most likely to stay that way for some time, neither squad could afford a second loss at this juncture of the schedule. Coach Lambeau faced the battle against Lions with all the trepidation of a Christian in ancient Rome's Colosseum. "One of the most dangerous teams in the National Football League" was how Lambeau described the Motor City eleven. Curly was so right, too. As John Walter put it, "a vast throng of 21,968 watched the home team's challenge for a Western division professional football title receive a severe cuffing. Detroit deserved its victory. It punched home a field goal by Regis Monahan in the first period, added a touchdown by Bill Shepherd early in the third, and then clung desperately to the advantage through an inspired Packer rally. The Lions made few mistakes." But the Packers made several errors. Three intercepted passes thwarted Green Bay scoring drives, and Detroit won, 17-7.

Fortunately for both Detroit (2-1-0) and Green Bay (3-2-0), Cleveland (2-3-0) pulled off a second straight upset, beating the powerful but overly confident Bears (3-1-0). This kept the division race wide open for everyone, including the idle Cards (1-4-0).

Meanwhile, the Eastern Division was in a turmoil as well. Washington (2-1-1), which had been unbeaten going into the weekend, was upset by the Giants (2-2-0) who moved into a third–place tie with idle Philadelphia (2-2-0). Brooklyn (2-1-1) pulled into a tie for the top spot by downing Johnny Blood's Pirates (2-4-0).

The Lambeau Years — Part Two

Lambeau decided it was time to step back and regroup his forces. Bunny Schoemann, the rookie center from Marquette, had suffered what turned out to be a career-ending injury in the second Cardinal game. To replace him and to shore up his ailing forward wall, Lambeau signed Carl Mulleneaux's big brother Lee. Also known as "Brute" Mulleneaux, the older sibling had played center for the New York Giants ('32), Cincinnati Reds ('33-'34), St. Louis Gunners ('34), Pittsburgh Pirates ('35-'36), and Chicago Cardinals ('38) in the NFL, and the Cincinnati Bengals in the American Football League of '37. Brute played his college ball at Arizona.

Schoemann wasn't the only casualty of the trip to Buffalo. The truth was never officially released, but Arnie Herber also suffered an injury that week, although his wasn't incurred on the playing field.

During the return train ride from New York, the hostility that had been brewing between some of the veteran players and some of the rookies finally surfaced, and a fight broke out. Herber objected to the fact that big Leo Katalinas was picking on Paul Miller, a man half his size. Katalinas told Herber to butt out, Herber refused, and a scuffle ensued. Herber swung and missed Katalinas with his right, smashing his fist into the wall. He then swung with his left and knocked Katalinas out cold. Herber's right hand was broken, putting him out of action. The situation became so bad that Assistant Coach Red Smith spent the rest of the trip playing cards in the baggage car. In relating the story to Jim Ford, Smith facetiously said that Curly Lambeau rode up front with the engineer as neither coach wanted to be caught in the middle of any brouhaha.

Now that they trailed the Bears by only a half game again, the Packers found new life when they faced the Brooklyn Dodgers in Milwaukee on the third Sunday of October. The Flatbushers weren't exactly loaded, but they did have All-Pro quarterback Duke Parker and future Hall-of-Fame player Beattie Feathers. Even so, they weren't enough to put a decent dent in the now formidable Packers. The Dodgers had scored only 13 points against Green Bay in their five previous meetings, all of which the Pack had won, while the Wisconsin eleven had amassed a total of 97 points. That ratio wasn't much different in their '38 meeting as the Packers walloped the Dodgers, 35-7, on TDs by Hinkle, Laws, Uram, Hutson, and Scherer.

The Packers (4-2-0) needed the win because the Bears (4-1-0) also won, practically eliminating the Cardinals (1-5-0) in a highscoring affair, 34-28. Detroit (2-2-0) took a step backwards when they lost to Washington (3-1-1) by the baseball score of 7-5. New York (3-2-0) kept pace with the Redskins by downing Philadelphia (2-3-0), while the Rams (2-3-0) and Pirates (2-4-0) were given a day off by Pittsburgh owner Art Rooney.

Not so oddly, the Packers' next opponent was the Pittsburgh Pirates. The two teams had met four times previously with the Packers winning all four by a total score of 150-24. Of course, this was before Johnny Blood became the player–coach of the Pirates.

Ever since the league schedule was announced, Blood had been aiming his team at the Packers and Curly Lambeau. Weeks before the game was to be played, John Walter quoted Blood in the sports editor's column, *Looking Up in the Realm of Sports*: "When I was playing in Green Bay Lambeau was always lamenting my shortcomings as a blocker rather than just as a runner, passer and kicker. Well, we play Green Bay in a few weeks and I just want to show Curly he was wrong."

Allegedly, to emphasize how badly the Pittsburgh management wanted to take their best shot at the Packers, Art Rooney cancelled the previous week's game with Cleveland just to let his injured players heal up. "We want to be in shape for the Packers!" said Rooney, according to Lambeau in a long distance telephone conversation he supposedly had with the Pittsburgh owner. Lambeau said he called Rooney to get his side of the dispute between Pittsburgh and Cleveland over the cancellation of their game. Also according to Rooney via Lambeau, "We have a strong team, but it is in bad shape. Several of our stars are badly battered. We feel that if we postpone the game (with Cleveland) until Dec. 4, our men will have recovered sufficiently to make a(n) exceptionally fine showing against the Green Bay Packers Oct. 23."

That was hardly the truth because the Pirates played an exhibition game against the Cincinnati Bengals *the night after they should have played Cleveland*. Lambeau was blowing smoke to arouse Green Bay fans into showing up for the Pittsburgh game and to get his players up for the fray. In reality, Rooney postponed the Cleveland contest because he saw a chance to make some needed money by playing the Bengals whose management had guaranteed him a profit.

Rooney needed the extra cash from the exhibition because he had a rather large payroll to meet. Besides having to pay Blood as both player and coach, he also had to pay Walt Kiesling as a player and a coach. But that wasn't the topper.

The number one college player in the country the year before was one Byron "Whizzer" White who was also very intelligent. White was so brilliant that he was offered a Rhodes scholarship, the top academic honor in the world in some circles. In order to keep White from running off to England for more schooling, Rooney signed him to a contract that called for a salary of $15,000 for one season, making White the highest paid player in the land. Rooney thought he had a gold mine in White, just like C.C. Pyle did with Red Grange a dozen years earlier. He was certain White would make his Pirates into an instant winner and fill the stands wherever they played. It just didn't turn out that way. As good as White was, he never received the same kind of press Grange got in college, thus the same kind of mystique that evolved around the Galloping Ghost failed to materialize with the future Supreme Court justice. Whizzer White was a financial bust for Rooney.

Rooney also failed to realize that, as good as White was in college, the pro game was different. In college, one man could really make the difference in a team, but not necessarily so in the pros where the talent was much more balanced from team to team. With White not proving to be so good with the Pirates, additional hype was needed to draw the crowds. That was Lambeau's reason for setting up his little smoke screen in the pages of the *Press-Gazette*.

Even with Lambeau's ploy, Whizzer White, and the return of Johnny Blood to Green Bay, Packer fans weren't fooled into turning out to watch an inferior team play their mighty favorites. A crowd of only 12,142 showed up at City Stadium to yawn through Green Bay's 20-0 victory. White was completely outplayed by Cecil Isbell who gained 98 yards on 13 carries to

White's 72 yards on 17 attempts. Isbell also completed four passes, while White had four intercepted.

The victory put the Packers (5-2-0) on top in the West as Cleveland (3-3-0) benefitted more from the week off than Pittsburgh (2-5-0) did. The Rams beat the Bears (4-2-0), while Detroit (3-2-0) also won to keep the divisional race interesting. Back East, Washington (4-1-1) and New York (4-2-0) won, separating themselves from the rest of the pack.

Having beaten the Bears twice in one season, the Rams were no longer an expansion team to be taken lightly, especially on their own field. Lambeau wasn't taking any chances with Cleveland. He knew one of George Halas' complaints about the Rams was how their blue-uniformed players seemed to get lost among Chicago's *navy blue*-jerseyed Bears. Curly wasn't about to tolerate any such mix-up with his team, so he put the Packers in new white jerseys just for the Cleveland encounter. The strategy worked because Green Bay took it to the Rams, 28-7, as Don Hutson once again had a three-touchdown day.

The Packers (6-2-0) received good news in the locker room after the Cleveland (3-4-0) fray; the Lions (4-2-0) had upset the Bears (4-3-0) in Chicago to put them a game and a half ahead of their top rival who just happened to be next on their schedule.

The promised aerial show that Mother Nature had deprived Bear and Packer fans of when the two teams met earlier in Green Bay still failed to materialize in near perfect football weather in Chicago in November. Instead, the 40,208 spectators had hardly settled into their seats when much of the action for the day was over. The Bears fumbled the ball away on the first play from scrimmage, and two plays later, Monnett hit Hinkle with a 15-yard scoring toss to put Green Bay ahead, 7-0. The Bears butter-fingered away the ensuing kickoff, and three plays after that Monnett hit Hutson in the end zone for another six. Although spotting the Packers a 14-0 lead, Chicago roared back to score 10 points in the quarter to close the gap to 14-10. Eddie Jankowski cracked over the goal on the first play of the second stanza to move Green Bay out to a 21-10 lead, only to have the Bears tack up seven more before the half ended. Hinkle split the uprights with a field goal in the third period, then the Packers held on to win, 24-17, and practically eliminated the Bears from the division race.

With the Bears (4-4-0) nearly out of contention, the Packers (7-2-0) faced only one more obstacle between them and at least a tie for the Western Division title: the Lions (5-2-0), their next foe on the field.

There was no doubt that Detroit was a good team; their record showed that. But the Lions weren't an overpowering squad like the Packers. Nearly all of the Motor City crew's wins had been by less than 10 points; one glaring exception being their 17-7 win over the Packers in Green Bay five weeks before. This loss to Detroit proved to be the rallying cry for the title hungry Packers as Cecil Isbell hit Clarke Hinkle with a 15–yard scoring toss on the first play of the second quarter, and the Pack never looked back as they rolled to a 28-7 win over the Lions in Detroit before 45,139 screaming fans.

Green Bay (8-2-0) had now clinched a tie for division honors, but Detroit (5-3-0) was still mathematically in the race. In order to win the title, the Packers had to beat Eastern Division leader New York (6-2-0) at the Polo Grounds the following week in their last game of the regular season.

The Giants had been on a roll since early in the season, having won five straight games. Coach Steve Owen knew his boys had to beat the Packers to keep their momentum going toward a division championship. To stumble once would give the Redskins all the opportunity they would need to pass New York in the standings. Owen impressed this fact on his players so well that they completely dominated the Packers, 15-3, in front of 48,279 appreciative New Yorkers.

The loss hurt the Packers (8-3-0) but didn't worry Lambeau. Detroit (6-3-0) still had two games to play over the next two weeks. If a playoff for the division title was needed, the Packers would have two weeks of rest while the Lions would have two weeks of bumps and bruises. When the Lions beat the Bears, 14-7, on Thanksgiving Day, Lambeau and his charges felt almost positively that they would be in a Western Division playoff game with Detroit. They were so sure of it that they began looking for — and arguing about — a playoff site more than a week before the Lions were scheduled to play their last game against the mediocre Eagles.

The schedule makers must have patted themselves on the back when the last day of the '38 season came around because both divisional races were still undecided and one might still remain undecided when the day was over. The New York Giants held a half game lead over the Washington Redskins in the Eastern Division, and they were playing each other. The winner of that game would gain the privilege of playing host to either the Detroit Lions or the Green Bay Packers for the NFL championship, depending on the outcome of the Lions–Eagles game and on the outcome of the Lions–Packers game if the Lions prevailed over the Eagles. To no one's surprise, the Giants mauled the Redskins, 36-0; but to the complete astonishment of every professional football aficionado, the heavily favored Lions fell to the Eagles, 21-7, negating any need for a playoff game and making the Green Bay Packers the champs of the Western Division.

Before the dust had even settled over the Polo Grounds after the Giants-Redskins contest, predictions of mild weather and a huge turnout for the title tilt were being made in all the newspapers. Curly Lambeau decided to keep his team in Green Bay for the first few days of practice and depart for New York on the Thursday before the game, traveling all day and night to the Big Apple. This decision was based on his desire to keep his plans for the Giants as secret as possible, especially since he had been planning for two weeks to play the Lions and suddenly had to switch to a strategy for attacking the New York defense and defending against the Giants' offense.

A real slam-bang thriller was staged for 48,120 fans, the largest crowd to turn out for an NFL title game up to that time. The Giants got off to a quick start when they blocked two Green Bay punts and turned them into nine points in the first quarter. Then Arnie Herber, back from the disabled list, launched a 50-yard pass to Carl Mulleneaux to close the gap to 9-7. The Giants tacked on another seven to open the margin to nine points again before the Packers mounted a scoring drive that culminated with Hinkle smashing over from six yards out to make the halftime score, 16-14. The Packers took the second half kickoff and marched down to field goal range, and Tiny Engebretsen split the uprights from 22 yards away to give Green Bay its only lead of the game, 17-16. The Giants stormed right back with a TD and PAT to make the score 23-17, and that's how it ended as neither team could dent the scoreboard again that day.

Green Bay had been invited to the wedding, but the Packers didn't get to go on the honeymoon as the Giants were the NFL champs for 1938.

§ § §

12

The Cream Also Rises

From 1929 thru 1938, the National Football League championship and its division titles, both Eastern and Western, had been captured each year except one by just four teams: the Green Bay Packers, New York Giants, Chicago Bears, and Washington (Boston) Redskins. These teams had become known as "the Big Four" of the NFL. As 1939 began, the status quo didn't appear ready for a change.

Curly Lambeau wasn't one to count his chickens before they hatched. Although he was confident that his Packers *could* defeat the Giants for the NFL title in '38, he wasn't positive that they *would* beat New York. The Packers were a very good team in '38, but they weren't a great team like his four previous league champs had been. To make them that way again, Lambeau knew he needed just a few more key people.

Lambeau's search for excellence began the day before the '38 title game with the Giants when the NFL moguls met in New York to hold the circuit's fourth annual draft of college players. The draft was expanded that year from 10 picks to 20. The Chicago Cardinals tied Pittsburgh with the worst won–lost record in the league, but it was the Western Division's turn to choose first. Cardinals owner Charlie Bidwill selected Ki Aldrich, a center from TCU.

The Packers had the ninth choice, and Lambeau used it to pick Larry Buhler, Minnesota's 220–pound powerhouse fullback. He followed up with Charley Brock, Nebraska's potent center. The rest of the draft list included Lynn Hovland, guard, Wisconsin; Francis Twedell, guard, Minnesota; Vincent Gavre, quarterback, Wisconsin; Dan Elmer, center, Minnesota; Roy Bellin, halfback, Wisconsin; Frank Balazs, back, Iowa; John

Brennan, guard, Michigan; Charles Schultz, tackle, Minnesota; Larry Craig, end, South Carolina; Paul Kell, tackle, Notre Dame; Johnny Hall, back, TCU; Charles Sprague, end, SMU; Bill Badgett, tackle, Georgia; Tom Greenfield, center, Arizona; John Yerby, end, Oregon; Willard Hofer, back, Notre Dame; and Chester Gunther, back, Santa Clara.

Drafting these men was one thing; signing them quite an other. As soon as Lambeau quit crying about being robbed of the '38 title by head linesman Larry Conover, he got down to the business of building his team for '39. The coach made straight for the West Coast and the college all-star and bowl games.

While in California, Lambeau got a good chance to look at some of the talent he had drafted. He was surprised by the abilities of some men and disappointed in others. One man he liked a lot was his top pick, Larry Buhler, but Lambeau didn't get to see Buhler perform in the East-West Shrine game as planned because shortly before he was scheduled to depart for San Francisco Buhler was involved in an automobile accident in St. Paul, Minnesota. To the relief of Lambeau and Packer fans everywhere, Buhler wasn't injured seriously and he announced upon leaving the hospital that he had every intention of signing with and playing for the Green Bay Packers.

Lambeau signed one draft choice — Chet Gunther — and a pair of free agents — Slats Wyrick, tackle, UCLA and Willard Sherman, center, Wisconsin-Whitewater — while in California.

On his return trip to Green Bay, he made a few stops along the way.

One wide spot in the road was Houston, Texas where Lambeau inked Frank Steen, an end out of Rice. Steen was a friend of Cecil Isbell. He didn't play professional football after graduating from college in '38 because he signed a baseball contract with the St. Louis Cardinals. Feeling it would be years before he would move up the baseball ladder to the Big Leagues, Steen gave up the game to play for the Packers.

Stopping off in Lincoln, Nebraska on his way north, the coach signed up another one of those legendary linemen who played for the Packers at one time or another. Charley Brock, the center that former Packer and local high school coach Tiny

Cahoon called one of the greatest centers he had ever seen in his life, put his name on the dotted line in late January.

Coming east, Lambeau paid a visit to Iowa City, Iowa and the campus of the University of Iowa to talk with draft choice Frank Balazs, the 210-pound fullback. The coach was impressed with Balazs' size and stature and felt quite confident that here was a man who wouldn't have any trouble making it in the pro game. With all the eagerness of a kid with a pocketful of quarters in a candy store, Lambeau bought himself a fullback.

For St. Valentine's Day, draftee Tom Greenfield, the center from Arizona, mailed in his contract. Lambeau was delighted to get another topnotch man for the middle of his line.

While in Chicago for the league's annual meeting in February, Lambeau signed 195-pound guard John Biolo of Lake Forest College. Biolo's college coach was Ralph Jones, the same man who had coached the Bears in the early '30s and who had installed the T-formation with the quarterback up close behind the center. Jones said Biolo was the best guard to ever play at Lake Forest and that he would prove to be a sound asset for the Packers.

As one of the Packers' representatives at the annual confab, Lambeau voted with the majority to give NFL President Joe Carr a new 10-year contract, to keep the league at its current 10 teams, to abolish barnstorming tours by pro teams after the regular season, and to reinstate Ken Strong who had been banned from the NFL for repudiating his contract with the New York Giants and jumping to the American Football League in '36. The coach was also able to make a player trade while in Chicago.

Carl and Martin Zoll played professional football for Green Bay before Curly Lambeau joined the team in 1919. Their little brother Dick was still wearing short pants when they were pounding the line for the undefeated and unscored upon unofficial state champions of 1918. Dick Zoll played his high school ball at Green Bay's West High, then went to Indiana University to play tackle for the Hoosiers. Coming out of college, he signed with the Cleveland Rams and played for them in '37 and '38. Lambeau was able to obtain Zoll's services by trading the rights to John Yerby, the Oregon end that

The Lambeau Years — Part Two 137

Lambeau had drafted, to the Rams.

Lambeau spent a few days back in Green Bay after the league meeting was concluded, then went on a tour of midwestern universities in search of more talent. In Minneapolis, he talked turkey with Charles Schultz and signed the Minnesota tackle to a Green Bay contract. In Chicago, Jack Brennan agreed to terms and Lambeau inked the Michigan guard to a deal. Then Lambeau was off on a cruise to Europe, saying football would be the farthest thing from his mind during his vacation.

Upon returning to the United States, the coach's thinking went straight back to the game he loved so much. In New York, he paid a visit to his son Donald who was attending Fordham and signed end Harry Jacunski who played three years for Fordham coach Jimmy Crowley, the Green Bay native who had played for Notre Dame as one of the "Four Horsemen" and who had played briefly for the Packers at the tail end of 1925.

Quite soon after Lambeau returned to Green Bay, the professional football world was rocked by the death of the NFL's head man, Joe Carr, who suffered a heart attack early in the afternoon of May 20 and died at the hospital several hours later. Carr had been involved in professional football since he founded the Columbus Pan Handles in 1904, and he had served as the NFL's president since 1921. With the possible single exception of George Halas, no man to that time could even come close to having done more to give the pro game major sport status than Carr. Although some of his methods might have been suspect, he always acted with the singular thought of doing what was best for the National Football League. Admiral William F. "Bull" Halsey could have had Carr in mind when he said, "There are no great men, only great challenges that ordinary men are forced by circumstances to meet." Building the NFL into a major league professional sport was one of the all-time great challenges in sports history, and Joe Carr met it more than admirably.

To replace Carr was Carl Storck, league vice-president and an official of the NFL since 1921. He assumed the duties of the president as provided in the league's constitution, then moved the organization's headquarters to his home town of Dayton.

At the annual meeting of the stockholders of the Green Bay Packers, Inc., that summer, it was deemed that the corporate heads were doing such a good job with the organization that all of them were re-elected to their respective posts, including the entire board of directors. Lee Joannes was entering his ninth year of leading the corporation. The only wet blanket on the thoroughly upbeat conference was the announcement by Joannes that the contemplated improvements to the west end of City Stadium had been postponed until uncertainty over the dispensation of President Roosevelt's WPA program could be determined. Then the meeting was turned over to Coach Lambeau for his view on the team's chances for copping the title in '39. Lambeau said *his 21st* squad of Green Bay Packers would be in the fight to the finish and just might get that crown a certain official had deprived them of the year before.

The author of the unbylined article about the stockholders' meeting made a very serious mistake when he wrote: "Green Bay enters its third decade of professional football history with the '39 team." (The name of the man responsible for this faux pas will probably never be known for certain because the entire sports staff of *The Green Bay Press-Gazette* of 1939 was deceased at the time of this writing.) The city of Green Bay had had professional football almost every year since 1896, and the current organization could trace its roots directly to the undefeated, unscored upon 1918 team, the Green Bay Whales captained and supported by Nate Abrams. The newspaper writer either didn't know this fact or he chose to ignore it.[*]

Just before the opening of training camp, John Walter wrote a most interesting story in the sports editor's column, *Looking Up in the Realm of Sports:*

"Howard Emich mails in the word from Madison that Green Bay football fans had better make themselves acquainted with the new movie, 'The Cowboy Quarterback,' which gives the Packers a lusty plug.

"Perhaps it would be better to wait and let the film gag take its Green Bay audience by surprise, as it did a throng in Milwaukee

---

[*] **See Chapters 1-3 of** *The History of the Green Bay Packers: The Lambeau Years — Part One.*

recently, but anyway, here's Howard's letter:

"While in Milwaukee over the week-end, I chanced to see Robert Wheeler's latest comedy, *The Cowboy Quarterback*.

"As a Packer fan well acquainted with and loyally proud of Curly Lambeau's scouting results, as well as the national fame of the Bays, I enjoyed the picture more than any other cinema offering in years.

"The Chicago *Packers* — Chicago, imagine — send their scout to Antelope, Wyoming, in search of Wheeler, a cowboy quarterback whose amazing gridiron exploits have become legendary in his native heath, news of his ability even reaching Chicago by devious means.

"The scout flies by airplane to within two miles of Antelope, begins to walk the remaining distance, but comes upon an old Indian squatting before a tepee (sic). Questioning reveals that no other paleface has held *pow-wow* with the cowboy quarterback, called Harry Lynn in the picture, and the scout gasps with relief while mopping his brow:

" 'Thank God, Green Bay hasn't beat me to it.'

"The crowd at the Warner theater shrieked with pleasure.

"To cut a feature story to newsreel length, Lynn goes to Chicago, runs wild all season to help the *Packers* to the Eastern Division championship in the pro league — yes, *Eastern* is right — but before the playoff against the Western champs, the California Ramblers, he is tricked by gamblers into an awkward position.

"He must remain out of the game or be branded *traitor* before his team. However, he gets into the game with 40 seconds to go, and needless to say scores the winning touchdown — but not before the heart-swallowingest fumble on the goal line you ever hope to see — and the *Packers* bring home the bacon, not to La Baye Verta, but to Chicago.

"Don't miss it!"

Everyone around Green Bay had a good laugh at that one. The *Chicago* Packers? It's amazing that neither George Halas nor The Green Bay Packers, Inc., sued the filmmaker for defamation of character, libel, slander, and whatever else their attorneys could think up.

Over the summer, Lambeau was able to sign nearly every veteran he wanted back from the '38 squad as well as a few more draft choices and free agents. Among the rookies were Fran Twedell, guard, Minnesota; Donald "Weenie" Wilson, back, Dubuque; Allen Moore, end, Texas A&M; Larry Craig, end, South Carolina; Paul Kell, tackle, Notre Dame; and Warren Kilbourne, tackle, Michigan. Craig, Twedell, and Kell were draft choices, while all the others came in as free agents.

When practice opened at the end of the first week of August, Coach Lambeau welcomed the largest squad of players in Green Bay history to date. Of course, not all of the 55 men would make the team that only had 30 spots to fill. According to Lambeau, only a few men could be guaranteed positions with the Packers. Don Hutson, Milt Gantenbein, Arnie Herber, Joe Laws, Cecil Isbell, and Clarke Hinkle were about the only men who felt confident that they would be in the lineup on opening day. The other 24 roster spots were up for grabs. Lambeau and assistant coach Red Smith would have their sleepless nights trying to figure out who to keep and who to let go.

After three weeks of intensive workouts, the Packers began their exhibition season. Johnny Blood, who had finally retired as a player, trained his Pittsburgh Pirates in nearby Two Rivers, Wisconsin that year. He and Lambeau cooked up a unique idea to have their two teams play a football doubleheader against each other so both coaches could get good looks at all their players under game conditions. Both games would be shortened to 10-minute quarters with shorter time periods between stanzas and between games.

In the first game, which featured mostly rookies and newcomers to their squads, the Packers and Pirates fought to a 7-7 tie. The second contest was all Packers, 17-0, as Lambeau used his veterans to crush Pittsburgh.

A little more than a week later the Packers traveled to Dallas, Texas to play a team of Southwest All-Stars in a sort of consolation game for the '38 NFL runner-up. Lambeau had already reduced his roster to 42 for the Pirates and further cut it to 37 for the All-Stars. The veterans started the game and ran up 31 points before halftime, then sat out the second half as the rookies did their part in the 31-20 victory.

The NFL season was slated to begin on September 10, the second Sunday of the month; but the Packers weren't on the schedule until the following week when they were set to host the Cardinals in Green Bay. The Chicago eleven opened against the Lions and were 21-13 victims, while the Philadelphia–Pittsburgh game was postponed for inclement weather.

By the time opening day arrived, Lambeau had his roster down to the required 30 players. Surviving the cuts were previously mentioned rookies Larry Buhler, Frank Steen, Larry Craig, Paul Kell, Charles Schultz, John Biolo, Jack Brennan, Tom Greenfield, Allen Moore, Warren Kilbourne, and Charley Brock. Frank Balazs, Fran Twedell, Weenie Wilson, and Harry Jacunski also made it but were on the disabled list when the season began.

Returning veterans included Baby Ray, Milt Gantenbein, Russ Letlow, Buckets Goldenberg, Bill Lee, Hank Bruder, Cecil Isbell, Clarke Hinkle, Don Hutson, Joe Laws, Pete Tinsley, Carl Mulleneaux, Tiny Engebretsen, Eddie Jankowski, Andy Uram, Arnie Herber, and Herm Schneidman. Earl Svendsen and Ernie Smith came out of retirement, and Dick Zoll and Clarence Thompson joined the Packers through trades with Cleveland and Pittsburgh. Dick Weisgerber was also with the team on opening day but was on injured reserve.

Among the missing were Wayland Becker, Frank Butler, Leo Katalinas, Nick Miketinac, Lee Mulleneaux, Darrell Lester, Paul Miller, Bob Monnett, Roy Schoemann, and Bernie Scherer. Becker was suspended from the team, then traded to Pittsburgh after the first game of the season. Scherer was traded to Pittsburgh over the summer. Katalinas, Miketinac, Schoemann, and Mulleneaux were cut, and the others retired.

The Cardinals and Packers were meeting for the 33rd time when the two teams took the field on opening day. Chicago had a new coach. The immortal Ernie Nevers was persuaded by Charlie Bidwill to give up college coaching and come back to the pros as the Cardinals head mentor. On the field, the series between the two clubs had been hard-fought but not of the type to create a real rivalry like both teams had with the Bears. This fact showed up at the box office where the games were staged before crowds that usually numbered less than half of what each one drew when playing the Bears. The Packers were trying to win their fourth straight from the Cardinals and sixth in the last eight games. Overall, Green Bay had won 17 while losing 12 and tying three to this date. The Packers were successful in this bid as they built up a 14-0 halftime lead on TDs by Carl Mulleneaux and Jankowski, then held off the rallying Cards in the second half to win, 14-10, in front of a sparse crowd of 11,792 fans.

The only team to hold a career won–lost edge over the Packers to this date was the Chicago Bears. In 40 previous meetings, the Bears had won 19 and there had been four ties. Just as he had always felt since the beginning of the two–division setup in the NFL, Lambeau figured the Bears were the team to beat if they were going to win a shot at the title. For three years running, the Bears had won the games in Green Bay, while the Packers had dumped Chicago four straight years in the Windy City. As they headed into their September 24 encounter, both teams were 1-0-0 and tied for first with Detroit. By Sunday night, the Packers were hoping to be alone on top of the division.

Chicago's lineup again read like a "Who's Who" in football when they took the field at City Stadium. Joe Stydahar was at one tackle spot, while the guards were Danny Fortmann and George Musso. George Wilson was one end, and Frank Bausch was at center. The backfield had Bernie Masterson, Ray Nolting, Joe Maniaci, Bill Osmanski, Gary Famiglietti, Jack Manders, and Sid Luckman. Luckman and Osmanski were just rookies in '39. They learned quickly though that the Packers weren't just the enemy two Sundays a year; Green Bay was Hell on earth, Curly Lambeau was the Devil incarnate, and the guys on the other side of the line were all demons who had to be exorcised by whatever means necessary to achieve victory. Of course, the young Packers were taught the same thing about Chicago, Halas, and the Bears by that master of football psychology Earl L. "Curly" Lambeau.

After playing a scoreless first quarter, the Bears racked up 13 points on touchdowns by Osmanski and Masterson and a PAT by "Automatic" Jack Manders who wasn't so automatic as he missed one point–after opportunity in the second quarter, and

The Lambeau Years — Part Two

Chicago headed into the locker room, feeling Green Bay was under their control at 13-0. Someone forgot to tell the Packers this because they came out of the dressing room for the third period as if they had the lead and merely had to put the finishing touches on their victory. Cecil Isbell started a third-quarter scoring spree with an 11-yard run to paydirt, culminating a 71-yard Packer drive. The Bears fouled up a lateral pass on their possession, and Milt Gantenbein fell on it on the Bears' 11. The Packers fought for every inch and got a first down on the one. After being repulsed once, Clarke Hinkle finally smashed his way over the goal to tie the game at 13-all. Tiny Engebretsen kicked his second PAT of the game, and Green Bay led, 14-13. The Bears were their own worst enemy again as Masterson threw an interception that Don Hutson hauled down. After the Packers stalled, Hinkle punted deep into Bear country, but the bungling Bruins mishandled the kick. The ball rolled into the end zone, and Tom Greenfield fell on it for Green Bay. One more Engebretsen PAT put the Pack up, 21-13. The Bears fought back with all the ferociousness that Papa Bear Halas could instill in them from the sideline, but all Chicago could do was put up one field goal in the fourth quarter. When the final gun sounded, the Packers had broken the Bears jinx, 21-16.

Cleveland had joined the NFL in '37 and was placed in the Western Division. In their previous meetings, the Packers had taken it to the Rams on all four occasions, outscoring Cleveland by a combined score of 124-41. Lambeau cautioned his Bear-mauled troops not to take the Rams too lightly, and they didn't — at least not for three quarters. At the end of the third period, Green Bay led, 24-14, behind TDs by Laws, Jankowski, and Herber and a field goal by Hinkle. But when the final gun sounded, the Rams were on top, 27-24, as Cleveland rallied to beat the Pack for the first time in history.

The loss left Green Bay (2-1-0) a full game behind Detroit (3-0-0), winners over the Cardinals (1-3-0), and in a tie for second with the Bears (2-1-0).

Lambeau backed up and regrouped for game four of the campaign. During the week, he released Fran Twedell and Frank Steen and picked up back Jimmy Lawrence on waivers from the Redskins. Lawrence had played with the Cardinals for three seasons before going to Washington in '39.

The Packers met the Cardinals in Milwaukee that Sunday before the largest crowd to ever witness a Packer game in the Cream City to that time. The head count came to 18,965. The fans saw a yawner for three quarters that turned into a heart-stopping finish in the final stanza. Green Bay built a 21-0 lead on TDs by Hutson, Hinkle, and Laws in the first, second, and third periods respectively. Then Chicago came to life scoring two quick touchdowns in the early going of the last quarter to cut the margin to 21-14. Hutson tacked on his second six-pointer at this juncture of the contest to make the score 27-14, only to see the Cards march right down the field and close the gap to seven points again. Lambeau went conservative at this time and ran out the clock to hold on to the 27-20 victory.

The Packers (3-1-0) and the Bears (3-1-0) moved up on the idle Lions (3-0-0), while New York (2-0-1) and Washington (2-0-1) remained tied for the Eastern lead.

Lambeau gave his veterans the next Sunday off when the Packers visited St. Louis for an exhibition game against their minor league affiliate. The Gunners of the lesser AFL — not to be confused with the major league AFL that had played in '36 and '37 — weren't much of a match for the younger Packers who soundly thrashed the Missourians, 31-0.

While the Packers (3-1-0) were enjoying the "rest" in the River City, the Bears (4-1-0) were stomping on the Cardinals (1-5-0) and the Lions (4-0-0) were slipping past Cleveland (1-4-0). At the same time, New York (3-0-1) and Washington (3-0-1) were showing the rest of the East why they were part of the "Big Four."

During the following week, Lambeau released Tuffy Thompson and signed veteran guard Gus Zarnas who had played for the Bears in '38 and had started the '39 season with Brooklyn before being released.

The fourth Sunday in October was "Showdown Day No. 1" for the Packers. The undefeated Detroit Lions were due into City Stadium. Tickets were in great demand, and Spike Spachmann's ticket crew was busy all through the week filling orders. When the sabbath final rolled around, 22,558 spectators — the second largest crowd in the city's history — rocked the stands as their favorites fell behind early, 7-0, then scored 26 unanswered points over the final three periods to win going away. Again, it was Hutson putting points on the board for the Packers — this time 13 on two TDs and a PAT — to lead the way. Andy Uram scored the other touchdown, and Engebretsen added five points with a field goal and two PATs.

While the Packers (4-1-0) were regaining a share of first place with the Lions (4-1-0), the Bears (4-2-0) missed a golden opportunity to take the top spot when they lost a close one to the Giants (4-0-1), co-leaders in the East with Washington (4-0-1).

On the eve of the team's departure for Milwaukee for their next game, Lambeau sent Jack Brennan and Warren Kilbourne to the Kenosha Cardinals, another affiliate in the minor league AFL. The move was necessitated by the return to health of veteran tackle Ernie Smith. Also, Lambeau felt the two linemen needed more seasoning if they were to play in the NFL.

Since New York did a good deed for Green Bay by beating the Bears, the Packers felt obligated to return the favor when the Redskins met them in Milwaukee the next week. Washington coach Red Flaherty had assembled a team that many considered to be much stronger than that of '38 when Washington finished a close second to the Giants in the East. This made for good hype, exciting fans all across the state to invade the Cream City for what was billed as a possible glimpse at the eventual NFL title game. A record 24,308 folks piled into State Fair Park in spite of a steady drizzle throughout the game to watch the Dairy State's favorite football team play. Very few of them went home wanting their money back as the Packers intercepted six passes and recovered two Washington fumbles to hold off the rampaging Redskins, 24-14. Hinkle, Bruder, and Laws scored the TDs, and Engebretsen added a field goal.

As October came to a close, the Packers (5-1-0) and Lions (5-1-0) sat atop the Western Division, two losses ahead of the Bears (4-3-0), losers to Detroit. Over in the East, New York (5-0-1) nipped Brooklyn (3-3-1) to effectively put the Dodgers out of the chase for the division flag.

"Out of the fat and into the fire." Or something like that. No sooner had the Packers beaten Detroit and Washington on successive Sundays than they had to pay a little visit to Chicago to face the half-crazed Monsters of the Midway, losers of two straight games.

This was "Showdown Day No. 2" for Green Bay. Like the Packers who wanted to end the Bear jinx in their park, the Bears wanted to end the Packer jinx in Chicago. The Packers hadn't lost to the Bears in Wrigley Field since '34. With only a few minor exceptions, the lineups were the same as when the two elevens met in September.

Joe Laws started the scoring in the first quarter when he returned a punt 72 yards for a TD to give Green Bay a 7-0 lead. The Bears evened things just seconds later on a long run from scrimmage. After an exchange of punts, Cecil Isbell found Milt Gantenbein in the end zone from 32 yards out to make the score at the end of the period, 13-7. Chicago came back in the next quarter to take a 14-13 lead that the Bears increased to 17-13 only a few minutes afterward. With less than a minute to go, Isbell hit Harry Jacunski with a scoring toss from 29 yards away to make the halftime score, 20-17, in favor of Green Bay. The Packers drove all the way down to the Bears' 10 on their first possession of the third quarter only to be thwarted when Bill Osmanski intercepted Herber's short pass and returned it to midfield. Hardly tired at all, Osmanski then ripped off a 37-yard gain from scrimmage to set up a Chicago TD that put the Bears ahead, 23-20. After both teams missed on field goal opportunities, the Packers were finally able to mount a 68-yard scoring drive that ended with Herber hitting Hutson in the end zone from 20 yards out to put Green Bay up, 27-23. On their next possession, the Bears started from their own 25 and marched up the field on Sid Luckman passes to the Packers' 10 where Osmanski went to work for the final TD of the afternoon, giving the Bears a 30-27 victory. The Packers didn't give up in the waning seconds as they drove down to the Chicago 33 when time expired.

The loss knocked the Packers (5-2-0) out of a tie for first with Detroit (6-1-0), but the Bears (5-3-0) kept their title hopes alive. In the East, Washington (5-1-1) and New York (5-1-1) were once again tied for the top spot.

In the aftermath of the game with the Bears, George Halas

accused the Packers and Lions of using illegal pass plays, although he stated that the miscues by the Packers might not have been intentional. Either way, Lambeau was hot over it. He denied it in the *Press-Gazette* and went on to say, "Furthermore, the Chicago Bears are the last team in the world to talk about unfair tactics on the football field. We have tolerated their rough, dirty play long enough, and now I am going to demand that Halas either apologize for his inferences in yesterday's (*Chicago*) *Tribune*, or try to prove them.... Halas' charges are like someone committing murder at the same time he is objecting to someone walking across his lawn."

Halas neither apologized for the remarks attributed to him nor tried to justify them in subsequent weeks. The truth was *Tribune* sportswriter George Strickler, who wrote the article where Halas allegedly accused the Packers and the Lions of cheating, took a little journalistic license by quoting Halas out of context and filling in the gaps with what he thought Halas meant to say. Much of the venom of Papa Bear's so-called accusations was aimed at the Lions as pre-game hype; the Bears were scheduled to play in Detroit the following Sunday.

Meanwhile, Lambeau put his players back to work. The winless Eagles were next up on their schedule, but the coach kept reminding his charges that Washington had only beaten Philadelphia by a single point, the same as the Giants. Translation: the Eagles were a tough team not to be taken lightly. Lambeau was right about that. The Packers built up a 20-3 lead on TDs by Andy Uram, Charley Brock, and Clarke Hinkle, then held on to win, 23-16, as the Eagles mounted a late attack to make a game of it.

Halas had his Bears (6-3-0) rolling now as they mashed Detroit (6-2-0) in the Motor City, letting Green Bay (6-2-0) back into a tie for first in the West. While in the East, Washington (6-1-1) and New York (6-1-1) remained tied for the lead as they headed for their season-ending showdown contest.

Lambeau faced the same situation of getting his gridders up for the game the next week when the Packers visited Brooklyn to take on the red-clad Dodgers. Washington had creamed the Dodgers, 42-0, the week before, but Lambeau warned his players not to be fooled by that. Brooklyn coach Potsy Clark had hated Lambeau and Green Bay since his days as head mentor at Portsmouth. Clark would pull every trick in the book to beat his avowed enemy. To prove his point, Lambeau put his team through heavy contact drills at their Travers Island, New York training site the week before the contest. He made his point completely as the Packers rolled over the Dodgers, 28-0, on touchdowns by Hutson, Bud Svendsen, Jacunski, and Isbell.

During the week, the Detroit management filed an objection to the Rams using Dutch Clark, the Cleveland coach, as a player against the Lions. Detroit claimed rightfully so that Clark still belonged to the Lions — as a player, although not as a coach. Clark understood why the Detroit people were behaving like that, so he used their ploy to fire up his own team to beat the Lions in Cleveland, 14-3.

With Detroit (6-3-0) losing, Green Bay (7-2-0) was left alone at the top of the Western Division, but this was no time for the Packers to relax. The Bears (7-3-0) had also won that week and were looking for Green Bay to stumble at either Cleveland or Detroit in the weeks ahead so they could meet the Eastern Division winner, either New York (7-1-1) or Washington (7-1-1), for the NFL crown.

In three short years, the expansion Rams had gained respect-ability in the NFL as witnessed by the early season upset of the Packers in Green Bay and their recent victory over Detroit. Cleveland's home attendance was growing each week, and when the Packers came to the Lake Erie city on November 26, a record crowd of 30,690 appreciative patrons showed up at Municipal Stadium to watch the Rams take the Pack to the wire before losing, 7-6. Joe Laws scored the tying touchdown, and Tiny Engebretsen kicked the winning extra point with less than two minutes to go.

The win guaranteed the Packers (8-2-0) a tie for first place in the Western Division's final standings. Green Bay's only re-maining challenger was the Chicago Bears (8-3-0) because Detroit (6-4-0) was eliminated from the race when the Lions lost their third straight game. Meanwhile, the Redskins (8-1-1) and the Giants (8-1-1) were primed for their final Sunday winner-take-all battle in New York.

All the Packers had to do was beat or tie the Lions in Detroit on the first Sunday in December to host the NFL title game. With their season already in the trash bin, the Lions had nothing left to play for except pride, which they did admirably. In the mud and rain at Titan Stadium, the Packers had to fight for every inch of turf to gain a 12-7 win over Detroit. Five first half fumbles stopped Green Bay scoring drives in their tracks, and the only scoring the Pack could do was a field goal by Tiny Engebretsen, while Detroit put a seven on the board. Baby Ray blocked a punt in the third quarter that slithered out of the end zone for a Green Bay safety to close the gap to 7-5. Then the Packers made one last attempt at the Detroit goal line, and Hinkle was the man of the hour as he torpedoed his way through the Lions for the winning touchdown.

While the Packers (9-2-0) were winning the Western Division laurels before 30,699 brave souls in Detroit (6-5-0), the Giants (9-1-1) got their prayers answered at the Polo Grounds as 62,404 fans watched a last minute Washington (8-2-1) field goal attempt go wide of the mark to preserve New York's stirring 9-7 win over the Redskins, setting up the second straight NFL title game between the Goliaths of Gotham and the Davids of tiny Green Bay.

Many Packer fans in the Green Bay area were irate over Lee Joannes and the executive committee's decision to play the championship game at State Fair Park in Milwaukee. Some regional grocers who bought their products from Joannes Bros. Wholesale Grocers told the truck drivers to turn around and take their groceries to Milwaukee; that's how upset they were over losing the title tilt to the Cream City. Rumors were in great abundance as to why the executive committee chose to play the game in Milwaukee instead of Green Bay. They ranged everywhere from Joannes and the boys — including Curly Lambeau — "taking a little something under the table from a small group of Milwaukee politicians and businessmen" to "the Packers were going to move to the Cream City" permanently the following year. Folks were saying that Joannes and Lambeau began making deals to move the game to Milwaukee long before it was even hinted at in the newspapers.

The directory of the Green Bay Packers, Inc., didn't put their stamp of approval on it until the Wednesday before the game.

They stated in a written press release that they came to that decision reluctantly because the people of Green Bay so richly deserved to have the contest in their own town. Also, Joannes thought the cost of the tickets for the tilt would be prohibitive to many Packer fans in the Green Bay area, so attendance wouldn't be what it should be for a game of such caliber. Joannes finally stated that he and the executive committee felt the Packers' Milwaukee fans should be rewarded for their continued support throughout the years.

The exact truth may never be known, but the decision to play at State Fair Park instead of City Stadium was the wiser and logical choice — from a business standpoint. State Fair Park had a seating capacity nearly 40% greater than the Green Bay field, and Milwaukee had proven that it would support the Packers. Also, the weather was a consideration not to be denied. The difference in the winter climate between the two cities can be immense on any given day. Most likely, Milwaukee would have better climactic conditions for the game which would induce more fans to turn out and would produce better play between the two combatants.

Whatever the reasons for choosing Milwaukee, the decision turned out to be a perfect one. The weather was almost ideal for football in December: clear skies and temperatures above freezing, although it was a little breezy. The playing field was in excellent condition: dry and soft as opposed to frozen. The stands were filled to capacity and then some as extra seating was placed on the oval track around the field: 32,279 patrons bought tickets. And the best of all: the Packers played a magnificent game.

Green Bay outplayed New York in every facet of the sport. Herber completed five of eight passes for 59 yards and a touchdown to Milt Gantenbein. Isbell was two of two for 37 yards through the air and a TD toss to Joe Laws. Eddie Jankowski bulled over the goal for a touchdown, and Ernie Smith and Tiny Engebretsen each hit on a field goal. On defense, the Pack snatched six New York passes out of the air and held the Giants to only 72 yards on the ground and 94 through the skies, many of those coming on desperation plays during the late going. But best of all, the Packers kept the Giants out of the end zone and off the scoreboard as Green Bay whitewashed New York, 27-0, for the widest margin of victory in an NFL title game to date.

When the sun set on Wisconsin on December 10, 1939, every pro football fan in the state knew their Green Bay Packers had won their fifth National Football League championship in 11 years. The Lambeau dynasty was alive and well.

§ § §

13

Resting on Laurels

If nothing else, Curly Lambeau was a superior judge of football talent. He could spot a real player in a midfield pile-up from the last row of the second deck of a stadium, and as soon as he picked his man out of the mass of tangled bodies, the coach was hot to sign the youngster to a Packer contract.

But when it came time for the draft, Lambeau had to rely almost totally on the word of other people. Sometimes that was good, and sometimes it wasn't so good. At the draft meeting of 1939 in Milwaukee the day before the Packers embarrassed the Giants for the National Football League championship, Curly Lambeau and the Packers had one of those times when the word of others was really bad.

Topping Lambeau's list of selections was Hal Van Every, a powerful halfback from Minnesota. After Cecil Isbell left Purdue for Green Bay, Lou Brock took over as the Boilermakers star back. Brock was the second man chosen by Lambeau. In order after these two were Esco Sarkkinen, end, Ohio State; Dick Cassiano, halfback, Pittsburgh; Millard White, tackle, Tulane; George Seemann, end, Nebraska; Frank Bykowski, guard, Purdue; J.R. Manley, guard, Oklahoma; Jack Brown, halfback, Purdue; Don Guritz, guard, Northwestern; Phil Gaspar, halfback, Southern Cal; Ambrose Schindler, halfback, Southern Cal; Bill Kerr, end, Notre Dame; Mel Brewer, guard, Illinois; Ray Andrus, back, Vanderbilt; Archie Kodros, center, Michigan; James Gillette, halfback, Virginia; Al Matuza, center, Georgetown; Jim Reeder, tackle, Illinois; Vincent Eichler, back, Cornell; and Henry Luebcke, tackle, Iowa. Only three men on this list made the Packers in 1940. Top choices Van Every and Brock and sixth pick Seemann were the only men to make the final cut.

The Packers started the new year of 1940 by playing the NFL All-Stars in Los Angeles on January 7. Lambeau took the team west just before Christmas and began preparing them for the game on their first day in California. Workouts were limited to two hours each morning from ten until noon. The rest of the time the Packers were either eating or playing — golf in the afternoon and "bridge" at night. While his players were enjoying themselves in group activities, Lambeau conferred with Pete Smith at MGM about putting the Packers in another film while they were in California. When they finally got down to playing the game at the Coliseum, the Packers took it to the All-Stars, 16-7.

Plans for a new major league American Football League had been formulating for over a year, and at the beginning of 1940, the loop appeared to be ready to get off the ground. Exactly which cities would get franchises was still up in the air in January, but the magnates of the NFL didn't care too much about where the AFL played as long as they kept their hands off the NFL's star players.

Consisting of Kenosha, St. Louis, Columbus, Cincinnati, Dayton, Los Angeles, and Louisville, the minor league American Football League did care. Its leaders didn't want the new circuit to play in or near any of its cities. To combat this, the little AFL expanded. On January 9, it was announced that Milwaukee was given a franchise.

This presented a problem for the Green Bay Packers, Inc. Construction of a new stadium was under consideration in the Cream City. If the new facility were to be built at North Holton and Capitol Drive, would the Packers be given preferential treatment when it came time to rent it? The same question applied to State Fair Park, if the new park failed to be built.

Milwaukee hotel man George M. Harris, the owner of the little AFL franchise, replied negatively when asked by reporters if he would demand first choice of playing dates at either field. He said he had absolutely no intention of trying to buck the Packers in Milwaukee. Even if both stadiums were available, he wouldn't schedule any games on dates when the Packers would be in town. Harris was smart to go this way because playing on the same day would only split the football audience and neither team would prosper for it.

Plans for the new stadium soon collapsed, but details for the new Milwaukee football team continued to fall into place. In fact, Harris moved ahead without delay. He got his Milwaukee Chiefs into the big league AFL, and he hired former Packer tackle Ivan "Tiny" Cahoon to be the head coach. Cahoon had been coaching high school football in Green Bay since the early days of his retirement as a player.

These two moves concerned the officers of the Green Bay Packers, Inc., but they were hardly going to lose any sleep over a league that had yet to play its first game. The Chiefs could play in Milwaukee. The Packers would, too. There would be peaceful co-existence — as long as the Packers continued to make money in the Cream City.

Soon after the Packers returned from California, trainer Dave Woodward was stricken by a heart attack and died on February 9. He had been the team's aches-and-pains man for six years, and before that, he had been the athletic trainer at the University of Minnesota for 16 years. Woodward was the first real trainer to be hired by the Packers.

At the annual meeting of NFL owners in April, George Marshall tried to have acting league president Carl Storck ousted from the top spot. A few weeks prior to the conference Marshall and George Halas had tried to interest *The Chicago Tribune* sports editor Arch Ward into taking the job, but Ward declined to accept the generous offer of a 10-year contract calling for $25,000 in salary per year. This left the owners in a quandary about what to do with Storck. A compromise was struck.

The biggest objection to Storck was all the power that would be placed in his hands. Among his duties was the job of choosing game officials. Marshall was still bitter over losing the Eastern Division title the year before, and he blamed referee Bill Halloran for the loss, claiming Halloran was "inefficient" during that game. Marshall wanted the job selecting game officials turned over to a committee of owners. Storck and his supporters were agreeable to this to keep Marshall in a peaceful mood.

As 1940 wore on, player contracts filtered into Lambeau's office in Green Bay.

George Seemann, the end out of Nebraska, and Bob Adkins, a back from Marshall, were the only two rookies signed before the league meeting in April. Immediately afterward, Fordham end Ray Riddick put his name on the dotted line. A few days later Hal Van Every, the Packers' number one draft choice from Minnesota, came to terms. Before the month was over, Lou Brock, the Purdue line-smashing halfback who was a distant relation to Packers' center Charley Brock, joined the Green Bay fold as did Georgia guard Howard "Smiley" Johnson and North Carolina State back Connie Mack Berry.

Dick "Red" Evans, an end from Iowa, signed in mid-May. At the end of the month, Lambeau inked Fred Shirey, a tackle from Nebraska who had turned down the Philadelphia Eagles the year before to go into the coaching ranks. The Packers obtained the rights to Shirey from the Eagles for their rights to draft choice Millard White. It turned out to be a good trade because White never played in the NFL and Shirey made the Green Bay squad in '40.

The Brooklyn Dodgers needed linemen, and the Packers could use another good back. A deal was made. Lambeau sent Bud Svendsen and the rights to draft choice Dick Cassiano to Brooklyn, and in return, Green Bay acquired the great Beattie Feathers, the holder of the single season rushing record — to that time — 1,004 yards in '34.

Lambeau had 35 men under contract by the middle of June. Only nine veterans — Don Hutson, Baby Ray, Bill Lee, Paul Kell, Cecil Isbell, Jimmy Lawrence, Larry Craig, Eddie Jankowski, and Clarke Hinkle — remained unsigned, and of these, the coach considered just three of them — Craig, Lee, and Jankowski — as potential problems. All three came to terms in due time.

When the stockholders of the Green Bay Packers, Inc., met in July, a new wrinkle was put into the organization that would prove to be a great mistake. Out of gratitude for winning the NFL title for the fifth time in 11 years, the stockholders agreed to create a second vice–presidency for the organization with the intention of filling the post with Earl L. Lambeau. Also, Lambeau was elected to the board of directors, supplanting Frank Walker. The directory then re–elected Lee Joannes as president, Fred Leicht as first vice–president, Frank Jonet as treasurer, and George Whitney Calhoun as secretary.

A few days after the annual meeting Lambeau announced he had traded long–time Packer Hank Bruder to Pittsburgh for guard Lou Midler who was in his second year in the NFL after playing college ball at Minnesota. Lambeau said that he was tired of Bruder's annual threats to retire and had drafted accordingly. Midler signed with the Packers a few days later.

Because the Packers were NFL champs, they were scheduled to play the College All–Stars at Soldier Field in Chicago in late August. To avoid being embarrassed again, Lambeau brought his players into camp early and began putting them through a rigorous training routine right from the start. Two weeks before the charity contest in Chicago the Packers held an intrasquad game that didn't do much to help Lambeau separate the men from the boys. In fact, it only confused the issue of Jimmy Lawrence who played spectacularly, surprising those who thought he would be among the first to be cut from the team.

Unlike the '37 College All–Star game in which the Packers nearly died from the heat because their brand new game jerseys couldn't "breathe" and they were humbled, 6-0, by the rookies, Green Bay took the field in Chicago ready to show the whole football world who the NFL champions were. The Packers came out passing and built an early lead that the All–Stars could never surmount. When all was done, Green Bay had won a decisive victory in an offensive affair, 45-28.

The following Monday the Packers took on the Washington Redskins in Milwaukee in their first NFL exhibition game. Nearly 15,000 fans turned out to see Green Bay take Washington into camp, 28-20. This game finally gave Lambeau some indication about who to keep and who to let go. He released three rookies and second–year man Warren Kilbourne. At the same time, veteran tackle and placekicker Ernie Smith quit the game to take over the family business in California.

As a final tune-up before the opening regular season game against the Eagles, the Packers hosted the Kenosha Cardinals of the little AFL. Just for the sake of old times, Lambeau put Johnny Blood into the Packer lineup. Blood was joining Kenosha that year as a player and assistant manager of the club. Green Bay held sway over the Cardinals, 17-0, and Lambeau saw where he could make more cuts on his roster.

Veteran quarterback Herm Schneidman decided to pack it in after five seasons in a Packer uniform to tend to his business in Quincy, Illinois. Lambeau then released rookie quarterback Glenn Olson, sending him to Kenosha along with Jim Gillette, Jimmy Lawrence, and Connie Mack Berry. Fullback Frank Balazs was put on the suspended list for "insubordination" when the team was in Milwaukee to play Washington. Actually, Balazs had gotten drunk and told Lambeau where he could put a football. Lambeau thought the suggestion was anatomically impossible, so he suspended Balazs for being so dumb.

With the squad now down to the new league limit of 33, the Packers were set to take on the Eagles in Green Bay. As the Eagles, Philadelphia had yet to beat the Packers in six tries, although some of the games were close. John Walter wrote in the *Press-Gazette* the week before the game that the 1940 Eagles, with little Davey O'Brien calling the signals, would be the best yet to visit Green Bay. He was so right as the Packers built a 27-6 lead after three quarters before having to squelch a Philly rally in the final minute to win, 27-20. Carl Mulleneaux hauled down two TD passes from Cecil Isbell and Arnie Herber; Isbell galloped 39 yards for another six-pointer; and Clarke Hinkle booted a pair of field goals.

After seeing limited action in the first game of the year, George Seeman was released and Beattie Feathers was farmed out to Kenosha. Others in the opening day contest were ends Don Hutson, Ray Riddick, Connie Mack Berry, Bob Adkins, and Dick Evans; tackles Baby Ray, Bill Lee, Fred Shirey, Paul Kell, and Charles Schultz; guards Russ Letlow, Gus Zarnas, Tiny Engebretsen, Smiley Johnson, and Buckets Goldenberg; centers Tom Greenfield and Charley Brock; and backs Larry

Craig, Joe Laws, Eddie Jankowski, Lou Brock, Dick Weisgerber, Hal Van Every, Andy Uram, and Larry Buhler.

Tickets to the next fray against the Bears were sold out three days before the scheduled contest. This "sad news" was announced on a billboard that Mrs. Barbara Bishop posted in front of the American Legion hall. The sign also advised the disgruntled many who missed out on the 1940 game to buy season tickets in '41.

Meanwhile, George Halas and Lambeau played their usual game of psychology in the newspapers of both cities, and everyone eagerly awaited the clash of what many considered at the time to be two of the greatest football teams ever assembled. Halas sent a telegram to Lambeau asking Curly to take it easy on his poor Bears and not run up the score. Lambeau sneered back, saying, "The Bears are coming up here to give us the going over of our lives, and if we let down for an instant, and believe any of this stuff from a team which has had five practice games and is primed to the hilt, we'll take a bad beating."

Came Sunday night, and Lambeau was wishing he hadn't been so right. The real Monsters of the Midway showed up at City Stadium and completely annihilated the Packers, 41-10, in front of 22,557 witnesses to the worst defeat in Green Bay history. The Packers buried themselves with their own mistakes. Seven Green Bay passes were intercepted by the Bears and turned into points soon afterward, with several new plays that Halas had designed specifically for this contest. The Pack outgained Chicago on the ground and through the air, but they could only penetrate the goal line once when Herber connected with Hutson for a third quarter score.

To make sure he wasn't caught off guard again, Lambeau, Red Smith, Hutson, and Bill Lee took the train to Chicago the following Wednesday to scout Green Bay's next opponent. The Cardinals were playing hosts to the Bears under the lights of Comiskey Park. The scouts came home worried as Jimmy Conzelmann's Redbirds whipped the Bears, 21-7.

Milwaukee fans honored their home town hero, Buckets Goldenberg at halftime of the 35th meeting — seventh in Milwaukee — between the Packers and Cardinals. The eighth year pro played his guts out as usual, and the Packers took out their frustration of the previous week on the Cards, 31-6. Isbell scored a pair of touchdowns, and Hutson and Laws crossed the goal once each as Green Bay beat the Chicago South Siders for the 20th time.

A break in the schedule gave the Packers the next Sunday off, allowing Lambeau a chance to do a little scouting of the Marquette–Wisconsin college game in Madison and the Rams–Bears game in Cleveland the day after. The coach got a good line on a few collegiate stars, and he was able to make a couple of trades. Green Bay traded tackle Fred Shirey to the Rams, then picked up tackle Leo "Moose" Disend, a third–year man who had played for Albright College before graduating to the pros, from the Brooklyn Dodgers.

The Rams had managed only one win over the Packers in six previous contests, and that win was in Green Bay in '39. Cleveland coach Dutch Clark was hoping for another upset when his Rams invaded Green Bay for the October 13 game. It wasn't to be, however, as the Packers connected on four touchdown passes — three from Isbell and one from Herber — to shear the Rams, 31-14. Carl Mulleneaux caught two scoring tosses, and Hutson and Handy Andy Uram snared one each.

With the season now five weeks old, the Packers (3-1-0) sat on top of the Western Division with the Bears (3-1-0). Detroit (2-2-1) held down third with Cleveland (1-3-0) in fourth and the Cardinals (1-3-2) in last. Out East, as Wisconsinites say, the powerful Redskins (4-0-0) appeared unbeatable, and second-place Brooklyn (3-1-0) looked much improved. The Giants (2-1-1) were still the Giants, and the two Pennsylvania teams — Pittsburgh (1-3-2) and Philadelphia (0-5-0) — were still dismal.

The Detroit Lions had won only one title since joining the NFL in 1930 as the Portsmouth Spartans, and that accomplishment was achieved in '35 two years after moving to Detroit. The head coach that year and every year before '35 and one afterward had been Potsy Clark. He left the Lions in '37 to take the helm of the Brooklyn Dodgers. After three seasons in Flatbush, he was back in Detroit directing the fortunes of the Lions once again.

Byron "Whizzer" White, who starred at Colorado then did a turn with the Pittsburgh Pirates in '38 before going off to

England with his Rhodes Scholarship in '39, was back in the NFL because of the war in Europe. But instead of rejoining Pittsburgh, White came over to the Lions to form a one-two punch with Lloyd Cardwell, the bruising back from Nebraska.

In 18 meetings of the two teams, the Packers had won 13, lost four, and there was one tie. A good crowd of 21,001 was on hand at City Stadium to watch the Lions up their win total to five as they downed Green Bay, 23-14. Once more the vaunted Green Bay aerial attack proved to be the Packers downfall as Detroit intercepted seven passes to go with the recovery of two Packer fumbles.

While Green Bay (3-2-0) was losing to Detroit (3-2-1), the Bears (4-1-0) were dumping Brooklyn (3-2-0) and the Rams (2-3-0) were burying the Cardinals (1-4-2) in the Western Division cellar. In the East, Washington (5-0-0) reminded the Eagles (0-6-0) why they were in Philadelphia, and New York (3-1-1) was doing likewise with the Steelers (1-4-2).

In five meetings with Green Bay since Pittsburgh joined the NFL in '33, the Steelers (nee Pirates) hadn't come close to beating the Packers on even one occasion. The Pack had out-scored the Steelers by a combined score of 170-24, and Green Bay had shut out Pittsburgh three times. Packer fans had little respect for the Pennsylvanians when they were the Pirates, and they had less for them now that Johnny Blood was no longer calling the shots for Art Rooney's team. Lambeau and the Packers had even less respect for the Steelers as the coach played most of the game with reserves and the veterans sat back on the bench enjoying Green Bay's 24-3 victory in front of 13,307 Milwaukeeans. Bob Adkins ran back an intercepted pass for one TD; Frank Balazs, finally out of Lambeau's doghouse, burst through the line for another; and Hutson pulled down yet another TD pass.

The Western Division standings began to take a definite shape that week with the Bears (5-1-0) on top, the Packers (4-2-0) in second, Lions (3-3-1) third, Rams (2-4-0) fourth, and the Cards (2-4-2) still bringing up the rear. The Eastern Division had the Redskins (6-0-0) still looking unbeatable in first place, the Dodgers (4-2-0) in second, Giants (3-2-1) third, Steelers (1-5-2) fourth, and Eagles (0-7-0) dead last.

Another reason for Lambeau to rest his veterans against the Steelers was the Bears were next on the Packers' schedule. He knew the team had to be at full strength if they were to have any kind of chance at downing the Monsters in Wrigley Field. Halas had managed to add two more greats to an already legendary team when he drafted halfback George McAfee out of Duke and center Clyde "Bulldog" Turner from Hardin–Simmons. Lambeau and the Packers had gotten a really good look at both of these men in the first encounter in Green Bay, and everyone had to admit that the two rookies made the Bears tougher.

There was one bright spot for the Packers as they headed to Chicago the Saturday before the game. George Musso would not be playing. The Bears' top–flight guard was injured, and his replacement was third–year man Aldo Forte. As it turned out, Forte played so well that Musso was hardly missed.

A full house of 45,434 cheering fans filled up the stands that first Sunday in November, knowing from the start that this was a make–or–break game for the Packers. A win by the Bears would just about wrap up the Western Division crown for them as it would leave the Packers a full two games behind with four games left to play. The pressure was on Green Bay more than Chicago because the Packers, even if they were to defeat the Bears, had all four of their remaining games on the road while the Bears had two at home. The likelihood of Green Bay winning all four and the Bears losing at least two had but two chances: slim and none.

With these thoughts buzzing through their heads, the Packers and Bears took the field. Green Bay kicked off, and the Bears went into their powerhouse man–in–motion T–formation attack. They drove down to just six inches short of the goal line before giving up the ball on downs. After a Green Bay punt, the Monsters came right back down the field but this time they scored to go up, 7-0. The Packers bounced back early in the second period to tie the game on a Herber–to–Hutson TD pass. Giving it all they had, the Bruins roared back again, returning the ensuing kickoff to the Green Bay 41. From there, they marched methodically toward the end zone, crossed the goal line, and went on top again, 14-7. For the remainder of the afternoon, the Packers held off every Chicago assault, driving the Bears backward much of the time, but Green Bay was unable to pierce the Chicago goal again. The halftime score stood up until the final gun. The Bears went to showers as happy winners.

Another Lambeau trait was his tenacity. The man was a pit bulldog when he wanted something. He would sink his teeth into whatever it was and not let go until all hope was absolutely lost. His Packers had been beaten twice by the Bears, but with four weeks to go in the season, Green Bay was still in the race — at least by the numbers.

The Cardinals had no mathematical chance to win the division title when they hosted the Packers the following Sunday, but the Lions still had hope as the Bears visited them in the Motor City. Down but not yet out, Detroit slipped by the Bears, 17-14, while Clarke Hinkle was scoring three touchdowns to lead Green Bay over the other Chicago eleven, 28-7.

Now with three games to go in the season, the Bears (6-2-0) didn't look so invincible atop the Western Division standings. The Packers' (5-3-0) chances of overtaking them still weren't good, but they had a better chance than Detroit (4-4-1) and Cleveland (4-4-0). It had been a week of upsets in the East, too, as Washington (7-1-0) missed a chance to wrap up the crown there when Brooklyn (5-3-0) beat the Redskins and New York (4-3-1) lost. The only clinching done that week was done by Pittsburgh (2-6-2) and Philadelphia (0-8-0). The Steelers beat the Eagles to guarantee fourth place for themselves and last place for the Quaker City crew.

With hope shining ever so brightly again in Green Bay, Lambeau chartered two airplanes for the Packers to fly to their next game in New York. Clarke Hinkle said often that Lambeau liked to go first class when the Packers traveled. Going by airplane wouldn't be just first class; it would also be the first time any NFL team flew to a game.

The team wasn't scheduled to leave for the Big Apple until Friday, but lousy weather — cold with high winds — made practicing one more day in Green Bay a bad idea. This should have been taken as the first omen of things to come.

The second bad break came during the flight from Chicago to New York. It was supposed to be a non–stop trip but turned out not to be. The Packers and all their equipment weighed so much that the planes used up extra fuel and were forced to land in Cleveland to gas up again. While they were on the ground, the United Airlines officials conferred with Lambeau about weather conditions in New York. A heavy fog had settled over the city, causing air traffic to pile up over La Guardia Airport. It was quite possible that the two chartered planes carrying the Packers could get caught in this jam up, which would cause a delay in landing of possibly two hours or force the planes to return to Cleveland. Either possibility was risky because the planes were using so much fuel that they might not have enough to stay in the air for two hours over New York or have enough to fly back to Cleveland. Lambeau considered the risks and chose to make the rest of the trip on the ground. Grumpily, the Packers boarded a train for Gotham, their record first flight as a pro football team only half completed.

If two omens weren't enough, the opening kickoff should have told Lambeau that his team was wasting its time pursuing the Bears. Larry Buhler took the ball on the one, ran it back to the 20, and was hit by three Giant tacklers. He coughed up the ball, and Lee Shaffer recovered it for New York. Three plays later, Shaffer hauled in a Len Barnum pass for the game's only touchdown and an early lead that held up the rest of the afternoon. Although the Packers led the Giants in every statistical category, New York was on the long end of a 7-3 score at sunset.

The toughest news of the day had still to reach the Packers when the final gun sounded at the Polo Grounds. They had lost; that much they knew. But they didn't know that the Bears had also lost and that they had blown a great chance to regain at least a share of first place.

On several occasions, Green Bay had completely dominated the expansion teams of Pittsburgh, Philadelphia, Cleveland, and Cincinnati when it had a team, but the Packers hadn't really clobbered any one of the older, established clubs since crushing the Portsmouth Spartans, 47-13, in 1930. Even then, the Spartans were new to the NFL. Feeling frustrated and full of revenge, the Packers headed for Detroit.

Entering the game, the Lions still had the faintest of hopes of overtaking Green Bay and Chicago. This was to be their last game of the year, and they knew they had to win to keep that thin ray of light at the end of tunnel alive. The light dimmed with each passing minute of play.

On their third possession of the game, the Lions' Whizzer White's pass was intercepted on the Green Bay 25 by Lou Brock who returned it to the Detroit one. Two plays later Isbell went over for the TD. Hutson added the PAT, and the Pack led, 7-0. The next time the Packers got the ball they marched 52 yards to score on an Isbell pass to Hutson from 13 yards out. The extra point went awry, and the score at the end of the first quarter was 13-0 Green Bay. The Lions had the ball to start the second period. Charley Price dropped back to pass, was rushed by Larry Craig, and fumbled. Carl Mulleneaux picked up the loose ball and ran it into the end zone. Hutson added another PAT, and the Packers lead was expanded, 20-0. The Packers stopped Detroit on their own 18 and took over the ball on downs. With military-like precision, Isbell led the team downfield in 11 plays to score on a 14-yard run by Eddie Jankowski and a PAT by Hutson to make the halftime score, 27-0, Packers.

Paul Kell recovered a Lion fumbled shortly after the second half kickoff to give the Packers the ball on the Detroit 24. The Lions held, and Bob Adkins' field goal attempt was wide of the mark. A bad punt by White gave the Packers the ball again in Detroit territory, this time on the 39. They moved down to the Lions' nine before stalling out, and Hinkle kicked a field goal to put Green Bay up another three, 30-0, by the end of the third stanza.

Hal Van Every got the next scoring drive started by intercepting another White pass and returning it to the Lions' 34. On the first play of the fourth quarter, Andy Uram danced 14 yards around right end to paydirt, and Adkins added the PAT to put the Packers ahead, 37-0. Van Every intercepted another pass by White on the Lions' next possession and returned it to the Detroit 44. Six plays later Jankowski racked up his second TD of the afternoon. The PAT was missed, and the Packers lead was now 43-0. The Lions finally kept a drive alive and scored the next time they had the ball to close the gap to 43-7. After stopping the Pack, Detroit got another shot at scoring, but Tom stopping the Pack, Detroit got another shot at scoring, but Tom Greenfield put an end to this threat by intercepting Dwight Sloan's pass on the Lions' 29 and returning it to the 25. With time running out, the Packers made a really unsportsmanlike move and threw the ball on three successive plays, the last one from Van Every being caught by Uram for a TD. Dick Weisgerber booted the extra point, and the Packers got out of town as quickly as they could with their 50-7 win.

This was Green Bay's last hurrah for the 1940 season. Although they had won, the Bears (7-3-0) also won, keeping a game ahead of the Packers (6-4-0). Green Bay needed the Bears to lose to the Cardinals, while they were defeating the Rams in Cleveland. The probability of that happening was not great. The Cardinals had gotten steadily worse as the season wore on, and the Rams had become better.

At Cleveland on the final Sunday of the campaign, Hinkle kicked a first period field goal to put the Packers ahead, 3-0, in the early going, but the Rams came back with 13 unanswered points in the second and third quarters. The Packers had to rally in the final period on a TD catch and PAT by Hutson and another field goal by Hinkle to tie the game at 13–all. A last second field goal attempt by Hinkle missed the mark, leaving the game knotted, 13-13.

The Bears held off the determined Cardinals in their season finale to win the Western Division crown, while Washington won the East, beating out Brooklyn by a single game.

For the Packers, it was another photo finish that saw them nipped by a nose at the wire.

§ § §

14

Close But No Cigar

As news of the conflicts in the Far East and Europe began to dominate the pages of the nations newspapers, the jargon of war overflowed into the sports sections, especially during football season. For example, a lightning-quick offense that utilized the pass as a large part of it was being compared to the Germans' *Blitzkrieg*. Football, unlike any other sport, resembled war with its two opposing teams fighting over a piece of real estate the same as two armies did.

When the Chicago Bears and the Washington Redskins met in the National Football League championship game in 1940, the Bears were being called "tanks" with their grind-it-out ground game, and the Redskins were said to be like "airplanes" because they could wreak havoc and destruction on the enemy from the air with Slinging Sammy Baugh throwing his devastating passes. On this one occasion, the Bears proved that "tanks" were superior to "planes" because they annihilated the Redskins, 73-0. Because bigotry was still an acceptable form of thought, one scribe wrote that the Bears were just making up for Gen. Custer at the Battle of the Little Bighorn. Chicago owner and coach George Halas said Washington had it coming after the things Redskins owner George Marshall had said about the Bears, calling them "crybabies" and "a first half team." Marshall needed to be taught a lesson, wrote Halas in his autobiography.

The biggest lesson to be learned from the title tilt was that the T-formation with the quarterback taking a handoff snap from the center and with another back in motion was far superior to the single-wing and double-wing formations employed by most teams throughout the country whether pro, college, high school, or just sandlot. The Bears' "T" seemed almost invincible. Those coaches who could see into the future were quick to copy it. Those who didn't realize that the "T" was the basic formation that would soon dominate football weren't long for the coaching ranks.

One exception to this growing trend in coaching was Curly Lambeau. He had been running the same offense for most of the 22 years since he first learned it at Notre Dame under the tutelage of the legendary Knute Rockne. His teams had won over 200 games (including exhibitions and non-league games) using the Notre Dame offense. All it needed was good men to make it run right, and Lambeau was a great at picking the right men for the job.

At the draft meeting in Washington held for the first time the day after the championship game, the Packers, drafting seventh, selected a Wisconsin back, George Paskvan, in the first round. He was followed in order by Robert Paffrath, back, Minnesota; Ed Frutig, end, Michigan; Herman Rohrig, back, Nebraska; Bill Telesmanic, end, San Francisco; Tony Canadeo, back, Gonzaga; Mike Byelene, back, Purdue; Paul Hiemenz, center, Northwestern; Mike Enich, tackle, Iowa; Ed Hefferman, back, St. Mary's; Dell Lyman, tackle, UCLA; John Frieberger, end, Arkansas; Ernie Pannell, tackle, Texas A&M; Bob Saggau, back, Notre Dame; Helge Pukema, guard, Minnesota; Robert Hayes, end, Toldeo; James Strasbaugh, back, Ohio State; Joe Bailey, center, Kentucky; and Bruno Malinowski, back, Holy Cross. Most of them signed contracts with the Packers for '41, but only Paskvan, Frutig, Rohrig, Canadeo, Lyman, and Pannell made the team.

John Walter made an observation in *The Green Bay PressGazette* that Lambeau was looking for a potential replacement for Clarke Hinkle at fullback. Hinkle, who had played nine bruising campaigns in the NFL, was rumored to be ready to retire. Walter surmised that Paskvan and Canadeo were the most likely candidates to succeed Hinkle in the starting backfield.

In early February 1940, Elmer Layden was hired as the NFL's first commissioner. Layden was one of the immortal "Four

Horsemen of Notre Dame" under Knute Rockne. He also served that university as head football coach and athletic director for seven years before accepting the NFL post. The owners gave Layden a five-year contract.

At the spring meeting of NFL owners, Carl Storck resigned as president of the league. This saved the magnates the trouble of firing him. This done they rewrote the league's constitution and gave the commissioner's office much more power than the previous document had given Joe Carr or Storck.

When Lambeau returned from the league conference in Chicago, he brought home an uncertain playing schedule for the fall. The problem, he said, was the Chicago Cardinals. Charlie Bidwill didn't want to play the Packers in Green Bay.

"I lose money every time I play at Green Bay," said Bidwill, "and I make money every time I play the Packers at Milwaukee."

The only two teams willing to come to Green Bay to play were the Lions and Bears. Both were good draws for the Packers because rivalries had built up with them over years. The Packers and Cardinals never developed this sort of competition for one simple reason.

The Cardinals were almost perennial losers, seldom contending for the Western Division title. They weren't the "big bad Bears" or "Gotham Giants" or the Spartans and later Lions of that number one whiner, Potsy Clark. No, they were the Chicago Cardinals who changed coaches and players as often as most people change their socks. Eleven different men had been the team's head coach from 1920 thru 1940, and only two of them lasted more than two years. Milan Creighton held the reins from '35 thru '38, and Ernie Nevers was top man for all of the '29 and '30 seasons and part of '31 before returning for one more shot in '39. The Cardinals had dozens of great players over the years, but few of them stayed with the team for more than two or three seasons because the money wasn't there to pay them. This lack of continuity showed itself in the standings. The Cardinals finished behind the Bears, Lions, and Packers every year from '30 thru '40 except '35 when they tied the Bears for third place in the division.

Since the Cardinals never contended with the Packers for the division honors, the fans of Green Bay just didn't care about them. They neither hated nor loved the Cardinals because the Chicago South Siders did nothing over the years to raise their wrath and cause them to turn out in droves at City Stadium to jeer and sneer at the Redbirds. The Bears were hated; the Lions were hated. The Giants? They were from New York, and there was nothing like showing up the big city boys. The Cardinals? They were to be pitied.

Bidwill wasn't alone in feeling this way about playing in Green Bay. The five Eastern Division powers — Tim Mara, Bert Bell, Art Rooney, Dan Topping, and George Marshall — didn't like it either. Mara's Giants and Marshall's Redskins drew well enough in Green Bay, but the cost of travel took a big bite out of their cut of the gate. Playing in Milwaukee was better because the crowds were usually just as large or bigger and because the visitors didn't have to travel that extra 100–plus miles to Green Bay. For the other three clubs, the crowds were always larger in Milwaukee.

The Packer organization had faced this same complaint in the '20s and had overcome their detractors by fielding winners year after year, making them a good draw on the road. But that was in the days when 15,000 *paying* customers in the Polo Grounds or in Wrigley Field were considered to be a great crowd. In '41, Mara, Marshall, and Halas expected their teams to draw an average attendance of 40,000 per home game. The Green Bay Packers, Inc., were confident of drawing an average of 20,000 for three games in City Stadium and an average of 25,000 for three games at State Fair Park in Milwaukee. Pittsburgh, Philadelphia, and Cleveland would have been quite happy with numbers like that, but they weren't the Green Bay Packers, five time winners of the NFL title. Give one of those cities a team like the Packers and they would draw like the Giants and Bears.

Bidwill, Marshall, and the rest of the complainers could make all the noise they wanted about the Packers moving to Milwaukee. The Packers weren't going anywhere as long as the franchise was owned by several hundred citizens of northeast Wisconsin who stood to gain nothing by a sale or transfer of the team to another city. Like it or not, the Packers were going to stay in Green Bay.

That still didn't mean the Cardinals had to play there, according to Charlie Bidwill. But Elmer Layden had another opinion. It was the Cards' turn to visit Green Bay, so they would play in Green Bay and like it.

That was the story on the surface, the tale spun in the pages of the *Press-Gazette* to cover up the real reason for scheduling a third regular season game in Milwaukee.

The underlying truth was the Milwaukee Chiefs of the American Football League had succeeded in diluting the drawing power of the Packers in the Cream City in 1940 and there was a growing fear in Green Bay that pro football fans in the Milwaukee area were switching their allegiance to the new club. Coach Tiny Cahoon's charges missed winning the AFL title by an eyelash, and another good year just might be all that it would take to dethrone the Packers as Milwaukee's favorite team.

Fueling the anxiety of Packer officials was the emerging business support the Chiefs were getting in the Cream City. Recognizing the potential of pro football as a moneymaking proposition, several businessmen in Milwaukee subscribed to a new stock issue for the Chiefs, modeling their organization after the Green Bay Packers, Inc., in most respects but with one important difference: the Milwaukee club wouldn't be a non-profit business.

To fight this growing menace to the south, Lambeau, Joannes, and their fellow conspirators in the NFL added another game in Milwaukee, hoping it would dilute the Chiefs' following and thus bring the upstart AFL club to financial ruin.

Of course, Lambeau and Joannes couldn't publish this fact in the newspapers. It's against the law to intentionally monopolize a business and destroy the competition. Instead of laying it on the line that the Packers had declared war on the Chiefs, Lambeau paraded Charlie Bidwill in front of Packer fans and used his alleged complaints as a coverup.

With the scheduling problem finally out of the way, Lambeau settled down to the job of signing up players for the season. He

The Lambeau Years — Part Two

figured on 30-35 veterans returning from the '40 campaign. They would be joined by at least a dozen draft choices and another 20-30 free agents just out of college. This would give him about 65-80 men in camp that summer. He felt sure that competition between that many men for only 33 jobs should leave him with a team that could compete with the powerful Bears for the division title.

Before opening camp, there were other matters to attend to. Lambeau arranged a new working agreement with the minor league Long Island Indians of the American Association. As part of the deal, former Packer Verne Lewellen was hired to coach the Indians.

Then there was the stockholders meeting in July. It was held in August. Joannes announced in the *Press-Gazette* that the weather was to blame. He was partially right. Lambeau was out sailing around the northern end of Green Bay when the foul atmospheric conditions forced him to seek a safe haven for his craft far from the city. When it was determined that he couldn't return in time to make the meeting, Joannes put it off for a week. After all, how could they hold a stockholders meeting without the *real* number one man in the organization there?

Once the stockholders did convene their conference, they re-elected all the corporation's directors for another year. The board then re-elected all the corporation's officers. Treasurer Frank Jonet gave his report, revealing "a favorable financial balance," and Lambeau said he expected the '41 team to be better than the '40 version. He based his expectations on the schedule more than anything else. The Packers would be playing Brooklyn in Milwaukee and Pittsburgh and Washington on the road. This meant no trip to New York, which he considered the hardest part of an eastern trip because the Big Apple had so many distractions for his players.

When camp opened in mid-August, Lambeau was a little shorthanded. Several veterans were missing. Some were hold-outs, while others had retired. Milt Gantenbein was among the latter, having found a job as end coach at Manhattan College in New York. Prominent among the former was Clarke Hinkle who was demanding top dollar for his services. Lambeau finally gave in and paid Hinkle $10,000 — a Green Bay record for that time.

Another holdout was Arnie Herber. He wanted more money, and Lambeau wanted a thinner Herber. As part of Herber's contract, he would be weighed the Saturday before each game, and every time he tipped the scales over 200 pounds, he would forfeit $50 of his salary. This clause was a first in the NFL.

The Packers played two exhibition games before the regular season opened in September. They tied the Giants, 17-17, at City Stadium, then nipped the Eagles, 28-21, in Milwaukee.

The Monday after the second pre-season contest was played Lambeau began cutting his roster down to the league limit of 33, and in so doing, he shocked Packer fandom. Among the released players was 11-year veteran Arnie Herber. Lambeau said he was forced to let Herber go because of his weight problem. He was reluctant to make the move but had to do it for the team. It was reported in the *Press-Gazette* that Herber was offered an assistant coach's job with the Long Island Indians, but he never coached there.

Besides the six draft choices — Paskvan, Frutig, Rohrig, Canadeo, Lyman, and Pannell — who made the team, the Packers' opening day roster included four other newcomers who were also rookies: Lee McLaughlin, guard, Virginia; Alex Urban, end, South Carolina; Bill Kuusisto, guard, Minnesota; and Mike Bucchianeri, guard, Indiana. The first three were free agents out of college, while rights to Bucchianeri were obtained from Philadelphia in a trade.

The veterans were Harry Jacunski, Baby Ray, George Svendsen, Pete Tinsley, Charley Schultz, Ray Riddick, Larry Buhler, Joe Laws, Clarke Hinkle, Don Hutson, Carl Mulleneaux, Larry Craig, Bill Lee, Tiny Engebretsen, Smiley Johnson, Tom Greenfield, Charley Brock, Eddie Jankowski, Lou Brock, Cecil Isbell, Frank Balazs, Hal Van Every, Andy Uram, and Bob Adkins.

The Detroit Lions under new head coach Bill Edwards were the first visitors to City Stadium in '41. Whizzer White and Lloyd Cardwell were still the big names in the Detroit backfield, and they proved to be as dangerous as ever. Even so, they were no match for Cecil Isbell's right arm and a slew of Green Bay runners who amassed 166 yards on the ground. Isbell completed 12 of 20 passes for 148 yards including a TD toss to Don Hutson. Tony Canadeo was one of the rushing stars, gaining 48 yards on nine carries and crossing the goal line once for his first Packer touchdown. The Packers also got field goals from Tiny Engebretsen, Clarke Hinkle, and Eddie Jankowski. Hinkle entered the game as the second leading rusher in the history of the NFL, only 12 yards behind Ace Gutowsky who played for the Spartans–Lions. Hinkle pounded the line for 34 yards and a new NFL career rushing record. The Packers completely dominated Detroit, 23-0, before an enthusiastic crowd of 16,734 fans. The attendance figure was a lot less than the *Press-Gazette* led its readers to believe would be present to watch the Lions and Packers when it ran of a pair of pre–game photos featuring ticket sales director Spike Spachmann and his assistant Mary Jane Charles at work in the sales office at the American Legion building.

The following week Tiny Engebretsen decided he couldn't carry out his assignments as a player any more and told Coach Lambeau so. The hefty lineman who came to the Packers from the Brooklyn Dodgers in '34 called it a career after nine full seasons in the league. After graduating from Northwestern, he signed with the Bears in '32, then played for Pittsburgh and the Cardinals in '33 before a brief stint with the Dodgers in '34. At the time of his retirement, he had kicked 48 PATs and 16 field goals for a total of 96 points, good for eighth on the Packers' all-time scoring list to that date. Not wishing to lose Tiny altogether, Lambeau hired him as a scout.

In another personnel move that week, Lambeau finally tired of Frank Balazs' drinking habits and sold him to the Cardinals. Of course, the coach didn't say that in the newspapers. He simply said that the development of George Paskvan made the move possible and that the team didn't need four fullbacks.

The undefeated Cleveland Rams were due to meet the Packers in Milwaukee the next Sunday. Dutch Clark had a backfield tandem of Parker Hall and Johnny Drake that many pro football experts thought was one of the best at the start of the '41 season. In their previous eight meetings since their series began in '37, the Packers had won six, lost one, and tied one with the Rams. Lambeau expected a tough game and got one — for three quarters. Rookie Tony Canadeo threw the first touchdown pass of his career in the first quarter, completing the scoring toss to Joe Laws. Hinkle caught a TD pass from Isbell in the final stanza, and Canadeo scored his second career touchdown later in the period. Herman Rohrig booted a 32-yard field goal to round out the scoring, and the Packers beat Cleveland, 24-7.

The Bears had yet to play a game in '41 when they visited Green Bay on the last Sunday of September. Once again, the Chicago roster read like an all-star team. Ken Kavanaugh, Joe Stydahar, Danny Fortman, Bulldog Turner, Aldo Forte, George Wilson, Sid Luckman, Ray Nolting, George McAfee, Bill Osmanski, and Norm Standlee could have starred for any team as individuals or in small groups. But unfortunately for the rest of the NFL, they all played for George Halas. Many were asking how anyone expected to beat the Bears.

Lambeau thought he had the solution when he assembled one of the greatest Packer teams of all time to face the Monsters of the Midway. They gave all that they got and then some as the lead seesawed back and forth for three quarters. The Bears led, 6-0, after one period, then built the margin to 15-0 before the Packers rallied with just two and a half minutes left in the first half when Isbell hit Hutson with a 40-yard scoring pass. Hinkle booted a field goal in the closing seconds to make the score 15-10 at the half. Green Bay took charge with a touchdown by Hinkle early in the third stanza to go ahead, 17-15; but the Bears came right back to go up, 22-17. The Packers threatened several times but couldn't put any more points on the board. Bob Snyder added a fourth quarter field goal to make the final, 25-17, in front of 24,876 fans.

The loss to the Bears was depressing, but it was only the third game of the season. The Packers had eight more to play and the Bears 10. Anything could happen.

The effects of the defeat at the hands of the Bruins were still troubling the Packers the next week when they met the Cards in Milwaukee. The career series between the two clubs now had the Packers with 21 wins, 12 losses, and three ties, but that was the past. For the present, Chicago coach Jimmy Conzelman was building a better Cardinal team. Their record had improved from 1-10-0 in '39 to 2-7-2 in '40. So far in '41, the Cards were 0-1-1, but they were playing better than their record indicated.

Clarke Hinkle gave the Packers the early lead, 7-0, on a one yard plunge, but the Cardinals came right back on their very next play from scrimmage to score on an 80-yard pass and to close the gap to one point. Chicago took the lead, 13-7, on a 76-yard pass play late in the second quarter. That score held up until the Packers mounted a scoring drive late in the game that culminated with a 14-yard scoring toss from Isbell to Lou Brock. Hutson added the PAT to give Green Bay the victory, 14-13.

With four weeks of the season gone, Green Bay (3-1-0) remained in second place behind the Bears (2-0-0) who mauled the third place Rams (2-2-0) that weekend. Detroit (0-2-1) and the Cardinals (0-2-1) brought up the rear. The Giants (3-0-0) led the East over Brooklyn (2-1-0), Washington (1-1-0), Philadelphia (1-2-0), and Pittsburgh (0-3-0).

In three years under Potsy Clark, the Brooklyn Dodgers reached the .500 mark only once and lost to the Packers twice. Jock Sutherland directed the Flatbushers to an 8-3-0 record in his first year as head coach but didn't play the Packers. The Dodgers had lost all five games in their series with Green Bay and wanted to snap the losing skein when the two met again in Milwaukee.

Isbell and Hutson teamed up on a scoring pass play of 34 yards midway through the first quarter to take an early lead, 7-0. Then Andy Uram broke away on a 90-yard punt return late in the period to increase the margin to 13-0. Hinkle added a field in the second to make the halftime score, 16-0. Hutson swept around left end for 18 yards and another TD in the third stanza to raise the lead to 23-0 before the Dodgers finally got on the board. Canadeo scored the last TD in the late going to make the final score, 30-7.

Attendance for the Brooklyn game was announced as 15,621, for the Cleveland contest 18,463, and for the Cardinals the crowd was estimated to be around 10,000. The average crowd was less than 15,000 per game. The year before the announced attendance for the Cardinal game in Milwaukee was over 20,000 and for Pittsburgh over 13,000, making the average better than 16,500. In '39, the two games in Milwaukee drew over 43,000 for an average of 21,500. In '38, the total draw was 33,000 for an average of 16,500, and in '37, it was 32,000 for an average of 16,000. The peak year was '39, the campaign before the Milwaukee Chiefs began play. The crowds dropped off dramatically in '40 and would have gone down even more in '41 if the third game with Cleveland hadn't been played at State Fair Park.

Although the Packers' management wouldn't admit it, the team's playing days in Milwaukee appeared to be numbered. Only a twist of fate could keep the Packers playing in the Cream City, but that was something Lambeau and Joannes would worry about later. The Packers still had the '41 season to complete first.

Lambeau chartered two United Airlines Mainliners the year before to travel to New York, only to have the flight cut short by bad weather on the East Coast, forcing the airplanes to land in Cleveland, which was only adding insult to injury. When it was time for the Packers to hit the road in '41, Lambeau again chose to travel by air, but this time the Packers would only have to go as far as Cleveland.

The Rams had lost three straight, the streak beginning with their loss to the Pack in Milwaukee. Even so, Lambeau feared Cleveland. The Rams were a hungry team, and they considered the Packers to be their number one rival, much the same as the Bears and Packers felt about each other. Lambeau worked his players extra hard during the week before departing for the Ohio city, and it was just as well that he did. Cleveland mounted an 80-yard scoring drive in the first period to go ahead, 7-0, only to have the Packers come right back and tie the game on an Isbell-to-Carl Mulleneaux TD pass. Green Bay took the lead, 14-7, in the third quarter on a Hinkle TD, but the Rams came back to tie it in the fourth. The Packers drove down to the Cleveland six before stalling with just over a minute to play. Hinkle was the only placekick holder in the lineup at the time,

The Lambeau Years — Part Two

so he knelt to hold for Hutson. The Alabama Flash kicked the first field goal of his career to give the Packers their fifth win of the season, 17-14.

The game was remarkable in only one aspect. Isbell set new standards for passing in Green Bay. He attempted 33 and completed 19 for 274 yards and had none intercepted. Those numbers would be good in any day or age, but for '41, they were absolutely incredible.

Since beating the Packers (5-1-0) by the mere score of 25-15, the Bears (4-0-0) had beaten the Rams (48-13), the Cards (53-7), and the Lions (48-0), giving the Monsters of the Midway a combined score of 175-35 over their four divisional foes. With the season only half over, pro football aficionados were beginning to wonder if the Halasmen would ever lose again. The Packers had fought them closely but still came up short. Had Green Bay improved enough to beat the Bears when they met for the second time? That was a good question but that would have to wait for an answer because the Lions in Detroit came first.

A good crowd of 30,269 fans turned out to see the Packers invade Briggs Stadium, but most of them went home disappointed. The Pack had beaten the Lions, 23-0, in their season opener, but the same result couldn't be expected in Detroit. No, the Lions had improved. But not enough. Hutson scored twice and Mulleneaux once on passes from Isbell, and Hinkle kicked another field goal as the Packers dumped Detroit, 24-7.

The Bears (6-0-0) won again to stay ahead of Green Bay (6-1-0) in the Western Division. Cleveland (2-5-0) lost another close one to be the first team eliminated in the West, and Detroit (1-4-1) and the Cards (1-4-1) were only a half game from being out of it. In the East, the Giants (5-1-0) lost their first game of the year to Brooklyn (3-3-0), and Washington (4-1-0) moved a little closer to the top. Philadelphia (2-4-0) still had an outside chance, but the Steelers (0-6-0) were already looking ahead to '42.

All along George Halas had said he feared Don Hutson more than any player in the NFL. Hutson was such a game-breaker that Halas designed special defenses just for him, and each one of them called for two Bears to cover him. Even so, Hutson often broke into the clear and caught the ball. Halas also said, in so many words, that without Hutson, the Packers were just another team, an eleven not much better than the Lions, Rams, or Cards.

It was make-or-break time for the Packers on the first Sunday in November when they took the gridiron at Wrigley Field to face the Bears. The Chicago fans knew it, too, as 46,484 of them created a new attendance record for the Bears. And what a game they saw!

The Packers scored first in the initial period when Isbell crossed the goal from one yard out. In the third quarter, Isbell hit Lou Brock for 36 yards and a TD to put the Pack ahead, 13-0. Later in the stanza, Hinkle booted a 44-yard field goal to increase the lead to 16-0. Through all this, the Bears had been completely stymied by a strong Packer defense that Lambeau had specially designed to halt Chicago's T-formation attack. By employing a seven-man line, the Pack was able to hold the Bears to a total of 25 yards in the first half. The stout line play forced the Bears to the air in the second half, and early in the fourth quarter it started paying off. Sid Luckman started connecting on his passes, opening up holes for the running game, and the Bears scored three minutes into the quarter to tighten the gap to 16-7. On their next possession, Chicago marched down the field again and put seven more on the board. The Bruins were at it again and had reached the Packers' 36 when Harry Jacunski broke through the line and stripped Luckman of the ball. Pete Tinsley fell on it to halt the drive. The Packers were forced to punt soon after, giving the Bears one more shot at scoring, but before Chicago could mount a threat, time expired.

It was hard to point out any one or two players as the heroes of the game, but Lambeau did say the Packers couldn't have won without Russ Letlow. It wasn't Letlow's play that was so important to the victory. It was his scouting reports. Letlow had been on the injured list for several weeks, and during that time, he covered the Bears' games every Sunday. His reports helped Lambeau come up with the defense that held the Chicago running game in check for three quarters.

Although there was a dispute with the officials in the closing seconds of the game, George Halas refused to complain about it in postgame interviews. Instead, he showed his sportsmanship and how much a gentleman he was when he said flatly that the Packers had earned their victory. Green Bay had beaten his Bears, and quibbling over the referee's decision that the Bears had used all their timeouts would only detract from the fact that the Packers were the better team that day.

The Packers had an open date in their NFL schedule the next week, but Lambeau filled it with an exhibition game with the Kenosha Cardinals in Kenosha. He took the second and third stringers to the game and still came away with a huge win, 65-2.

The Bears (6-1-0) got back on the winning track, but now they were in second behind the Packers (7-1-0). The race in the East was a three-team affair. The Giants (6-2-0) were on top with Washington (5-2-0) in second and Brooklyn (5-3-0) in third. Philadelphia (2-5-1) had joined Pittsburgh (0-7-1) in looking ahead to next year.

The Cardinals gave the Packers everything they could handle in their first meeting in Milwaukee earlier in the year, and Lambeau expected much of the same when the two squads were scheduled to meet in Green Bay on November 16, which would be the latest date for a home game since the Packers joined the NFL. "It was not until well into the fourth quarter, after Don Hutson made a spectacular dash around end for a touchdown, that the Packer supporters could relax," wrote Ray Pagel in the *Press-Gazette*. Hutson scored Green Bay's other touchdown, and Hinkle added a field goal to give the Packers a tough 17-9 win to keep them atop the Western Division standings.

The Packers (8-1-0) had hoped that Washington would prove to be a stumblingblock for the Bears (7-1-0), but the Redskins still couldn't handle the "T" as Chicago hammered them, 35-21. The loss put Washington (5-3-0) a game and a half behind New York (7-2-0) and left them with only scant hope of catching the Giants.

In six previous encounters, Pittsburgh hadn't come close to beating the Packers even once. They still couldn't in '41. Hal Van Every had the biggest scoring day of his career when he posted three touchdowns to lead the Pack to a 54-7 rout of the Steelers in Pittsburgh. Hinkle scored another pair of TDs, and Hutson, Alex Urban, and Ernie Pannell crossed the goal once each.

Green Bay (9-1-0) had one game remaining on its schedule, while the Bears (8-1-0) had two. The Packers would be facing the Redskins, and Chicago would visit the Eagles, then finish up against the Cards. More and more, it looked like the two rivals would have to play a third game to decide who would play the Giants for the NFL title.

Since the beginning of their regular season series with the Redskins in '32, the Packers had beaten them five times while losing two and tying one. Half of those games were played before Sammy Baugh came into the league, but his addition to the team hadn't been much help for Washington against Green Bay. The Pack had won three of the four contests. Also, the Packers had defeated the Redskins in the NFL championship game in '36. All but one of the games had been relatively close. Lambeau expected the '41 game to be the same way, and he wasn't disappointed.

Washington built a 17-0 lead in the first half on TDs by Frank Filchock and Bob Seymour and a field goal by Bob Masterson. Down but not out, the Packers roared back in the third quarter behind Hutson and Isbell who connected on a pair of TD passes to close the margin to 17-13. The passing combo teamed up again in the early going of the fourth quarter to make the score 20-17 in Green Bay's favor. On the ensuing kickoff, Ray Hare took the ball in Washington's end zone and ran it out only to be surrounded by blue and gold Packers, then ran back into the end zone where he was tackled for a safety. A late Washington threat was thwarted by the Packers, and the final score had Green Bay on top, 22-17.

As expected, the Bears (9-1-0) mauled the Eagles to stay close to the Packers (10-1-0) who had completed their regular season, then the Monsters of the Midway took the measure of the Cardinals, 34-24, in a seesaw battle that saw the Cards blow a latev lead. The playoff game between the Packers and Bears was on.

The headlines in the *Press-Gazette* stated how Lambeau was confident his Packers could take the Bears again. To counter

The Lambeau Years — Part Two

The headlines in the *Press-Gazette* stated how Lambeau was confident his Packers could take the Bears again. To counter this, the newspaper reported how the Bears were predicting a victory margin of 40 points or more over Green Bay. Sid Luckman stated the Bears' case when he said, "The Packers tricked us once this season with their seven–man line, but they are not going to do it this time."

Whereas the Packers had the far superior passing attack, the Bears were that much better on the ground. As the Bears had proven against the Redskins in the 1940 title game, a solid rushing game will wear down and defeat a team that relies on the pass. It happened again at Wrigley Field a year later.

Hinkle scored an early touchdown to give the Packers the lead, 7-0. Then the Bears went to work. They scored 30 unanswered points before halftime, then coasted to victory, 33-14. The Packers were greatly disappointed over losing, but they had no one to blame but themselves. They threw five interceptions and fumbled away the ball three times. Lambeau's seven–man line failed at almost every turn as the Bears rambled for 267 yards on the ground.

To add insult to injury, Commissioner Elmer Layden fined Lambeau $100 for allowing two of his players to wear jerseys with numbers that didn't correspond with the game programs. That would stick in Lambeau's craw more than the loss of the division crown because the mix–up on the numbers was the league office's fault, not Lambeau's and the Packers'. As soon as Lambeau angrily pointed out this fact to Layden, the fine was dropped.

It had been a great year for the Packers, but not quite great enough. And now the country was at war. What next?

§ § §

15

Year with an Asterisk

In *Halas On Halas*, Papa Bear George Halas wrote: " . . . Then over the loudspeakers came a voice: 'Ladies and gentlemen: The Japanese have bombed Pearl Harbor.' Everyone was stunned. I didn't know what to do. We decided the game should go on. Very few people left . . . "

The date was December 7, 1941, and the Bears were playing the Cards on the last Sunday of the regular season at Comiskey Park. The announcement might have "stunned" Halas as he wrote, but he didn't stay stunned. He quickly re-tuned his senses to the contest at hand. This was evidenced by the fact that during the rest of the game he repeatedly rushed onto the field to argue with officials and was subsequently fined $100 by Commissioner Elmer Layden for the infractions. Not until after the Bears had beaten the Cardinals did Halas consider what war might mean to him, the National Football League, and professional sports in general.

A wave of patriotism broke over the country, and men — including George Halas, owner of the Chicago Bears and other enterprises — and women from all walks of life volunteered for the armed forces. President Franklin D. Roosevelt and Congress had seen the future in 1940 when the first peace-time draft of young men for military duty was instituted, but it hadn't affected that many professional athletes prior to the attack on U.S. military and naval installations in Hawaii. When the war finally did come, it became only a matter of time before the number of draftees would be dramatically increased, and this was certain to have a detrimental effect on professional sports.

The Green Bay Packers felt the military draft for the first time in November of '41 when Bob Adkins received his induction notice from Uncle Sam. He was given a physical, then told he would be notified when to report. Shortly after Japanese torpedo planes sank or severely damaged every battleship tied up in Pearl Harbor, Adkins was called to duty.

Although there were reports of Japanese submarines and airplanes being sighted off the coast of California and the country as a whole was the verge of invasion hysteria, cooler heads prevailed and order was maintained throughout the nation. Giving the people a sense of normalcy was the best way of dealing with a possible panic.

The leaders of the NFL decided it was best that the playoff game between the Packers and Bears and the league championship contest should be played as scheduled, if for no other reason than it was their patriotic duty to continue as if nothing were wrong. Therefore, Layden and the NFL's magnates went through the motions of the college player draft.

Topping Coach Lambeau's draft list was Urban Odson, a 247-pound tackle from Minnesota. The rest of Green Bay's draftees for the '42 season were Ray Frankowski, guard, Washington; Bill Green, fullback, Iowa; Joe Krivonak, guard, South Carolina; Preston Johnston, fullback, SMU; Joe Rogers, end, Michigan; Phil Langdale, tackle, Alabama; Gene Flick, center, Minnesota; Tom Farris, quarterback, Wisconsin; Jimmy Richardson, halfback, Marquette; Bruce Smith, halfback, Minnesota; Flash Applegate, guard, South Carolina; Tiny Trimble, tackle, Indiana; Tom Kinkade, halfback, Ohio State; Fred Preston, end, Nebraska; Bob Ingalls, center, Michigan; George Benson, fullback, Northwestern; Horace Young, back, SMU; Henry Woronicz, end, Boston; and Woody Adams, tackle, TCU. Of these men, only Bob Ingalls was to play for the Packers in '42; Preston and Benson joined the Army and Frankowski joined the Navy. Frankowski and Smith would join the Packers in '45, and Urban Odson would play for Green Bay in '46. Krivonak, Johnston, Farris, and Benson would play pro football elsewhere after the war.

Because of the Japanese invasion scare on the West Coast, the usual post-season bowl games played in California were moved to so-called safer playing sites. Also, travel was restricted, and this limited Curly Lambeau's scouting and signing forays into the hinterlands. There was little for him to do but correspond with prospective players and hope to sign them. He was able to make a trip to California once the invasion scare had passed in early '42, and that was when he did the bulk of his work.

At the same time, he was powerless to protect the team he had. The unmarried men were prime candidates to be drafted, and the many of married players felt it was their duty to their country to serve in the armed forces.

Hal Van Every's career in pro football came to a halt when he was the first man to enlist in the Army Air Corps. Lee McLaughlin went into the Navy, but Charlie Schultz was rejected by the army because of high blood pressure. Others entering the service were Eddie Jankowski, Ed Frutig, Bill Johnson, Carl Mulleneaux, Alex Urban, and Tom Greenfield. Pete Tinsley was rejected by the Navy because of a hearing defect.

Realizing that the game was outgrowing his abilities to handle so many players at one time, Lambeau added a new coach to his small staff. He hired former Green Bay player Eddie Kotal to be the Packers' backfield coach. Kotal had been the athletic director and football coach at Central State Teachers College in Stevens Point for the past 11 years.

Not long after Kotal again became part of the organization, Lambeau signed Ted Fritsch, Kotal's top backfielder at Central State Teachers. Fritsch was an all-conference fullback in his junior and senior years.

In late February, Lambeau was quoted in the *Los Angeles Times*:

"Our Green Bay squad lost 10 of 33 players to the service, and it is possible our club won't be as strong as it was last season. But the other teams were hit, too, and I think you will find the losses pretty evenly distributed. The caliber of play may not be quite as high throughout the league, but it still will be worth seeing."

When practice for the NFL teams began in early August, five teams had training sites in Wisconsin. The Packers were in Geen Bay as usual; the Bears at St. John's Military Academy in

Delafield; the Giants at Superior; the Cardinals at Carroll College in Waukesha; and the Eagles at Two Rivers. The Redskins headed west to San Diego, while the other four teams stayed closer to home. The Lions set up camp at Charlevoix, Michigan; the Steelers at Hershey, Pennsylvania; the Rams at Hiram, Ohio; and the Dodgers at Princeton, New Jersey. Ray Pagel, who had taken over for John Walter as sports editor of the *Press-Gazette*, reported that approximately 100 NFL players from the year before were in the armed forces. Hardest hit was Green Bay.

At the annual stockholders meeting of the Green Bay Packers, Inc., a few changes were made in the roster of corporate officers. Fred Leicht stepped down, leaving Lambeau as the only vice-president. Frank Jonet took over the duties of the secretary as secretary-treasurer, and George Whitney Calhoun *officially* became the club's publicity director, a post that had always been his since before Curly Lambeau became a part of pro football in Green Bay in 1919.

Lambeau reported that he had lost 16 veterans to the services and 18 of his 20 college draftees. Although he would never say so, Lambeau was scraping the bottom of the barrel for any talent he could find. He told the stockholders that the men he had signed were as fine as any he had contracted in the past. This was pure bunkum.

Throughout the summer, Lambeau contracted players, as usual. Actually, he was signing bodies to fill the void being left by the veterans and draftees who had entered the services. Among these were some local men who had played college ball. Chuck Sample of Appleton played fullback at Toledo, then for Verne Lewellen and the Long Island Indians of the American Football Association in '41. Art Albrecht of Manitowoc went to Wisconsin but was ineligible for the team.

Some of the other men Lambeau signed were Jim Finley, a guard who had dropped out of Michigan State his senior year; Ben Starrett, a back from St.Mary's who had been signed by Pittsburgh but had been shipped out to the Wilmington Clippers of the AFA; Don Miller, a back from Wisconsin; Joel

Mason, an end from Western Michigan who had been tried out in '41 by the Cardinals and released; and Bob Kahler, a back from Nebraska who had failed to make the Packers in '41 and was sent down to Long Island. These were just some of the *replacements* for the regulars who had gone off to war. Fortunately for the Packers, most of the other teams were having the same problem finding players.

Putting together a team wasn't the only problem Lambeau and the Green Bay Packers, Inc., were having. More than ever, the eastern teams were complaining about the difficulty of traveling to Green Bay to play. In fact, many of them didn't even want to go to Milwaukee for a game; they tried to talk Lambeau into scheduling games in Buffalo or Cincinnati or even Toledo in order to avoid going to Milwaukee. But true to the people who had supported him and the Packers for over 20 years, Lambeau insisted on six home games — three in Green Bay and three in Milwaukee. He got the trio of contests for City Stadium but had to sacrifice one game in the Cream City. This was a minor concession to the eastern owners that he was quite willing to make because the American Football League had folded and the Milwaukee Chiefs were no longer a rival for fans in southern Wisconsin.

Once again, this was the story in the *Press-Gazette*. Behind it lay certain facts that were only whispered about in close circles of Packer insiders.

With one very important exception, the rest of the magnates of the NFL wanted the Packers to move to Milwaukee completely or to a city like St. Louis or Cincinnati. By moving to St. Louis, the rivalry with the Bears would still be alive, or a new one could be built between Cincinnati and Cleveland. If either of those options was too drastic, then Milwaukee would have to do.

Of course, Lambeau fought any notion such as this with every resource at his disposal and with the support of George Halas. As the two oldest members of the league's hierarchy in terms of service, Lambeau and Halas carried a lot of weight, especially Halas because he was in Chicago, the NFL's second largest city. It might be said that Halas helped to keep the Packers in Green Bay and the Cardinals in Chicago for selfish reasons, but even if that were true, keeping both franchises in their respective cities turned out to be good for the league in the long run.

Lambeau was no fool, of course. He used this outside threat to his advantage back home. He privately let the right people know that if attendance didn't continue improving he would be powerless to stop the league from moving the franchise to Milwaukee or worse. By keeping the Packers in Green Bay, Lambeau would benefit in two ways. As the club's unofficial general manager, more ticket revenue meant he could pay his players a little more, which meant they would be more apt to remain in Green Bay for longer playing careers. This would mean that the Packers would continue to be perennial winners, which was good for Lambeau. As the head coach of a winner, he would receive regular raises in pay from the grateful stockholders of the Green Bay Packers, Inc. For the time being at least, it was to Lambeau's advantage to keep the Packers in Green Bay.

To help him achieve this, the Green Bay Association of Commerce took it upon themselves to launch a massive oneday season ticket sales drive. Under the direction of Don Fairbairn, William Servotte, and Earl S. Ward, the members of the association met for breakfast at the Beaumont Hotel on September 10, then they swept the city looking for potential ticket buyers. The results were an additional 1,437 season tickets being sold to raise the total for the year to close to 4,000, which was almost 1,100 more than the year before.

Of course, Lambeau and the Packers did their part in making the ticket drive a success. Green Bay dumped the Dodgers at Brooklyn, 21-16, in the first exhibition game of the season, then thumped the Army All-Stars at State Fair Park in Milwaukee, 36-21. In between those two tilts, the Redskins did a number on the Packers at Washington, 28-7. Giving the Packers a big boost in these games and with season ticket sales was the play of home grown boy Ted Fritsch. Hailing from Spencer, Wisconsin, he scored a pair of TDs and kicked a field goal against the All-Stars to excite Packer fans.

After the final cuts, the Packer roster included veterans Ernie Pannell, Bill Kuusisto, Buckets Goldenberg, Tony Canadeo,

Joe Laws, Don Hutson, Larry Craig, Bill Lee, Baby Ray, Pete Tinsley, Russ Letlow, Charley Brock, Lou Brock, Andy Uram, Dick Weisgerber, Harry Jacunski, and Cecil Isbell. The other rookies to make the team that haven't already been mentioned were Paul Berezney, Earl Ohlgren, John Stonebraker, Fred Vant Hull, Joe Carter, Milburn Croft, Hale Hinte, and Bob Flowers.

The Packers opened the season with the Bears in Green Bay. It was their 47th meeting, and Chicago held an edge in the series, 23-19 with four ties. The war had taken its toll on the Bears but not, it seemed, like it had on the Packers. The only big guns missing from the Chicago roster were George McAfee, Norm Standlee, and Bob Swisher. Just about everyone else was back, and that meant trouble for the Packers.

Press-Gazette reporter Art Daley covered the game and summed up the outcome in two paragraphs:

"The Packers had the Bears down, 28 to 27, going into the fourth quarter when Frank Maznicki booted a 17-yard field goal to put the Bears in front, 30 to 28. There were only six minutes left, after an exchange of punts, when hell and high water really broke loose.

"The Bears gobbled up only three minutes of actual playing time in destroying any thoughts or hopes of Packer fans for victory. They recovered a fumble and intercepted a pass, and that, brothers, was the end of the game so far as the Packers were concerned."

Before a crowd of 22,007, the Bears took home the bacon, 44-28, in spite of a brilliant game by Isbell and Hutson. The Packer passer completed 19 of 31 passes for 261 yards and two touch-downs, and Hutson caught eight passes for 147 yards and a pair of scores. On the negative side, four of Isbell's tosses were picked off by the Bears, three of them being converted into points.

For the first time in several years, Andy Turnbull, the man most responsible for the Packers remaining in Green Bay and in professional football, spoke out publicly about the play of the team. In several quotable paragraphs in the sports editor's column, Turnbull lashed out at the lack of spirited play by the Packers, saying they were just as good as the Bears, if not better, but had fallen victim to the myth that the Halasmen were invincible. As if verbally whipping the players weren't enough, Turnbull gave the football fans of Green Bay a good going over, too, by accusing them of complacency that had carried over to the team. He exhorted them all to get "really mad when the Packers lost a ball game."

Lambeau knew who the real boss of the Packers was, and he promised the team would play harder the next week against the Cardinals.

During the week, the coach released guard Jim Finley, and Don Miller was called to military duty. To replace Finley, Lambeau signed Arnold Winters. Bill Lee went off to war just before the Packers met the Cardinals in Chicago.

In a thoroughly awful affair, the Packers were able to beat the Cards, 17-13, in a Sunday night game in front of 30,000 fans in Comiskey Park. Trailing, 13-3, going into the final quarter, Green Bay came to life in the late going. Isbell hit Hutson with a five-yard scoring toss to close the gap to 13-10, then Charley Brock stole the ball from a Chicago rusher and ran 20 yards to paydirt for the last score of the day.

To fill the two empty roster spots on the Packers, Lambeau hired end Keith Ranspot and tackle Royal Kahler the next week. Ranspot had played for SMU, then signed on with the Los Angeles Bulldogs for a couple of years before playing the '41 season for the Cardinals and the first couple of games with the Lions in '42. Kahler was the older brother of Packer back Bob Kahler, and like his sibling, he attended Nebraska before turning pro with the Steelers in '42, "quitting" Pittsburgh after just two games to join the Packers. To replace Kahler on the Steelers' roster, the Packers sent Art Albrecht to Pittsburgh.

The Packers met the Lions in Milwaukee the next week before a crowd estimated to be around 19,500. Not that many folks saw the Packers wallop the Motor City crew, 38-7, because Milwaukee officials were inflating the figures to keep the games in the Cream City. In this lopsided win, Hutson caught a pair of TD passes, and Uram, Chuck Sample, and Ranspot also scored six-pointers.

Ticket Director Ralph C. Smith announced early in the week that there were plenty of seats left for the Cleveland game at City

Stadium the next Sunday, but few fans heeded the call. Only 12,847 showed up to see the Packers come back from a 21-17 halftime deficit to win going away, 45-28. In an aerial circus, the Packers completed 27 of 39 passes for 330 yards, and the Rams completed 16 of 28 for 254 yards. Hutson caught his sixth and seventh TD passes of the year, and Sample, Isbell, Canadeo, and Laws also scored. Oh, yes. Hutson also caught 13 passes for 209 yards, a new NFL record.

The Packers won their fourth straight when they waxed the Lions in Detroit, 28-7, the following week. Surprisingly, Hutson didn't catch any touchdown tosses, but he did kick two PATs. Joe Carter, Sample, Lou Brock, and Uram scored the six-pointers. Uram's TD came on a 98-yard kickoff return in the fourth quarter.

For the first time since '33, the Packers and Cardinals did not play in Milwaukee. Their initial meeting of the year was in Chicago, and the second one was set for City Stadium. It was the Packers' last home game in Green Bay, and they gave the small crowd everything they came to see. How small was it? It was so small that the newspaper didn't print the attendance figure. Hutson had another incredible day, catching five passes for 207 yards and three touchdowns. Hutson's TDs were 35, 73, and 65 yards long. But he wasn't the only man having a great day. Andy Uram also caught three touchdown passes of 64, 36, and 62 yards. For the day, Uram hauled in four passes for 174 yards. Doing most of the tossing was Cecil Isbell, who connected with Hutson for all three of his TDs and with Uram for two of his. Isbell was 10 of 21 passing for five TDs and 333 yards. Hutson also set a Packer record by kicking six extra points. Oh, yes. The final score was 55-24, which is remarkable in that the Packers trailed, 17-7, early in the second quarter. Ray Pagel took a line from a war song and adapted it to the Packers. While he feared being irreverent, he still wrote: "Praise the Lord and pass to Hutson."

Hutson did it again the following week when he scored three more touchdowns against Cleveland as the Packers dumped the Rams, 30-12, in Cleveland. This was the third time in his career that Hutson crossed the goal line three times in one game against the Rams.

With only four games to go, the Packers and Bears had eliminated the rest of the Western Division competition from the race. The Bears (7-0-0) were still undefeated, while the Packers (6-1-0) had only lost to the Bears. Many wondered if Green Bay could repeat their unexpected '41 victory over the Monsters of the Midway in Chicago when the Pack traveled to the Windy City for their mid-November showdown with the Bruins.

Lambeau designed a new defense that was supposed to stop Chicago's vaunted running attack, and it did — for the first half. The Packers held the Bears to just 34 yards on the ground in the first two periods, but Chicago still scored 21 points. The Packers were their own worst enemies as the Bears converted an interception and a recovered fumble into a pair of TDs, and the third six-pointer came on a long bomb. The Bears added another 10 points in the third quarter as their ground game got going, and they scored once more in the final stanza before the Packers got a token TD near the end of the game. Chicago more or less wrapped up the division title that Sunday, 38-7.

As far as the division race was concerned, the Packers were through. They had little chance of overtaking the Bears, so they merely went through the motions of playing their last three games. Hutson scored another 15 points against the Giants as the Pack tied New York, 21-21, in a game where the great jazz singer Al Jolson paid $70,000 for the game ball when it was auctioned off for the benefit of Army relief. Hutson scored all seven points as the Packers shut out Philadelphia, 7-0; and he scored six more points on three PATs and a field goal as the Packers nipped the Steelers, 24-21, for what the *Press-Gazette* called the "little championship" as both teams were in second place in their respective divisions.

For the year, Hutson caught 17 touchdown passes and kicked 33 extra points and one field goal for a total of 138 points — a record that would stand until broken some years later by another Packer, Paul Hornung. Also, his 17 TD receptions was a mark that would stand for four decades, and his 33 PATs was a record for one season. Hutson pulled down 74 passes — another one-season record — for 1,211 yards — also a record for one season. The truly amazing thing about Hutson's records was they were achieved in an 11-game season. Broken down in terms of points per game, yards per game, etc., Hutson's marks were 1.545 TDs per game, 12.545 points per game, 6.727 receptions per game, and 110.09 yards per game. Numbers such as these ranked his '42 season among the greatest years of the greatest pass receivers to ever play the game.

But Hutson's '42 season does deserve an asterisk beside it. There is no doubt that Hutson was already the premier pass receiver in the NFL in '41, the last full campaign before the involvement of the United States in World War II. Prior to '42, none of Hutson's statistics in any category came close to those he put up that year. This is understandable in that he was playing against the best in the land from '35 thru '41. But in '42, almost half the league was made up of replacement players, men who wouldn't have made it in the NFL if so many regular stars and many of the best college recruits hadn't gone into the armed forces.

Hutson wasn't the only great Packer of '42. Cecil Isbell led the league in passing by completing 146 of 268 passes for 24 TDs and 2,021 yards. His number of completions, TD tosses, and yards were new single-season league marks, but he was playing against the same war-time replacements that Hutson was. Isbell's marks deserve an asterisk the same as Hutson's even though he was as highly regarded by his contemporaries before the '42 season as he was after it.

Of course, Hutson and Isbell would have had a great year without the war, but their statistics probably wouldn't have been as good as they were. Time would prove this to be true of Hutson but not of Isbell, but only because '42 was his last season in pro football.

§ § §

16

The Year of Uncertainty

When 1942 came to an end, Nazi Germany still controlled most of the territory it commanded at the start of the year and Imperial Japan was in control of more than it had under its flag on New Year's Day. The Allied High Command knew both wars could go either way yet and that 1943 would be a pivotal year in determining the outcome.

The leaders of the National Football League felt the same way about professional football. With the armed forces drafting established players and prospective players, the magnates wondered if there would be enough men to fill the ranks of all 10 teams in the loop. In fact, there was concern about the number of magnates that would be available because Cleveland owner Dan Reeves and Bears owner George Halas had enlisted in the service. This concern was so great that they postponed the annual draft of collegiate talent from December until the following April.

In the interim, the 10-1-0 Redskins defeated the 11-0-0 Bears in the NFL title game, 14-6; and the rumor mills about the league's future were grinding out one tall tale after another.

One story making the rounds that had a sound basis to it was the one about reducing the size of the league from 10 teams to eight or even six for the '43 season. Primary among the teams that were being mentioned for elimination from the loop for the duration of the war was Green Bay. Once again the eastern owners wanted to drop the Packers from the NFL rolls, and once again George Halas came to Green Bay's rescue. He let his fellow owners know that he wanted the Packers to remain in the league at all costs.

When the league meeting did get underway at the Palmer

House in Chicago in early April, Dan Reeves shocked everyone by withdrawing the Rams from the league for the coming season and possibly for the duration of the war. Cleveland's roster of players was then divided among the remaining nine teams by drawing names out of a hat. Lambeau drew the names of Chet Adams, Mike Holovak, Jim Shepherd, Bert Davis, and Dick Kieppe. Only Adams ever played for the Pack.

Then the regular draft was held. Lambeau took Dick Wildung, tackle, Minnesota; Irv Comp, halfback, St. Benedictine; Roy McKay, halfback, Texas; Nick Susseoff, end, Washington State; Ken Snelling, halfback, UCLA; Buddy Gatewood, center, Baylor; Norm Verry, tackle, USC; Bobo Barnett, guard, Baylor; Bob Forte, halfback, Arkansas; Van Davis, end, Georgia; Tom Brock, center, Notre Dame; Ralph Tate, halfback, Oklahoma A&M; Don Carlson, tackle, Denver; Mike Welch, halfback, Minnesota; Ron Thomas, guard, USC; James Powers, tackle, St. Mary's; Harold Prescott, end, Hardin Simmons; and Ed Forrest, center, Santa Clara. Of these men, only eight of them ever played for the Packers.

The two biggest items to come out of the conference was the new roster limit of 28 players and a free substitution rule. Both were the direct result of the manpower shortage.

Because the situation concerning exactly which teams would be playing in '43 was yet to be resolved, a schedule wasn't made up at the April league meeting. This necessitated a second meeting in early summer for the purpose of drawing up a slate of games. When the June confab rolled around on the calendar, it was decided that the Philadelphia and Pittsburgh franchises would merge for '43 and play as the Phil–Pitt "Steagles" for lack of a better name. This left the NFL with eight clubs, four in each division, balancing the schedule to 10 games with each team playing a round–robin slate within its division and playing each team in the other division once.

With the league situation now settled, Lambeau went about the business of signing players, but before he could get very many signatures on contracts, his plans for the coming campaign were dealt a severe blow. Cecil Isbell and Don Hutson announced their retirements from the game. Isbell got a new job as backfield coach at his alma mater Purdue, and Hutson planned to go into business. Lambeau was in a panic. There went 80% of his offense.

Fortunately for the Packers, Hutson's "retirement" was only a ploy for more money. He succeeded quite well because he became the highest paid player in the league that year. When Lambeau announced the signing of Hutson, he said, "Don feels he owes it to football to continue. Most of his off–the–field life has resulted from his work on the gridiron. The game needs Hutson and we feel that Don, besides being a definite help to the Packers, will play a big part in building home front morale as a result of his past record and great playing." This was another Lambeau smoke screen to cover up the fact that Hutson had bested him in negotiations and to conceal the fact that Hutson was just as mercenary as the next fellow. Lambeau didn't want everyone to know that Hutson put his pants on one leg at a time like every other guy around; Hutson was legendary and had to stay that way — *for the good of the game.*

With Hutson in the fold, Lambeau had to find someone to get the ball to the six–time All–Pro selection and the NFL's two–time Most Value Player Award winner. Lou Brock, Tony Canadeo, Ted Fritsch, and Ben Starrett were back with the team for '43, but none of them could come close to passing the way Isbell had. No, Lambeau needed a first class passer, and he felt he had one in Irv Comp. The coach had Comp work overtime with Hutson during training camp so the rookie could learn some of the veteran end's moves.

Once again a one–day season ticket sales drive was attempted, and it proved more successful than ever before. A total of 125 workers turned out to do the job, and these people were divided into teams. Each team was then given the name of an NFL club in order to spur competition among them. The result was excellent. The drive netted sales of 3,390 tickets for the two–game home slate that year. Harry Masse's *Philadelphia Eagles* sold 412 tickets to lead the pack, and his two best salesmen were Les Kelly and Dan McGuire who combined to sell 211 tickets. Rodney Stewart, Walter Robbins, Lee F. Lodl, and Norm Wall were first thru fourth in the "selling to the highest percentage of potential customers" competition.

At the annual stockholders meeting of the Green Bay Packers, Inc., all the officers were re-elected as was the entire board of directors.

The Packers met the Washington Redskins in Baltimore for an exhibition game in early September and defeated the defending NFL champions, 23-21, on a Don Hutson field goal in the late going. With the victory, Lambeau served notice on the rest of the league that the Packers were ready to reach the heights of pro football once again.

Green Bay scored in every quarter when they downed Phil-Pitt, 28-10, in an exhibition game in Pittsburgh the next week. Although the Packers won decisively, Lambeau was displeased with his defensive line for allowing the Steagles to rush for over 300 yards.

The war came a lot closer to Green Bay the next week when news was received that Don Hutson's brother Robert was killed in action. Hutson learned of his brother's death when his mother telephoned him to tell him that his father had passed away. The senior Hutson's demise was unexpected as there was no previous indication that he was in poor health. Don prepared to leave the team immediately for his parents' home in Pine Bluff, Arkansas. Announcement of the Hutson family tragedy was made just three days before the Packers' opening game of the season at City Stadium against the Bears. When proper travel connections for Hutson to go home for his father's funeral and return to Wisconsin in time for the game on Sunday couldn't be made on such short notice, he decided to stay in Green Bay.

When the Packers opened the season, the roster included Hutson, Baby Ray, Bill Kuusisto, Charley Brock, Pete Tinsley, Paul Berezney, Harry Jacunski, Larry Craig, Tony Canadeo, Lou Brock, Ted Fritsch, Joel Mason, Dick Evans, Tiny Croft, Forrest McPherson, Chet Adams, Glen Sorenson, Buckets Goldenberg, Sherwood Fries, Bob Flowers, Tony Falkenstein, Joe Laws, Andy Uram, Bob Kahler, Jim Lankas, Don Perkins, Ben Starrett, and Irv Comp.

McPherson was an NFL veteran tackle who had played with the Bears in '35 and with the Eagles from '35 thru '37 that

Lambeau had talked out of retirement. Evans returned to the Packers after a couple of years with the Cardinals. Sorenson was a rookie guard out of Utah State. Fries was a rookie guard out of Colorado A&M. Falkenstein was a rookie halfback out of St. Mary's. Lankas had played for the Eagles in '42 after graduating from St. Mary's. Perkins was a product of Platteville State Teachers College and had played for the Milwaukee Chiefs in '41.

When George Halas went into the Navy, he left Luke Johnsos and Hunk Anderson, his two assistant coaches, to share the head coaching duties of the Bears. Johnsos handled the offense, and Anderson took charge of the defense. The arrangement worked in all but one respect; neither man was Halas and neither one could inspire a team the way Halas could. Without pointing any fingers, Sid Luckman said that that was the reason the Bears lost the '42 title game to Washington.

The Bears lost a lot of stars to the war effort just the same as the other teams did, but there was one major difference with the Chicago eleven. There were more stars to pick from in the first place. George Musso, Danny Fortmann, Bulldog Turner, George Wilson, Bill Osmanski, Hampton Pool, Luckman, Scooter McLean, and Gary Famiglietti were still wearing navy blue and orange that fall, and to top that off, Bronko Nagurski came out of retirement to play tackle for the Monsters of the Midway. With a lineup like that, the rest of the league wondered if the Bears would go undefeated in the regular season again in '43.

Magnates in the NFL weren't the only people wondering about the Bears in '43. The War Manpower Commission also had a few questions about the Chicago players. In a front page story, the *Chicago Sun* reported that an investigation was underway "to determine whether members of the Chicago Bears professional football team have the necessary certificates of availability to leave essential war jobs to play football." WMC Regional Director William H. Spencer wanted to learn "how and why such certificates were issued." His probe was prompted by published reports that several Chicago players had left jobs in shipbuilding plants and farms to play football and several people had inquired why this was allowed.

All of the Bear players who were mentioned in the investigation were cleared of any wrong-doing, but a few them were unable to obtain such certificates the next year.

The Packers proved right off that the Bears weren't invincible when they fought Chicago to a 21-21 tie. It was a seesaw battle that saw the Bears go up by seven in the first quarter only to have Green Bay match them in the second. The Bears jumped ahead in the third stanza, and the Packers came right back to tie it at 14. In the final period, Chicago moved ahead once more but couldn't stop Canadeo from hooking up with Hutson for the tying tally late in the game. The tie was the fifth in the series that began in 1921 and that was led by the Bears, 25 wins to 19 for the Packers.

Only 15,563 cash customers and an estimated 2,500 service men who were admitted free turned out at Comiskey Park in Chicago the next week to watch the Packers thump the Cards, 28-7. Irv Comp threw his first touchdown pass of his career to Mason in the first quarter, then threw his second only minutes later to the same receiver. Fritsch rushed for a TD, and Lou Brock hit Harry Jacunski with a scoring toss. Hutson booted all four PATs and raised his career scoring total to 537 points.

The Detroit Lions and their new coach Gus Dorais, the man who helped popularize the forward pass at Notre Dame with Knute Rockne three decades earlier, were on tap for the Packers the next week. By virtue of having the worst record (0-11-0) in the NFL in '42, the Lions had first choice in the draft, and they took Fighting Frankie Sinkwich, the three-time All-American back from Georgia. The Lions won their first two games of '43 over the Cards and Brooklyn before losing a close one to the Bears.

Lambeau expected a fierce battle with Detroit but didn't get one. The Packers won for the 20th time in the 26-game series between the two teams, 35-14. A nice crowd of 21,396 turned out at City Stadium and saw Fritsch, Comp, and Lou Brock cross the goal once each and Uram twice. Hutson kicked all five PATs to give him an even dozen without a miss on the year.

Due to a lack in confidence in Comp as a passer, Lambeau had changed his offensive strategy at the beginning of the year. Instead of using the air waves to gain ground, the coach opted for the infantry attack on the opposition. After three games, Hutson had only eight receptions, which was good enough for second place among the league's top receivers but was a poor showing for the All-Pro end. If that wasn't such a great oddity for Packer fans, then having four of the league's top eight rushers was. Canadeo led the NFL with 187 yards gained; Laws was fourth with 139; Fritsch, fifth, 125; and Comp, eighth, 114. Comp was also fourth in passing, but he had only thrown 21 passes, while Canadeo, who was eighth, had thrown 29. Both of them had completed 11 thus far.

In nine regular season meetings since '32, the Packers had beaten the Redskins six times, lost to them twice, and tied them once. Their only post-season contest in '36 was also a Packer victory. George Marshall exhorted his boys to put a halt to that trend before they were slated to play the Pack in Milwaukee. The pep talk worked because the tough Redskins massacred the Packers, 33-7, before 23,058 disappointed fans as Sammy Baugh and Andy Farkas had field days offensively, and the Redskins stopped the Packers at every opportunity.

Cartoonist Lou Grant of *The Milwaukee Sentinel* depicted the feeling around Packerland after the Washington debacle. He had Lambeau as a patient in a hospital bed with a block of ice on his hurting head, a black eye, a bandaged arm, and his right leg in traction. Holding his hand was a Packer fan who looked worried. The chart on the end of the bed had a graph line going down hill, and the diagnosis read: Acute Baugh-itis with an inflamed Farkas. A pot-bellied doctor was telling a well endowed nurse, "... now this is a patient I want you to watch very carefully. The poor chap was found wandering in a dazed condition out near State Fair Park last Sunday. Obviously the victim of a brutal beating. He's been delirious, thinks he's General Custer being massacred by the Indians. Keeps calling for Isbell. And the little guy visiting him looks kind of sick too!!"

The following week Lambeau received word that Ade Schwammel, the big lineman who had played for the Packers in the mid-'30s, was able to get a leave of absence from his job in San Francisco to play for the Packers again. Schwammel joined the team in time for the Lions' game in Detroit but did not play.

The rest of the Packers did play, and the result was much the same as the first time around. Green Bay waltzed all over the Lions, 27-6. Lambeau finally got Hutson back into the offense as the Alabama Flash caught his second TD pass of the year. Comp began to pay dividends, too, as he completed 14 of 18 passes for 201 yards.

Since they started playing the Giants in '28, the Packers had beaten them nine times, lost to them nine times, and there had been one tie. The two teams had also split their two post–season games. Oddsmakers had New York favored to beat the Packers at the Polo Grounds, especially after Charley Brock was hospitalized with an appendectomy just a few days before the contest was scheduled to be played. Being underdogs irked the Packers as they rallied in the fourth quarter to defeat the Giants, 35-21. Hutson caught two more TD passes, and he booted five more PATs to give him 21 straight for the year.

It was do–or–die week in Chicago as the Packers faced the Bears for their best shot at the division crown. Chicago's record still had but one blemish on it, the tie with the Packers; while Green Bay had the loss to the Redskins as well as the split decision with Chicago. A second loss in the seventh week of the season would mean sure disaster for the Packers.

The *Press-Gazette*'s headline told the whole story:

Bears Demolish Packer Title Hopes in Chicago Tilt, 21-7.

The Packers had a good day rushing the ball; the Bears had a better one. Green Bay did fine going through the air; Chicago did better. The Pack was tough on defense; the Bruins just a little tougher. It was the Bears' day; it wasn't the Packers'.

Green Bay took out its frustrations over losing to the Bears by plucking the hapless Cardinals, 35-14, the next week in Milwaukee. Hutson had a Hutson–type day when he caught six passes for 86 yards and three TDs, and he kicked all five Packer PATs to give him 27 straight. Canadeo had a decent day, too, passing 11 times, completing eight for 110 yards, and rushing for 39 yards on eight carries.

With just two weeks to go in the race, the Bears had clinched a share of the division title but had two tough games to go against Washington and the Cardinals. Meanwhile, the Packers would be facing the Brooklyn Dodgers and the Phil–Pitt Steagles.

The Dodgers were 2-6-0 when the Packers came to town, and they had never defeated the Wisconsin eleven in six previous tries. Hutson and company made it seven straight wins over the Flatbush squad, 31-7. The All–Pro end caught another pair of TD passes and kicked four PATs and a field goal. Oh, yes. He broke another one of his own records when he caught eight passes for 237 yards breaking his old mark of 209 yards set in '42 against the Rams.

On that same Sunday, the Redskins gave the Packers a faint glimmer of hope when they dumped the Bears. The Packers moved up a game on Chicago and still had a mathematical chance of catching the Bears. That chance went out the window when the Bears dumped the Cardinals, 35-24, on the last Sunday in November, while the idle Packers listened to the game on the radio.

The Packers had one more game to play against Phil–Pitt at Shibe Park in Philadelphia. Green Bay won, 38-28, in a real offensive show by both teams, and the story of the contest was once again Don Hutson. He caught another pair of TD passes and booted five more PATs to set yet another record by making 36 consecutive extra points in one season.

For the fourth straight year, the Packers finished second in the Western Division behind the Chicago Bears. Bears first; Packers second — this was beginning to sound like a broken record. Before the year of 1943 was over, Lambeau vowed he would do something toward bringing an end to Green Bay's string of second place finishes.

§ § §

17

Lambeau's Last Hurrah

During the middle of the '43 campaign, Don Hutson announced that he would retire from the game at the end of the season. Lambeau loathed losing a man like the Alabama Flash. Of course, Hutson was the greatest receiver to ever catch a pass to that time, but he was more than the Packers' star player. He was also a leader on the team.

Everything that Johnny Blood was in personality, Hutson wasn't.

Blood was unmarried during his playing days. He drank to excess frequently. He was loud and boisterous but in a pleasing way that made him popular with his teammates. He was a leader who led by using a lot of rah–rah to get the boys to rise to the occasion. He *blew in his pay*, as old–time cowboys used to say, on wine, women, and all the merriment he could endure for as long as the money held out.

Don Hutson was the quiet sort. He was married before coming to play for the Packers. He didn't drink, and he didn't chase women, much to the chagrin of those football groupies in the Green Bay area who chauvinistically counted bedded Packers as rungs on a social ladder. He was a leader by example, which was always positive and for the good of the team.

On the field, their talents may have been very close to being equal. Clarke Hinkle related how Hutson, a rookie who had yet to take a beating in a single NFL game, and Blood, the veteran of 10 pro campaigns already, ran a foot race – a dash of 40 yards or so – at training camp in '35. Hutson won, naturally, but only by a step. In his prime, Blood was considered to be one of the best receivers – if not the best – in the league. Many of the same things that were written about Hutson had already been written about Blood: He could go up with two defenders clinging to him and come down with the ball; he could elude tacklers with a twitch of his hips; he had speed to spare; he had sure hands.

Blood and Hutson were only different in that they played in different eras primarily. Pro football — and the ball itself — was just beginning to change to favor the passing game when Blood entered the twilight of his career. Many of the major changes were already made when Hutson graduated from Alabama; he benefited from them and at the same time justified them with his level of play.

The one trait that separated them was Blood's playfulness. He was hard to take seriously, whereas Hutson was almost always taken seriously because of his actions, not so much his words, although he often had a positive word to fit any occasion, whether a teammate needed an emotional lift or a gentle nudge in his character.

When Johnny Blood was offered the Pittsburgh job in '37, Lambeau did nothing to stop him because he felt Blood wasn't all that necessary to the success of the Packers. When Hutson said he would be hanging up his cleats at the end of the '43 season, Lambeau was in a panic about how to keep him around because Hutson was vital to the future of the Packers. If he couldn't have Hutson the player, then he wanted Hutson the man to be a part of his coaching staff.

On December 11, 1943, Lambeau signed Hutson as an assistant coach and scout for the Packers. This filled the void left when Eddie Kotal was called into the service. Five days later, Red Smith quit.

Richard "Red" Smith was a native of Combined Locks in the Fox River Valley southwest of Green Bay. He graduated from Kaukauna High School, then attended Lawrence College in Appleton before going to Notre Dame where he played varsity football under Knute Rockne. After graduating from the South Bend, Indiana university in 1927, he played baseball for the New York Giants, then joined the Packers that fall. He continued playing pro baseball in the summer and football in the fall until 1930 when he accepted the posts of football coach, baseball coach, and athletic director at Seton Hall College in Orange, New Jersey. In '33, he was named an assistant to Dr.

Clarence W. Spears at the University of Wisconsin in Madison. In '36, he returned to Green Bay to become Lambeau's line coach, and he became a part–time coach for the Milwaukee Brewers baseball team. In '41, he was signed to manage the Green Bay Bluejays baseball team of the Wisconsin State League, and in '42, he was hired to manage the Columbus Club bowling alleys. The next year he was hired as a full–time coach for the Milwaukee Brewers.

When Smith's resignation was announced in the *Press-Gazette*, Lambeau was quoted as saying, "Pro football has been growing so rapidly and duties of coaches have increased to such a great extent that it is desirable to have a year around assistant. Because of Red's baseball connections, which he felt he could not give up, he decided to resign."

That was for public consumption. Behind closed doors, Smith resigned because Lambeau gave him an *ultimatum* to give up his other jobs or give up being a Packer coach. Not that Lambeau wanted Smith to stay on his staff. He didn't need Smith; he had Hutson now who was the perfect assistant type for Lambeau. Smith wasn't; not any longer at least.

When Smith became Lambeau's assistant in '36, he was eager, docile, and in awe of his boss the living legend. In time, Smith came to realize that his hero wasn't infallible, that the things Mike Michalske, Cal Hubbard, and Johnny Blood were saying about Lambeau just might be true, that maybe the great football genius wasn't always right. Once he was sure Lambeau was human, Smith began second–guessing the Packer mentor; first privately, then openly to Lambeau's embarrassment.

Coinciding with this attitude was Smith's own rise in fame and popularity, brought on by his personal successes away from football. When he was handed the reins of the baseball Bluejays, he sorted through four dozen applicants for enough men to make up a winning team, then led them to one pennant and one very close second place finish. As a reward for his success on the field, the Brewers hired him to coach under manager Charley Grimm.

Because of jealousy over Smith's continuing success and because his megolomaniacal ego was being bruised by Smith's second–guessing — the same personal reasons that he fired

Johnny Blood a decade earlier — Lambeau gave Smith two choices: give up everything else or give up the Packers. Lambeau felt fairly confident — and hoped — that Smith wouldn't give up his baseball job and his position with the Columbus Club. Of course, Lambeau wouldn't have made such a move if he hadn't already hired Don Hutson as an assistant.

For his part, Smith refused to do either because he could see right through Lambeau. He argued that he had faithfully fulfilled his duties as line coach for eight years with the Packers while he held down other jobs and that he didn't see any reason why he couldn't continue to do so in the future. At this point, Lambeau threatened to fire him. Smith suddenly realized he was in a no-win situation. If Smith stood his ground, he was fired, and Lambeau could say just about anything he wished as a reason for the dismissal and the *Press-Gazette* would back him up. If he quit his other two jobs, how would he make ends meet financially and wouldn't he be closing the door on a career that might have a better future than the one he was seeing in football? His only alternative was to quit, to bow out of the Packer picture as gracefully as possible — then regroup.

It took Red Smith less than three months to get back into football. On February 28, 1944, the New York Giants hired him to be their line coach under Steve Owen. Smith was one up on Lambeau, but the last laugh was still to be had.

The New Year began on a sour note for Lambeau and Packer fans everywhere. Tony Canadeo was called back into the Army.

At the winter meeting of the NFL moguls, expansion was the main topic of conversation.

A new franchise in Boston was approved in '43, but the applicants couldn't find enough men to fill out a roster in order to play that season. That problem still wasn't solved.

Another group wishing to put a team in Buffalo applied for admittance into the league. Actor Don Ameche led a group wanting a franchise in Buffalo the year before. The application would have been accepted if not for one string that Ameche attached. He wanted permission to move the team to Los

Angeles when the war was over. George Halas vetoed this request because he had promised Charlie Bidwill that he would support a move of the Cardinals to Los Angeles after the war. The Buffalo group was told they would have to wait until April before a decision could be made.

Los Angeles and San Francisco also had potential owners at the January confab. Their applications were tabled when Commissioner Layden told them that they would have to continue playing among themselves until the war ended.

In the meantime, the NFL now consisted of 11 teams because Cleveland was returning to the gridiron in '44 and the Philadelphia and Pittsburgh teams would be regaining their own identities. The awkwardness of having an 11-team league was the reason for postponing a decision on Buffalo's application. It was felt that if the Boston Yanks could find enough players to field a team and if Buffalo could also put together a roster, then the league would go with 12 teams. If not, then some other plan would have to be considered.

A sidelight — involving George Strickler, the NFL's press agent and Chicago sportswriter, who would have a bearing on future events in Packer history — cropped up in mid-January concerning charges made by Strickler against two Big Ten Conference schools. In a December 27, 1943 *Time* magazine article, Strickler charged Wisconsin with offering a salary to Ted Fritsch to play football for the Badgers. He also made the same complaint against Iowa concerning the enrollment of Richard Ashcom of the Lions in that university's medical school.

The truth of the matter was Fritsch was given a job by a dairy operator named Duane Bowman while Fritsch was attending post-graduate classes at Wisconsin in the summer of '43. Fritsch had a 4-F draft status because of a perforated ear drum, thus his availability to play for the Packers. Having already played pro football, Fritsch wouldn't have been eligible for college ball anyway. For him to play under another identity would have been ludicrous for the same reason. Because he was a Packer, he would have been instantly recognized by thousands of fans and someone would have come forward and blown the lid off the scandal.

Strickler knew this, of course, but he was one of those reporters who *caused* news to be made when no one else was making any. To apply a "mod rocker" term from 1960s England, Strickler was a *mixer*, a person who stirs up trouble because he can't stand peace and quiet. Strickler was a headline writer who wanted to be a headline maker.

Big Ten Commissioner Major John L. Griffith cleared Fritsch, Ashcom, Wisconsin, and Iowa of any wrongdoing, but he also let the man who started the ruckus off the hook by saying Strickler merely reached a wrong conclusion when he learned of Fritsch's and Ashcom's situations. Griffith should have made a stronger denial and said something about Strickler reaching such a stupid conclusion on such flimsy evidence. But he didn't, and Strickler continued to "poke the bee's nest" whenever things were quiet on the sports page.

At the spring meeting of the NFL leaders, no decision was made over how many teams would participate in the coming campaign, but all applications for franchises were tabled until the war ended. This disappointed Sam Cordavana of Buffalo, Abe Wattner of Baltimore, Ernie Nevers of San Francisco, Anthony Morabita of San Francisco, Don Ameche of Los Angeles, and a group identified as "Miami sportsmen."

The rules committee came up with some startling new changes for the pro game. Free substitution was further encouraged when the owners decided the players no longer had to report to an official when entering a game while play was stopped. Coaching from the sidelines was finally approved, and a player was allowed to come to the bench for instruction during a time-out. The last major change was the elimination of the kickoff out of bounds. Henceforth, a team kicking off out of bounds would be assessed a five-yard penalty and would be forced to kick again.

Then the draft was held. Just as they had the year before, the magnates were more interested in obtaining the rights to certain players for that time when the war would end than they were interested in getting talent for the coming season. In '43, only 23 of the 300 men drafted played in the league that fall.

Lambeau made Michigan guard Mervin Pregulaman his top

choice, then took 29 more players. Only Bill McPartland, a tackle from St. Mary's, ever played for the Packers. An example of what a hit-or-miss affair the draft was in those days was Lambeau's choice of Kermit Johnson who had played in the AFL of '36 and '37. Somehow Johnson was listed as a graduating senior from Mississippi State.

A schedule was worked out at the meeting for an 11-team league. Because of the odd number of clubs, Philadelphia was designated a "roving" team. Instead of being tied to playing every team in the Eastern Division twice, the Eagles would play every team in the NFL once, giving them 10 games. The rest of the clubs would play each team in their own division twice and one team from the other division once and the Eagles, giving every team 10 games. It was a nice thought, but it didn't last more than 24 hours.

On the last day of the conference, Charlie Bidwill and Art Rooney decided on a merger of their teams for the '44 season. The new aggregation was to be known as "Cards-Pitts" but wound up being called Card-Pitt. This put the league back to 10 teams, and everyone was happy again except Lambeau because he wanted only eight teams in the league in order to keep the talent from being too widely distributed.

In June, Lambeau committed a sacrilege of immense proportions. He hired George Trafton, the former Chicago Bears center who had started so many fights with the Packers during his playing days, as the Packers' line coach. The *Press-Gazette* reporter tried to defend Lambeau's choice by stating Trafton was an archenemy of Bears' coach Hunk Anderson. Their enmity allegedly stemmed from a college boxing match at Notre Dame. Trafton recalled that Anderson approached him before the fight and said he thought they should fight to a draw because they were teammates on the football squad. Trafton agreed to the proposal, but Anderson must have forgotten it because he came out swinging and knocked Trafton out of the ring with a haymaker. Trafton, angered by the unexpected double-cross, jumped back into the ring and thrashed Anderson to win the school heavyweight title.

It was a great story but hardly verifiable. It would be unequivocally believable if not for the fact that Anderson and Trafton lined up beside each other for four years when they played for the Bears in the '20s. George Halas was never one to keep two guys on the same team who couldn't get along together. The boxing tale was probably true, but it probably wasn't the reason for Trafton's hatred of Anderson. There was more to their feud than that — or at least Trafton's part of it.

Trafton always wanted to coach football but not until after his playing days were over. Hunk Anderson quit the Bears after the '25 season and went back to Notre Dame to coach under Rockne. When Rockne died in a Kansas plane crash, Anderson was passed over for the head coaching job, and Elmer Layden was hired. Anderson stayed on as line coach. After the '32 season, Ralph Jones quit as head coach of the Bears. Halas wanted to hire Anderson to lead the Bears, but Hunk already had a good job and he expected to replace Layden one day. Trafton and his mother, who was a minority stockholder in the Bears, wanted him to be the Bears' new coach. Halas took the application under advisement until he found the money to buy out George's mother. As soon as Mrs. Trafton was gone, so was George and his application. Halas said he wanted Anderson or he would take the reins himself. Trafton resented Anderson, Halas, and the Bears for the snub.

Any bad blood between Anderson and Trafton might have begun in college, but the corker came much later.

Trafton got the Green Bay job by insulting the team. He had a chance meeting with Lambeau at a restaurant in Chicago, and the two former foes began talking football.

"What's wrong with that club of yours?" asked Trafton. "They don't scrap back like that old Green Bay crowd. Why right now, in this dinner jacket, I could chase those mugs out of the park."

Lambeau glared back at the 47-year-old Trafton and said, "You've got a job. Show up in Green Bay August 20."

Trafton showed up for the first practice that summer and was greeted by three dozens hopeful players. Returning to the Green Bay fold for '44 were Joel Mason, Baby Ray, Bill Kuusisto, Charley Brock, Pete Tinsley, Ade Schwammel, Harry Jacunksi, Larry Craig, Irv Comp, Joe Laws, Ted Fritsch, Lou

Brock, Don Perkins, Tiny Croft, Glen Sorenson, Bob Flowers, Paul Berezney, Bob Kahler, Ben Starrett, and Forrest McPherson. Newcomers were Roy McKay, fullback, Texas; Paul Duhart, back, Florida; Ray Wehba, end, USC who had played with the Dodgers in '43; Bob Kercher, end, Georgetown; Dick Bilda, back, Marquette; and Charley Tollefson, guard, Iowa. Mike Bucchianeri, the big guard out of Indiana who had played for the Packers in '41 before seriously injuring a knee, was finally healthy enough to play again.

This crew faced the Redskins in an exhibition in Baltimore and was soundly thrashed, 20-7. Five days later they went up against a Navy eleven coached by Jimmy Crowley and came away winners, 25-14. Then they traveled to Buffalo to play the new Boston entry into the league and completely dominated the Yanks, 28-0. The last encounter featured the return of Don Hutson who had come out of retirement when Lambeau found his team sorely lacking in good receivers.

As the Dodgers, Brooklyn failed to defeat the Packers in nine tries. Owner Dan Topping hoped that trend would change when he renamed his eleven the Tigers for '44. No such luck. In the season opener for both teams, the Packers tamed the Tigers in Milwaukee, 14-7, on touchdowns by Hutson and Lou Brock. A small crowd of 12,994 turned out on a very hot day for September.

Buckets Goldenberg retired at the end of the '43 season the same as Hutson had, and like Hutson, he couldn't stay away from the game he loved so much. He ended his retirement just in time for the Packers' annual battle with the Bears at City Stadium.

Hunk Anderson and Luke Johnsos, the Bears' co–coaches, whined about the fact that the Packers had more veterans on their squad than Chicago did, and they were quite correct. The Packers had 22 men on their roster who had NFL experience, while the Bears only had 14 returnees from their '43 squad.

Chicago's inexperience showed up in the fourth quarter of the game. After falling behind, 28-0, in the first half, the Bears rallied in the third and fourth quarters to tie the Packers, 28-28, with just a few minutes remaining on the clock. Fritsch took the ensuing kickoff after the Bears' fourth straight touch–

down and returned it to the Packers' 48. Lou Brock gained five yards on one run, then was stymied on the next. A third down pass was intercepted by Luckman, but Chicago was called for holding before the theft. Green Bay got the ball back and a first down on the Bears' 42. Brock then swept left end with a host of blockers to convoy him down the field. The only man in his way was Luckman, and Brock lowered his head and ran right through the erstwhile tackler. Hutson converted to put the Packers ahead again, 35-28. Chicago tried a desperation pass that Fritsch intercepted and returned 55 yards for one more TD, making the final, 42-28. No single Packer had a particularly outstanding day as the whole team contributed to the winning effort. Brock and Fritsch scored two TDs each, and Hutson and Comp had one apiece. Hutson extended his consecutive PAT string to 44 with six conversions.

For the first time in five years, the Packers had defeated the Bears in City Stadium. The last time was '39 when Green Bay won all the marbles. Many wondered if the victory over Chicago was a portent of things to come in '44.

The Lions were next for the Packers. Lambeau made it public the day before the game in Milwaukee that many of his players were still hurting from their contest with the Bears. After taking a 27-6 beating, Detroit coach Gus Dorais wondered how good Green Bay might have been had the whole team been healthy. Hutson had complained of sore feet all week and didn't practice. Fortunately, they were feeling just fine on Sunday afternoon as the fleet-footed end pulled down nine passes for 88 yards and a touchdown. Hutson's PAT streak came to an end at 46 after his own TD in the third quarter.

Art Rooney and Charlie Bidwill could have used a little more imagination when they decided on a name for their merged teams. Instead of Cards-Pitts or Card-Pitts or Card-Pitt, depending on which published title one preferred, they could have called their mixed aggregation the Chi-Pitt Steel Cardinals, which would have made those boys sound tough at least.

Phil Handler and Walt Kiesling were co-coaches of Card-Pitt, which seemed all right on the surface, but it left the players undecided about whose orders they should follow. This indecision haunted the team all year long, starting with their contest in Green Bay. Short on talent and not very well prepared for the game, the Card–Pitt squad took it on the chin, 34-7, from the Packers. Hutson, Starrett, Lou Brock, and Perkins scored the touch–downs; Hutson getting two on passes from Comp. Hutson also caught 11 passes for 207 yards. Comp was coming on as an NFL passer, completing 13 of 23 for 220 yards.

The Green Bay (4-0-0) victory over Card–Pitt (0-2-0) wasn't the only good news that day for Packer fans. Cleveland (2-0-0) dumped the Bears (0-2-0) that very same afternoon. The two game lead over Chicago caused a lot of Green Bay supporters to start planning a post–season trip to somewhere in the East.

When the NFL schedule was being made out that summer, the slate makers had to concern themselves with the availability of playing fields and space on trains. Also, the league had an obligation to the country to play a certain number of exhibition games for the benefit of those men and women in uniform. For all three reasons, the Bears and Redskins, Card–Pitt and Giants, and Eagles and Rams played exhibitions on the Sunday the Packers were thrashing Detroit. The Packers were set to take their turn at doing their patriotic duty when they were scheduled to meet the Eagles in Nashville the Saturday after they demolished Card–Pitt. Fortunately, the game didn't count in the standings because Philadelphia crushed Green Bay, 38-13.

While Green Bay (4-0-0) was playing the Eagles (1-0-1) for the war effort, the Rams (3-0-0) were winning again, downing Detroit (1-2-0). The Bears (1-2-0) chalked up their first victory that Sunday over hapless Card-Pitt (0-3-0). In the East, the Giants (2-0-0) beat Brooklyn (0-3-0), and Washington (1-0-1) beat Boston (0-3-0).

The slate makers rolled another natural the following week when the unbeaten Rams visited the unbeaten Packers at City Stadium. When looking back over the two teams' schedules to date, both had played the same trio of teams in their own division and the Packers had played one game outside their division against Brooklyn. In comparing the results, the Packers were easily the favored team for the match with Cleveland because they had defeated the opposition by greater scores than the Rams had. Also, they were playing in Green Bay, which was a plus for the Packers. But the final ace up Lambeau's sleeve was the temporary return of Tony Canadeo to the lineup. Corporal Canadeo was home on furlough from Fort Bliss, Texas, and he was free to play for the Packers for a few games anyway.

New coach Aldo Donelli directed his Cleveland team to an early TD, then watched as the Packers roared back with 14 points of their own on touchdowns by Starrett and Laws. The Rams tied the game at 14–all before Comp hit Lou Brock with an eight–yard scoring toss to put the halftime score, 21-14, in Green Bay's favor. Fritsch tacked up a TD in the third period to put the Packers up, 28-14, but the Rams came back early in the fourth to tighten the score, 28-21. Green Bay sealed the victory at 30-21 when the Packers chased a Cleveland runner deep into the end zone and forced him over the end line for a safety. Canadeo had a big day running the ball, gaining 107 yards on just 12 carries for the first 100–yard day in his NFL career. Fritsch gained 76 yards on 10 carries to complement the "Grey Ghost from Gonzaga." Hutson was Hutson again, catching seven passes for 87 yards and rushing for 49 yards on three attempts.

Green Bay (5-0-0) now had undisputed possession of first place in the Western Division. Cleveland (3-1-0) was still in second, and the Bears (1-2-1) and Lions (1-2-1) remained tied for third after playing each other to a tie. Card–Pitt (0-4-0) remained hapless, losing to the Eastern Division–leading Giants (3-0-0). Philadelphia (2-0-1) dumped Boston (0-4-0) and Washington (2-0-1) beat Brooklyn (0-4-0) to keep the race in the East interesting.

After enjoying home cooking for their first five games, the long–dreaded road trip was set to begin with a visit to Detroit for an October 29 meeting with the Lions. The Packers won a narrow defensive struggle, 14-0, on touchdowns by Laws and Fritsch.

While the Packers (6-0-0) were winning over the Lions (1-3-1), the Bears (2-2-1) were beating the Rams (3-2-0), and in the East, Philadelphia (3-0-1) and Washington (3-0-1) were moving into first place by defeating the Giants (3-1-0) and Card–Pitt (0-5-0), respectively. The Boston Yankees (1-4-0) won their first game ever by downing Brooklyn (0-5-0).

A golden opportunity to pound a nail in the Bears' coffin for '44 presented itself the first Sunday in November. The Packers headed into Chicago confident they would eliminate the Bruins from the division race and complete their first season sweep of the Bears since '35. Unexpectedly, Green Bay let their chance slip away.

When the two teams met in September, the Bears were playing their first game of the regular season after just one exhibition game, while the Packers were playing their second game of the campaign after three practice tilts. Green Bay also had the advantage of playing on their own field in front of a sellout crowd of about 25,000 fans. Even so, they barely beat the Bears.

It was now five weeks later, and the Bears had played another exhibition game against a tough Washington team and had racked up four more league contests, winning two, losing one, and tying one. With each passing game, they had gotten better, while it seemed that Green Bay had leveled off. With a crowd of 45,553 behind them, the Monsters of the Midway rose up and crushed the team that *Press-Gazette* reporter Art Daley so fondly called the "Pachyderms" in a story he wrote about George Trafton some weeks earlier. Bears 21, Packers 0.

Green Bay (6-1-0) got a break when the Rams (3-3-0) lost their third straight, losing to Washington (4-0-1) who remained in a tie with Philadelphia (4-0-1), victors over Boston (1-5-0), for first place in the East. The Giants (4-1-0) continued to hang tight behind the leaders, beating Brooklyn (0-6-0), and Detroit (2-3-1) stayed in the Western Division race with an easy win over CardPitt (0-6-0).

The Packers magic number for clinching a tie for the division flag was two when they played Bears, and it was still two when they traveled to Cleveland the next Sunday. With the Rams, Giants, and Card–Pitt left on their schedule, many Packer backers were confident Green Bay could win at least two of the three contests, beginning with Cleveland, a team that appeared to be coming apart at the seams. They were right about the Rams. The Packers had started them on their way to disintegration in October, and now they had the chance to eliminate Cleveland from the divisional race. Of course, the same op–

portunity had presented itself in Chicago the week before, and look what happened.

Lambeau seldom let his teams play poorly two games in succession. Displeased by his offense in Chicago, he put in overtime to get it ready for Cleveland. The extra work paid superb dividends as Hutson had one of his "Cleveland kind of days," catching six passes for 94 yards and a pair of TDs. Teammates Joe Laws, Paul Duhart, and Irv Comp also scored, Laws getting a pair of six-pointers. Hutson kicked all six PATs to finish off the scoring in Green Bay's 42-7 win.

Green Bay's (7-1-0) win eliminated both Cleveland (3-4-0) and Detroit (3-3-1), winner over Card-Pitt (0-7-0) again; but the Bears (4-2-1) were still in the chase after beating Boston (1-6-0). Out east, Washington (5-0-1) trimmed Brooklyn (0-7-0) to move a half game ahead of Philadelphia (4-0-2) who tied the Giants (4-1-1).

When Red Smith left the Packers and signed on to coach the line for the Giants, one of the first things he told Steve Owen was that he knew where the Giants could find themselves a first class passer if they needed one. Owen needed one. The Giants signed former Packer great Arnie Herber to a contract.

Herber wasn't exactly riding the bench and doing nothing in New York. The week before the Giants played hosts to the Packers he rallied his team from a 21-7 deficit midway through the final quarter to gain a tie with the Eagles. Herber wasn't much help on the field when the Packers met the Giants at the Polo Grounds, but he and Smith were instrumental in New York's win, 24-0, over Green Bay. The two former Packer players had been aiming for this game all season, and having been part of Lambeau's teams for a combined total of 21 years, they were well versed in the Packer mentor's tactics. It was this knowledge that they passed on to the New York players which led to Green Bay's defeat.

Green Bay's (7-2-0) loss didn't hurt much more than Lambeau's pride because the Lions (4-3-1) clawed and ripped the Bears (4-3-1) in Chicago, eliminating the Bruins from the race and giving the Western Division title to the Packers. The situation in the Eastern Division was clouded when the Eagles (5-0-2) romped over the Redskins (5-1-1) to put them in a second-place tie with New York (5-1-1).

The Packers had one more game to play in their season, and they won it handily, defeating Card-Pitt, 35-20, in Chicago on two TDs each by Hutson and Duhart and one by Perkins. The game was sort of anticlimactic since the Packers already had the division title.

The real story of the last ten days of November was the sudden verbal brouhaha that erupted in the pages of newspapers from New York to Green Bay. Arthur Daley, sports editor of the *New York Times* (not to be confused with reporter Art Daley of the *Press-Gazette*), wrote an article about Lambeau for *Colliers* magazine titled "The Wizard of Green Bay" in which he stated Don Hutson and Cecil Isbell hadn't been on speaking terms during Isbell's last season with the Packers. Lambeau denied this part of the story emphatically, saying Isbell and Hutson had always been the best of friends, citing several examples of their friendship as proof of his statement. Hutson and Isbell were also quoted in the *Press-Gazette*, affirming Lambeau's statement.

At the center of the story, claimed Lambeau, was Red Smith. Lambeau said he had called Daley in New York twice and asked him who had told him such a preposterous tale about Hutson and Isbell. Daley, according to Lambeau, didn't hesitate to tell him it was Smith. Lambeau further stated in the Green Bay paper that "Red Smith made trouble for us when he was here and we attempted to protect him. But when he violates the first principle of sportsmanship by giving out deliberate falsehoods, it is time to call a halt."

Chapter two of this incident occurred the next day when Russ Davis reported in the *Press-Gazette* that Lambeau had received an anonymous telephone call right after returning to his hotel room after the New York game. The caller told the coach not to train his team at Bear Mountain the next time they came to New York because every one of his practices had been scouted. He didn't say who had been scouting the Packers, but subsequent statements by Lambeau made it clear the Giants' coaches had been watching from the hill overlooking the practice field or from a window of a building near the practice site. Davis quoted Hutson as saying that it was possible because the Giants had been "shifting to meet those new plays of ours... and we hadn't run them off against any other team in the league this year."

Round three came a week later when Smith's denial of Lambeau's charges and Daley's denial that he had told Lambeau that Smith had related the story about Hutson and Isbell appeared in the *Press-Gazette*. Smith sent a letter to the newspaper so there would be no misquoting him.

"Enclosing a copy of a letter from Art Daley. I hope this will correct any idea that Lambeau misinformed the public about. Little boys always come home to cry and this time it is the coach and not the players. They are all a fine bunch and we have a lot of respect for them.

"Again Lambeau used his masterful art of twisting words and was not man enough to take a loss. Our club was ready and we just beat, fair and square, a good Packer team.

"Regarding Lambeau's statement, all the years I spent in Green Bay, I never had any trouble with any players, Don Hutson, whom I have the greatest respect for, or Lambeau as a coach. Everyone in the Packers organization, the press, the radio and the fans, treated me wonderful and I have only the deepest respect for them all."

In Daley's letter to Smith, he wrote:

"In case you missed the enclosed clipping (meaning the story where Lambeau made his charges) — which you probably haven't — here it is. I must say that I was shocked by it. I did speak twice to Curly Lambeau, although I never before knew that private conversations were subject to use in the public prints.

"The first time I spoke to Curly your name never was mentioned. The second time he specifically asked me if I had spoken to you. I told him that I had talked to many persons and had picked up considerable information throughout the many years I had covered professional football.

"Apparently, Curly chose to jump to conclusions he wanted to jump at. According to all traditions of the craft, newspapermen never reveal their sources of information. I think, perhaps, that is answer enough."

Lambeau replied to the Daley and Smith missives by sticking to his story. When asked why he waited until *after* the game to make his charges, Lambeau said he had planned on doing it the Friday *before* the game, but he didn't say *why he didn't do it that Friday*.

The *Press-Gazette* confused the issue at hand somewhat by printing a few erroneous facts. One had Isbell's last season with the Packers as '41, and the other had Smith resigning from the Packers in February '44. Isbell's last season was '42, and Smith resigned in December '43.

Before the next salvo exploded in print, the regular season was played out. After beating the Packers, the Giants nipped Brooklyn while the Bears crushed the Eagles and Washington slipped by Boston. This put the Giants (6-1-1) into a tie with the Redskins (6-1-1) for first, and the Eagles (5-1-2) slid into second. Then New York (7-1-1) beat Washington (6-2-1) by a field goal to take over first place, and the Eagles (6-1-2) got back into second place. The Giants (8-1-1) crushed the Redskins (6-3-1) the following week and won the right to play the Packers for the NFL title. The Eagles (7-1-2) finished a close second.

Just before the title game was to be played at the Polo Grounds on December 17, United Press International released a story by Jack Cuddy that related how Smith hoped to get the last laugh on Lambeau by virtue of a New York win over Green Bay. Cuddy made a faint attempt to repeat the circumstances around the now celebrated feud between Lambeau and Smith but hardly got at the real meat of the matter. Instead, he poked fun at Midwesterners and their brand of English to a degree that must have irritated many of them. He did offer one quote by Smith:

"I do not choose to comment upon my previous relations with Lambeau; I cannot recall having any difficulties with him or with the Packer club. I will break down and confess, however, that I hope we beat hell outta them Sunday."

Cuddy did remark that the Midwestern reporters who were in New York to cover the game did say that Lambeau and Smith "had been at loggerheads" during most of Smith's tenure with the Packers. Cuddy then displayed some of his Easterner's ignorance and prejudice by being derisive of the expression "at loggerheads" instead of expanding on the statement by the other reporters.

The Lambeau Years — Part Two

With this last bit, the verbal feud was buried. Not by Lambeau or Smith, but by Andy Turnbull. He recognized something that surely many readers of the *Press-Gazette* must have also seen: Lambeau was lying through his teeth. Smith calling him a little boy who went home to cry about the loss to the Giants was accurate because Lambeau didn't say word one about the Hutson–Isbell story while he was in New York, either before the game or after it. He waited until he was back in Green Bay where he had the *Press-Gazette* to back him up. Daley told the truth about newspapermen not revealing their sources. Anyone who knew anything about journalism must have realized that a reporter revealing a source was tantamount to professional suicide. Daley would never do that; he didn't get to be sports editor of the largest newspaper in the country by betraying his sources. The final proof of Lambeau's prevarication came from the Belgian himself.

In the story by Russ Davis about the Packer practices being scouted by the Giants, Davis reported that Lambeau got the call tipping him off an hour after the game. Lambeau denied this could have happened because "We don't do that in this league." After thinking about it, he realized that the Giants had been in all the right places at all the right times to stop Packer drives that day, and the only way they could have done that was by having prior knowledge of the Green Bay game plan. The only way to get that was to spy on the Packer practices. Lambeau had been had, so he struck back. He tried to disgrace Red Smith by accusing him of spreading the Hutson–Isbell story.

The feud might have continued but for one factor. The Packers avenged their earlier loss to the Giants by beating New York, 14-7, for the NFL title. Lambeau had gotten the last laugh on Smith with the win because the Packers seemed to be *in all the right places at all the right times to stop the Giants*. He never said who did his dirty work for him, but Lambeau did say that he had "friends in high places" in New York. Lambeau proved two could play the spy game.

The '44 season could have been written in Hollywood and made into a movie. It had all the elements of good entertainment, and for Packer fans, it had a perfect ending.

§ § §

18

One War Ends...

As the year 1945 opened, the Allies felt sure of victory in both theatres of war, and at home, many people had the feeling that a return to normalcy was just around the corner. Realists and historians thought otherwise. They knew that nothing would be the same as it was before the war. The geography and politics of the world would be reshaped, and many of the inventions of war, such as the jet airplane, would find peace–time applications that would forever change the lives of people everywhere.

The same was true in the National Football League. World War II had brought about some new innovations that would forever change the sport. But most importantly, it was proven that, in spite of travel restrictions and gasoline rationing that also limited movement, Americans loved the pro game more than ever and would turn out by the tens of thousands to watch a single contest, even if the combatants were both losers.

During the last few years before the war, the practical commercial use of television was just getting under way. The war stopped its progress for the moment, but those visionaries who could see into the future theorized that one day television would be a mountain of gold waiting for the right people to mine it. Oddly, it was radio that proved this theory to be true.

Before the war, commercial radio had grown enormously, but it hadn't reached its full potential yet. The war helped to bring about another surge in radio's popularity because people had two basic desires that it could fill. Radio brought the war news to every person within earshot of a speaker who wanted to know about the latest battle, and with entertainment programs, it took listeners away from their worries, especially those concerns about loved ones who somewhere else in the world fighting for their country. Because America was on an around-the-clock war work schedule, radio became a 24-hours-a-day business, creating a bigger demand for programming. Part of this demand was filled with sports, live broadcasts of baseball games and football games air-waved coast-to-coast and even to servicemen overseas who needed that ethereal umbilical cord to the States. The increased demand for programs, especially sports events, started small bidding wars between the various networks who were competing for advertising dollars. As the competition grew, so did the listening audience; and gradually each began feeding on the other.

Smart money saw this and said, "If people are going to get this excited about *listening* to something happen, how are they going to react when they can *see* it happening, too?"

Of course, the visionaries knew the commercial exploitation of television wasn't going to happen the day the Germans and Japanese surrendered. There was time yet to lay the groundwork for several different methods for getting a piece of the TV pie.

Since before the war, the owners of the National Football League had discussed the eventuality of expansion. Eight teams split into two four-team divisions or 10 teams divided into two five-team divisions was good for the game because it produced two winners who vied for the overall title and it was easier to promote a fourth place club in a five-team division than it was to promote an eighth place team in a 10-team league. But there were so many more cities across the country that wanted pro football. How could they all be accommodated and the game remain topflight?

The men who had been around for some time, like George Halas, Curly Lambeau, and Tim Mara, knew that expansion for the sake of expansion could be ruinous to the NFL. This was proven in '20s when the league handed out franchises like New Dealers would hand welfare checks a decade later. Even in the '30s when prosperity seemed imminent, expansion was still precarious; one of three teams — Cincinnati — added in '33 failed to make it through two seasons and the Portsmouth and Boston franchises had to shift to Detroit and Washington, respectively, to survive. By the time Cleveland was admitted to the league for the fifth time, the magnates had come to realize that stability was all important for the circuit. Before allowing the Rams to play with the big boys, the moguls made certain that the ownership had the money to support the franchise through thick and thin.

Just prior to the war, potential owners from several cities came knocking at the NFL's door. Prominent among the callers were groups and individuals from Buffalo and Los Angeles. There were also applicants from Boston and Minneapolis. Most of the NFL leaders saw that one day their league would have teams in those cities but not in '41, '42, or '43. They finally took in Boston in '44 and planned to add another team in '45.

Since the inception of the NFL, three American Football Leagues had come and gone, none lasting more than two years. Each one of these loops was made up of impatient entrepreneurs who were told by the NFL owners that they weren't expanding today and to get in line for tomorrow. The first AFL took this snub and fought back to its own ruin by paying exorbitant salaries to players who weren't worth it. The second AFL didn't fight back and died due to lack of interest. The third AFL was dealt a death blow by the war.

Some members of the NFL owners club realized that it was only a matter of time before a group of businessmen with sufficient capital would come along and start a league that could compete with the NFL for the best available talent in the country. Halas, Lambeau, and Mara were not among their number. They believed professional football was a closed club presided over by the NFL. There would be no admittance without the permission of the NFL's owners. Halas, Lambeau, and Mara were convinced that no other league could survive without recognition from the NFL; three AFLs proved that. The expansion of pro football was okay and even desirable — *but only on their terms.*

When the NFL magnates met in January of '45, the main subject of conversation was expansion. Boston had been added in '44, while the Chicago Cardinals and Pittsburgh Steelers had merged for the year. The two established clubs weren't expected to remain as one for '45. This meant the league now had 11 teams, which was an awkward number when scheduling time came around. Most of the owners opposed adding a 12th team due to the manpower shortage, but George Marshall of Washington said, "If we can play with 11, we can play with 12 teams." The majority felt that it was premature to expand until the government made up its mind about a piece of legislation before Congress. The bill stated in certain terms that all men of fighting age had two choices: serve in the armed forces or work in a defense related job. Professional sports didn't qualify as the latter, which meant all pro leagues would be suspended for the duration of the war.

The league meeting was adjourned until April.

Lambeau hired a new assistant in late January. Walt Kiesling, the former Packer player, had been the head coach at Pittsburgh after being Johnny Blood's assistant for two years. Then he was co-coach with Bert Bell when Bell and Rooney traded franchises for a couple of years. After Bell went back to the front office, Kiesling assisted Buff Donelli for a season. Then he co-coached the Steagles with Greasy Neale and co-coached Card-Pitt with Phil Handler. Tired of bouncing in out of positions of authority, Kiesling resigned from the Pittsburgh organization and signed with the Packers.

Just before leaving on a trip to scout talent, Lambeau addressed the Elks Club in Green Bay. As part of his talk, he named his all-time Packer eleven. For center, he chose Charley Brock; guards, Mike Michalske and Buckets Goldenberg; tackles, Cal Hubbard and Baby Ray; ends, Don Hutson and Lavvie Dilweg; fullback, Clarke Hinkle; halfbacks, Verne Lewellen and Cecil Isbell; and quarterback, Red Dunn as a ball handler and Larry Craig as a blocker.

Once he got out to California Lambeau was quoted as saying he was all for a new league when he was asked about the new All-America Conference that was still in the forming stages. He qualified his approval:

"If it's not one of these fly-by-night leagues that promise a well-known college player a lot of money and then give him only a small percentage of the profits."

He then added for the benefit of his California friends: "On the whole I think it would be a swell thing, and there's room for more."

When Lambeau returned home later in the month, he announced the release of George Trafton as line coach. In making the announcement known, Lambeau *said Trafton had been told of his release in mid-January* — just before Walt Kiesling was hired — *but that news of his release was withheld from the press so Trafton could hook up with another club without any undue publicity.* "If times were normal," said Lambeau, "we would have more than three coaches on our staff and undoubtedly would have kept George on as a fourth member. I think a great deal of his ability and am sorry that circumstances are such that he is leaving us."

This was another Lambeau smoke screen. When he went to the league meeting in Chicago in early January, Lambeau took Hutson and a part-time scout, Bob Conrad, with him. He didn't take Trafton because he intended to fire him before the league meeting but didn't until he was sure he had a replacement. After conferring with Kiesling in Chicago, Kiesling accepted the job but said he had to get a release from Art Rooney first. As soon as Kiesling was released by Pittsburgh, it was announced that he had signed on with the Packers. Lambeau then left for California and was more or less out of touch with people in Green Bay until his return in late February when he announced Trafton's release.

Trafton was burned by Lambeau for the same reasons that Red Smith had been. The former Bear was getting too much press, meaning Lambeau was getting less. Also, as the two men became more familiar with each other as the season rolled along, Trafton began making suggestions that went contrary to Lambeau's way of thinking. This ruffled the Belgian's feathers considerably, but as always, he kept it to himself until the time was right for him. That time came after Trafton had signed a one-year lease on an apartment in Green Bay and after his wife became too pregnant — she was due in March — for them to move.

When the NFL leaders met again in April, they finally made

some decisions about the coming campaign. The ability to decide something was facilitated by the pronouncement by President Franklin D. Roosevelt that baseball — and therefore, football — was a good thing for the country and the war effort.

The owners decided to play the '45 season with 10 teams again because of a fly in the ointment. Branch Rickey of the Brooklyn Dodgers of the National League of Baseball pulled the rug out from under the Brooklyn Tigers of the NFL when he told their management they could only rent Ebbetts Field for one more year because he wanted to have a pro football team — in one of the three new leagues being planned at this time. Brooklyn owner Dan Topping decided not to rent the Dodgers ballpark for '45 and tried to lease Yankee Stadium but was stopped by the Maras of the NFL Giants because they had territorial rights in Manhattan. This left the Tigers without a home for '45, which necessitated a merger for the '45 season between the Boston Yankees and the Tigers into a team to be known as "The Yanks" that would play four home games in Boston and one at Yankee Stadium in New York — with the Maras' blessing.

Beyond '45, the owners voted to expand to 12 teams in '46, but they put off any decision on where the new team would be located until after the Brooklyn situation was settled permanently. The only other business to be conducted was the player draft and the making of the '45 playing schedule.

Lambeau's first pick for the Packers was fullback Walt Schlinkman from Texas Tech. Of the other 29 men he selected, only Clyde Goodnight, end, Tulsa; Don Wells, tackle, Georgia; Lloyd Baxter, center, SMU; Nolan Luhn, end, Tulsa; and H.J. "Ham" Nichols, guard, Rice, would ever play for the Packers.

At a banquet sponsored by several Green Bay service organizations in early August, Lambeau and the Packers were honored for winning the '44 title. The coach was asked to say a few words, and he stood up and gave much of his standard rah-rah rhetoric except for one little paragraph that said more than he surely must have intended it to say. He was trying to share the credit for all that had been accomplished through the years in regards to the Packers with some of the people who deserved a lot more credit than he was giving them.

"Without the help of Andy Turnbull," he said, "we don't know what would have happened to the team. *The public will never know what he did in the early days* (Author's italics.) nor do we know what we could have done without his co-operation and assistance."

Lambeau was so right about the public not knowing what Turnbull had done and was still doing. Few people appreciated his many contributions to the organization in its early days, even when he was doing them, because Turnbull was not the kind of man who liked being in the limelight. He left that to Lambeau, and unfortunately for history's sake, Lambeau received more credit than was actually due him, especially in the beginning. Of course, this was mostly Turnbull's doing, too. He knew that in order to keep the Packers playing in Green Bay he had to rally the community behind the team and to do that he needed a focal point for the fans. Curly Lambeau, popular home town football hero, fit the billing perfectly.

The war in Europe had been over for three months, and recent developments in Japan gave everyone hope that the war there would soon be concluded. Already, the Army and Navy were discharging some personnel. Lambeau was hoping some of the dischargees would be men to whom Green Bay had the NFL rights. Green Bay had 44 players in the armed forces.

Lambeau, Hutson, and Kiesling welcomed 35 gridders to the first workout in early August. A few days later the Japanese surrendered, and the NFL restored the player limit to 33 from the war-time 28.

The Packers played the College All-Stars at Soldier Field in Chicago on August 30. A crowd of 92,753 fans turned out to watch Hutson score 11 points as Green Bay won, 19-7. This exhibition was followed by games against Philadelphia, Pittsburgh, and Washington. The Eagles nipped the Packers, 28-21. Green Bay stomped the Steelers, 38-12; and the Redskins dominated the Pack, 21-7. The highlight of these contests was the return of Johnny Blood to Green Bay. The Vagabond Halfback was home on leave from the Army. Lambeau added him to his staff to put some fun into training camp, calling Blood his "morale coach."

The first service veteran to be discharged and to return to the fold was Carl Mulleneaux, the big end from Utah who had 13 TD receptions to his credit as a Packer. Ray Frankowski, a guard from Washington who was drafted in '42, got his walking papers from the Navy and joined the team. He was the first draft choice lost to the armed forces to play for the Packers. Ed Frutig, the Michigan end who had played with the Packers in '41 before going off to war, came back to play in Green Bay again.

Lambeau's roster at the beginning of the season featured returnees Baby Ray, Glen Sorenson, Charley Brock who was now the team's captain, Pete Tinsley, Larry Craig, Irv Comp, Joe Laws, Ted Fritsch, Joel Mason, Don Hutson, Carl Mulleneaux, Ed Frutig, Forrest McPherson, Tiny Croft, Mike Bucchianeri, Charlie Tollefson, Bill Kuusisto, Bob Flowers, Roy McKay, Lou Brock, Don Perkins, Buckets Goldenberg, Alex Urban, and Ben Starrett. Newcomers included Ray Frankowski, Ken Keuper, Clyde Goodnight, Paul Lipscomb, Nolan Luhn, Ed Neal, Solon Barnett, and Russ Mosely.

More than two weeks before the Packers were scheduled to open the season at home against the Bears, the game was sold out. The *Press-Gazette* announced this fact with a photograph of Bernice Briese, assistant to Ticket Director Ralph C. Smith, putting up a "sold–out" sign outside the Packers' ticket office at the Legion Building. Both teams worked out in secrecy as they prepared for their opener at City Stadium. They practiced working with the new rule changes. Unlimited substitution would be allowed in '45 whereby teams could send players into the game without calling timeout, and the hash marks on the field were moved in another five yards from each sideline in order to put just a little more offense into the game.

In a game that saw the Packers get all the breaks, Green Bay downed the Bears, 31-21. Fritsch scored a pair of TDs and booted a field goal. Roy McKay and Don Perkins scored a touchdown each, and Hutson kicked four PATs. Chicago dominated all the statistics except two: turnovers and penalties. The Packers intercepted one pass and recovered a critical Bear fumble. The Bears were flagged for six major penalties for 89 yards, while the Packers were caught violating the rules five times for 49½ yards. Sid Luckman's big day of 14 completions in 24 tries for 237 yards went for nought.

Ernie Pannell gained his release from the Navy and put on a Packer uniform the next week. Joining him was a shipmate from the same PT boat command. Bernie Crimmins had played guard at Notre Dame before serving his country.

Defense gave Green Bay its first victory of '45, and it provided the second, too. The Lions met the Packers in Milwaukee and intercepted six Detroit passes, but that was only a part of the story. Roy McKay, the halfback from Texas who had spent most of the '44 season on the injured list, showed Packer fans he had an arm equal to Irv Comp's flipper. Trailing, 7-0, just one play into the second quarter, McKay hit the master receiver, Don Hutson, with a 59–yard bomb to tie the game. After Comp and Clyde Goodnight teamed up for a 46–yard score, McKay found Hutson again, this time for 46 yards and a TD that pushed the score to 21-7. The Lions threw an interception, and McKay immediately found Hutson for six points from 17 yards out to make the score 28-7. Still in the second period, Fritsch intercepted a Lion pass and returned it 69 yards to make the score 35-7. There was more time on the clock before the half. The Packers got the ball back, and McKay hit Hutson with a six-yarder for their fourth TD of the stanza to give the Packers 41 points for the quarter — a record for points scored in a quarter by a team. Hutson was the owner of 29 of those points — also a record for points scored in a quarter by a single player. The Packers weren't through yet. Lou Brock tossed a TD pass to Comp, the play covering 59 yards, in the third frame. Charley Brock got into the act in the fourth quarter, returning an intercepted pass 31 yards for a touchdown. Goodnight also racked up a safety, and Hutson converted seven of eight PAT attempts to make the final score, 55-21. All but seven Packer points were the direct result of pass interceptions and fumble recoveries.

The Packers and Rams were tied for first place in the Western Division when they met in City Stadium on October 14. Green Bay had won 12 of their 14 previous meetings with one game ending in a tie. Those games were all played before Bob Waterfield became the Rams quarterback. Waterfield was eight of 17 passing for 135 yards and two TDs and four meaningless interceptions. He directed a spirited attack that refused to die in the late going, overcoming a 14-6 Green Bay lead going into the final stanza to defeat the Packers, 27-14, and the Rams took over sole possession of first place.

As he did so often in the past, Lambeau looked for scapegoats after the loss to Cleveland. Sometimes he complained in the newspapers that the officiating had cost the Packers the game, and on other occasions, he remained silent and just released a few players. This was one of those times when he chose to let some men go. Frankowski and Urban "left" the team for personal reasons according to Lambeau. Urban's wife was ill in Ohio, so he quit to be with her. Frankowski said he wasn't in shape and was finding the grind too much after three years in the service. Urban's pro football career ended with the Cleveland game, but Frankowski went on to play for three more years, although not with the Packers.

Green Bay's next opponent was the undefeated Yanks. The two met in Milwaukee before a crowd of 20,846 fans. Hutson caught a pair of TD passes — one each from Comp and McKay — and kicked five PATs as the Packers walloped the Easterners, 38-14. McKay also had a big day running the ball, gaining 97 yards on nine carries and rushing for a TD.

The Packers (3-1-0) remained a game behind the Rams (4-0-0) who were beginning to look invincible. Detroit (3-1-0) was tied with Green Bay, but the biggest surprise of all was the Bears (0-4-0) were off to their worst start ever. Even the lowly Cards (1-4-0) were ahead of the Bruins in the standings, the Redbirds only win coming over the Northsiders, snapping a 29–game losing streak that stretched back to the '42 season.

Those same lowly Cards were the last visitor to City Stadium in '45. Three Hutson TDs and one each by Nolan Luhn and Fritsch kept the Chicago Southsiders near the bottom of the division as the Packers won handily, 33-14. Comp had a big day passing, completing nine of 12 for 185 yards and two TDs, both to Hutson.

The victory put the Packers (4-1-0) back into a first place tie with Cleveland (4-1-0) and the surprising Lions (4-1-0). The other surprise team of the year, the Bears (0-5-0), was still buried in the cellar.

There's nothing like a little hate to get the blood pumping, and the Bears found out that was all they needed to break their losing streak. The Packers paid them a visit at Wrigley Field, and the Monsters of the Midway rose up and struck them down — but not without a fight. Green Bay took an early lead, 14-0, in the first quarter, only to see the Bears come roaring back in the second with 21 points. The Packers also tacked 10 markers on the scoreboard in the second frame to make the halftime score, 24-21, Green Bay. The second half was a defensive duel that Bears won because they scored the only points of the third and fourth quarters to beat the Packers, 28-24. Comp, Craig, and Goodnight had touchdowns for the Packers, but the real story of the game was how the Bears kept Hutson bottled up and how they mauled the Packers unmercifully. Comp was forced to leave the game after scoring his TD in the first period, and McKay suffered a broken nose, the loss of two teeth, and a variety of bruises and cuts.

After their first loss to Cleveland, Charles F. "Chili" Walsh, the Rams' general manager, predicted the end of the "Big Four" in the NFL. He said in no uncertain terms that '45 would be remembered as the year that not one of the "Big Four" — meaning the Packers, Bears, Redskins, and Giants — won the NFL title. He even went so far as to say that Cleveland, Detroit, Boston, and Philadelphia were on the rise and would become the new "Big Four" in the league.

Lambeau disagreed with Walsh, and he told his troops that they had better prove him right when they played the Rams in Cleveland the next Sunday or some of them would be left a little light in the wallet. The Packer coach threatened to fine or suspend any player who didn't "put out." He said that some of the older players were playing only part of the time and this was giving the younger players the wrong impression about how a champion should play.

McKay, Comp, and Goldenberg were too hurt to help the team that week. Without the two best passers on the team, Hutson was barely noticeable on the field in Cleveland. The Rams scored early and often to take a 20-7 lead in the first period that stood up until the end, effectively eliminating the

The Lambeau Years — Part Two

Packers from the division race. Once again it was Waterfield who led the Cleveland attack with his passing and punting.

The loss dropped the Packers (4-3-0) two full games behind Detroit (6-1-0) and Cleveland (6-1-0) with just three games to go. The best the Packers could hope for was a tie because the Rams and Lions still had to play each once more. For the Packers to even tie for the crown, they had to win all three games, while Cleveland and Detroit were losing at least two games each. This was possible but not likely because one of Cleveland's remaining games was at home against the Cardinals.

As usual, Lambeau dumped players after the loss. This time Don Perkins, Mike Bucchianeri, and Forrest McPherson got the axe. Coming back to Green Bay was Chuck Sample, the Appleton product who had just received his discharge from the Army. Also leaving the team was Buckets Goldenberg who had sustained a foot injury against the Bears and he decided it was time to hang up his cleats for good.

As the Packers continued their road trip, traveling to Boston to meet the Yanks, more rumors concerning the fate of the franchise were quelled when the Green Bay Packers, Inc., gave Lambeau a new contract that would keep him at the head of the team through the year 1949. With the announcement, Lambeau made a statement that would come back to haunt him in due time. He said:

"There have been rumors in the past about the Packers moving out of Green Bay. *I don't have the power to move them, and even if I did have the power, I would never do it.* (Author's italics.) I was born in and have lived in Green Bay all my life and I have no intentions of moving. My home is here and will always be here. *I don't plan on being away from the city any more than I have during the last five years." (Author's italics.)*

In reference to the new powers given him by the corporation to represent it in all league matters, he stated:

"*To date, the executive committee and I have always worked in harmony.* (Author's italics.) They've been generous in giving me the right to vote and I appreciate it. *I shall always strive 100 per cent to protect the interests of the Packers.*"

This last item would also come back to cast a huge shadow on

Lambeau in the future.

But before that day came, Lambeau had a season to finish.

The Packers crushed the Yanks again, this time by the score of 28-0. Lou Brock scored a pair of TDs, and Hutson put six on the board. Bernie Crimmins scored a touchdown when he scooped up a fumble and ran 13 yards to paydirt with it.

As expected, the Rams (7-1-0) dumped the Cards (1-8-0) to stay two games up on the Packers (5-3-0). However, the Lions (6-2-0) lost to the Giants (2-4-1) in an upset. All Cleveland had to do to win the Western Division was dump the Lions in Detroit on Thanksgiving Day, and this they did with relative ease.

The Packers finished their season by beating the Giants, 23-14, at the Polo Grounds, then lost to the Lions, 14-3, in Detroit.

The loss to Detroit left the Packers in third place, the first time they had failed to finish either first or second in the division since '34 when they were third that year. It was just the beginning of the slide.

§ § §

Summary

Although Curly Lambeau's association with the Green Bay Packers would continue for another four years, for all practical purposes, the love affairs between Packer fans and Lambeau and between the stockholders of the Green Bay Packers, Inc., and their head coach were over.

Few people in 1945 realized how drastic the changes facing the National Football League would be in the years to come. None of the NFL moguls took the All-American Football Conference seriously in the beginning, figuring the upstart league was nothing more than a flash in the pan just as the American Football League of 1936-37 and the American Football League of 1940-41 had been. But after a while, some of the magnates began to see that the AAC meant business and that the new circuit could and would have an effect on their teams. The one man who failed to see how much the AAC might mean to his team was Curly Lambeau.

Whereas every other team in the NFL was based in a city that had a population of more than 500,000 people and a metropolitan population of over a million, Green Bay was still a small city with a big heart and Milwaukee was a good sized city that was more baseball oriented than football conscious. Every other club in the league could share its population with a team in a rival loop and survive. The Packers couldn't. Every other NFL team could get into a bidding war for a player's services with a team from the competing league and survive. The Packers couldn't. A lot of men in pro football in '45 could see this even then. But not Lambeau.

Curly Lambeau was looking ahead to the next season, but he was looking through those oft-mentioned rose-colored glasses. He was seeing his Packers and the NFL in a future that was based on the past. The league had met challenges from outsiders before and came away in great shape. The Packers had suffered through worse seasons than they had in '45 and gone right back to the top the next year. Lambeau looked at the talent he already had on his team and the talent he thought he had coming back from the war, and he saw an invincible squad similar to that of his '29, '30, '31, '36, '38, '39, and '44 teams. His '46 Packers would be loaded and ready to go wild game hunting, especially for Bears and Rams, the two teams he figured would give his Packers the most trouble.

What Lambeau refused to see was '45 was the end of an era. Not just for the Green Bay Packers but for the NFL as well. Don Hutson announced his retirement during the season, and this time he meant it. Not for many years would one man once again make such a difference in his team. Hutson put in a full 11 years, and that was enough. He was well past his prime, and everybody knew it except the man who should have seen it clearer than anyone else.

Not only was Hutson hanging up his cleats, so was that iron man of the backfield on both offense and defense, Joe Laws, who had a dozen campaigns worth of clippings in his scrapbook. Although Laws didn't make a big deal of his retirement, Lambeau should have seen it coming the same as he should have seen Hutson's. But he didn't. And why didn't he?

By '45, Curly Lambeau had built a fantasy world around himself where he saw himself as God's gift to professional football. He had come to believe that he hadn't just founded the Green Bay Packers but that he did it all by himself. He seemed to forget that Green Bay had a pro football team before he joined it in 1919 and that had he gone back to Notre Dame that fall Green Bay would most likely have had a pro football team anyway. It's been conceded in the first volume of this series that Lambeau provided the impetus for those first two meetings of the 1919 team, held on August 11 and 14; however, it was also pointed out that he desired to have the meetings that early because he was getting married on August 16 and he planned to use his honeymoon trip to pick up a few games for the Green Bay squad, which he did by arranging contests with teams from Milwaukee, Chicago, and Beloit. But this did not make him the founder of the Green Bay Packers.

One argument that was given to this author that Lambeau

was the founder of the Green Bay Packers was that not until 1919 was the Green Bay team known as the Packers. That made as much sense as saying that the New York Jets didn't exist before Sonny Werblin changed the nickname of the same franchise from the Titans to the Jets or that the Houston Astros didn't exist before their name was changed from the Colt .45s or that the Chicago Cubs didn't exist before 1902 because the Chicago team in the National League of Baseball Clubs was known as the Colts and before that the White Stockings. Admittedly, the Green Bay team of 1918 wasn't a business concern, but neither were the Green Bay teams of 1919 and 1920. Not until '21 did the Packers become a real professional football business when John and Emmett Clair were granted a franchise in the American Professional Football Association which became the NFL the following year. But even if the founding date of the Packers were to be pinned on that August 1921 day when the franchise was granted, then *the Clairs* would be the co-founders of the Packers, not Curly Lambeau.

Of course, Lambeau conveniently overlooked the Clairs' contribution to the history of the Packers, just as he forgot that Nate Abrams, his boyhood chum, had brought the two sides of Green Bay together again in 1918 to form the Green Bay Whales and that it was this team that Lambeau merely *joined* in 1919.

Another oversight on Lambeau's part was his career as the coach of the Packers. It's written everywhere except here that Curly Lambeau was the founder and only coach of the Packers from 1919 thru 1949. This simply wasn't so. The first coach of the Green Bay Packers was Bill Ryan, the high school coach who came back from World War I and was hired to coach the 1919 Packers. In 1921, the Clairs hired Joe Hoeffel, Lambeau's high school coach, to run the team. Not only was Lambeau not the first coach of the Packers but he wasn't even Green Bay's first NFL coach. In fact, Lambeau didn't coach the team officially until '22 when he owned the Packer franchise under the guise of the Green Bay Football Club, Inc. When he surrendered the franchise to the Green Bay Football Corporation in '23, he also lost his job as coach and didn't get it back until '24.

But by '45, the only man around the NFL who knew any better about Lambeau's career was George Halas, but Papa

Bear wasn't about to dispute anything Curly claimed because he had a few skeletons to hide in his own closet. There was one man who could dispute Lambeau's claims, but to do so would be tantamount to calling himself a liar. George Whitney Calhoun, that holder of the public trust as a member of the fourth estate, knew the whole truth about Lambeau and the beginnings of the club, but he had gone along with Curly for too many years to change his tale now. As far as he was concerned, the Packers were founded by good old Curly — but allegedly *only on a suggestion made by Calhoun over a glass of beer.*

This Packer mythology was only partially to blame for convincing Lambeau that *he was the Green Bay Packers incarnate.* The other villain that turned his head was that siren of the West called Hollywood, but the complete tale of that affair must wait for the next volume in this series. Suffice it to say that Lambeau "went Hollywood" long before anyone in Green Bay realized it.

None of the above should do anything to detract from Curly Lambeau's accomplishments as the head coach of the Green Bay Packers. He was the man at the helm when the Packers reigned over the pro football world six times in 16 years. The Chicago Bears might have won more division titles in those years and only one less NFL championship, but their head man, Halas, was at the reins only three times when the Bears sat atop the league. In fact, Halas would only win six NFL titles during all his 38 years as head coach of the Bears. Lambeau won his six in 31 campaigns in the NFL. No other coach in the history of the NFL had yet to match these two giants at the time of this writing.

Lambeau was a great judge of talent. He knew a football player when he saw one.

Lambeau was also a great motivator. He could get a team to play way over its collective head, sometimes by yelling himself hoarse and at other times by not saying anything, just looking and shaking his head.

Lambeau was also an innovator of the game. He was the first NFL coach to emphasize passing as a regular part of his game plan instead of using it as a last ditch effort to win. Unlike Halas in the early days who thought throwing the ball was close to being a criminal offense, Lambeau went to the air early and often because he knew it was easier to advance the ball over the heads of the opposing team than it was to try to grind it out through them.

Yes, Lambeau was a great coach — in his day. Trouble was, at the end of '45 he didn't realize that his day was over. He thought he could sit on his laurels and skate by on his reputation. He was pushing 50 really hard, but that didn't mean he was washed up. He could still learn — if he wanted to. Trouble was, he didn't want to. Lambeau thought he had all the answers, even when new coaches like Paul Brown were coming up with lots of new questions. Football had seen all the changes it would ever see and that was that as far as Lambeau was concerned. In '45, he was a man set in his ways, but he didn't know it. He was also a man who was receiving his due in respect and honor from his colleagues in the coaching ranks and from those men in the fourth estate who wrote story after story about the genius of Green Bay. That was another Lambeau problem: he was beginning to believe all his press clippings.

December 31, 1945 wasn't just the end of the year. It was the end of an era. Hutson and Laws were gone. World War II was over. The nuclear age had begun. The jet age had begun. Television, supercharged car engines, four–lane divided highways, rock'n'roll, and a professional football war were just over the horizon. The world would never be the same again, and Curly Lambeau, the Green Bay Packers, Inc., and all Packerdom were about to learn this the hard way.

This portion of *The History of the Green Bay Packers* closes here because the National Football League, Curly Lambeau, and the Packers were about to enter a new era in their collective histories. The NFL was about to face the greatest challenge of its 26-year existence with the establishment of Arch Ward's All–America Conference. Lambeau was soon to learn that his popularity in Green Bay was as fleeting there as it was in Hollywood. And the Packers, that is, the Green Bay Packers, Inc., were to come within an eyelash of passing permanently into history.

To add the next dozen years of Packer history after '45 to the first 25 Packer seasons would be an injustice. They were separate eras and must be treated as such. For as the one was bright and glorious, the other was dark and ignominious. Therefore, the two shall remain as much apart in this series as they were in history.

§ § §

Bibliography

Books

The Baseball Encyclopedia, Sixth Edition, Revised, Updated & Ex-panded, edited by Joseph L. Reichler, Macmillan Publishing Co., Inc., 1985
George Halas and the Chicago Bears, George Vass, Henry Regnery Company, 1971
The Green Bay Packers, Pro Football's Pioneer Team, Chuck Johnson, Thomas Nelson & Sons, 1961.
The Green Bay Packers, The Story of Professional Football, Arch Ward, G.P. Putnam's Sons, 1946.
Halas on Halas, George Halas with Gwen Morgan and Arthur Veysey, McGraw-Hill Book Co., 1979
History of American Football, Allison Danzig, Prentice-Hall, Inc., 1956.
The NFL's Official Encyclopedic History of Professional Football, Macmillan Publishing Co., Inc., 1973
Official 1985 National Football League Record & Fact Book.
The Packer Legend: An Inside Look, John B. Torinus, Sr., Laranmark Press, 1982
The Pro Football Digest, edited by Robert Billings, Digest Books, Inc., 1978
The Scrapbook History of Pro Football, Richard M. Cohen, Jordan A. Deutsch, Roland T. Johnson, and David S. Neft, The Bobbs-Merrill Company, 1977.

Newspapers and Periodicals

The Chicago Tribune.
The Green Bay Gazette.
Green Bay Packers Media Guide, 1987.
The Green Bay Press-Gazette.
The Milwaukee Journal.
The Milwaukee Sentinel.
The New York Times.
Collier's

§ § §

Index

— A —

Abrams, Nate — 138, 235
Acme Packing Company — 12, 34
Adams, Chet — 194
Adams, Woody — 183, 196
Adkins, Bob — 155, 157, 160, 164, 172, 182, 183
Akron, Ohio — 47
Alabama, University of — 39, 78, 79, 95, 183, 203
Albrecht, Art — 185, 189
Albright College — 159
Aldrich, Ki — 134
Alk, Samuel — 75
All—America Conference — 223, 233, 237
Ameche, Don — 205, 207
American Football Association — 171, 185
American Football League (includes all organizations of this name) — 98, 111, 116, 127, 136, 153, 154, 157, 170, 186, 208, 222, 233
American Legion (Sullivan Post) — 76, 158
Amherst Junction, Wisconsin — 39, 40
Anderson, Heartly "Hunk" — 42, 197, 208—210
Andrus, Ray — 152
Antigo, Wisconsin — 121
Applegate, Flash — 183
Appleton, Wisconsin — 13, 64, 185, 203, 231
Apsit, Marger — 41
Arizona, University of — 127, 135, 136
Arkansas, University of — 120, 167, 194
Army All—Stars — 187
Ashcom, Richard — 206, 207
Atkinson, L.C. — 74, 75

— B —

Badgett, Bill — 135
Bailey, Joe 167
Baker, Jack — 13
Balazs, Frank — 134, 136, 141, 157, 160, 172, 173
Baldwin, Baldy — 109
Baltimore, Maryland — 196, 207, 210
Banet, Herbert C. — 112, 118
Barnett, Bobo — 194
Barnett, Colleen — 12
Barnett, Solon — 227
Barnhardt, Frank — 121, 123
Barnum, Len — 163
Barrager, Nate — 20, 24, 57, 64, 81, 82, 98
Bartanen, Walt — 121, 123
Battles, Cliff — 41
Baugh, Sammy — 166, 180, 199
Baum, Ceil C. — 74, 75
Bausch, Frank — 142

Baxter, Lloyd — 225
Baylor University — 194
Beaumont Hotel — 187
Becker, Wayland — 97, 104, 112, 122, 141
Bedore, Edward A. — 123
Bell, Bert — 32, 51, 52, 64, 94, 95, 169, 223
Bellin, Roy — 134
Beloit, Wisconsin — 234
Benson, George — 183
Bent, Willard J. — 33—35, 76
Berard, C.M. — 32
Berezney, Paul — 188, 196, 210
Bero, H.J. "Tubby" — 33, 77, 82
Berry, Connie Mack — 155, 157
Bertrand, George — 75
Berwanger, Jay — 95, 96
Bettencourt, Larry — 96, 97
Bidwill, Charlie — 32, 53, 59, 68, 95, 134, 141, 168—170, 206, 208, 211
Bielefeldt, Oscar — 74, 75
Bilda, Dick — 210
Big Ten Conference — 206
Biolo, John — 136, 141
Bishop, Barbara — 158
Blaisdell, Neil — 22
Blood (McNally), Johnny — 18—24, 38—40, 46, 48, 50, 52, 53, 57, 60—62, 78, 83, 84, 86, 90, 98—100, 110, 112—114, 121, 122, 126, 128, 129, 140, 157, 160, 202—205, 223, 226
Boex, Milan — 113
Bonaparte, Josephine — 101
Bonaparte, Napoleon — 101
Borak, Fred — 121
Borchert Field — 44, 45
Boscobel, Wisconsin — 12
Boston, Massachusetts — 111, 205, 222
Boston Braves — 30
Boston College — 183
Boston Redskins (See Washington Redskins)
Boston Shamrocks — 116
Boston Yanks — 206, 210, 212—215, 218, 222, 225, 229—232
Bowman, Duane — 206
Brennan, John "Jack" — 135, 137, 141, 145
Brett, Ed — 121, 123
Brewer, Mel — 152
Briese, Bernice — 227
Briggs Stadium (Detroit) — 177
Brock, Charles — 134, 135, 141, 147, 155, 157, 172, 188, 189, 196, 200, 209, 223, 227, 228
Brock, Lou — 152, 155, 158, 164, 172, 175, 178, 188, 190, 195, 196, 198, 210—213, 227, 228
Brock, Tom — 194
Brookfield, Illinois — 56
Brooklyn Dodgers (baseball) — 225

The Lambeau Years — Part Two 241

Brooklyn Dodgers — 31, 33, 46, 47, 49, 50, 52—54, 66—71, 79, 84, 87—91, 94, 97, 99, 103—105, 110, 114, 115, 117, 120, 126—128, 144, 145, 147, 155, 159, 160, 162, 165, 171, 173, 175, 177, 179, 185, 187, 198, 201, 210, 212—216, 225
Brooklyn Tigers (See Brooklyn Dodgers)
Brown county, Wisconsin — 18, 32, 43, 61, 75
Brown, Jack — 152
Brown, Paul — 78, 237
Bruder, Henry "Hank" — 24, 39, 42, 48—51, 57, 62, 64, 67, 71, 75, 81, 85, 87, 90, 98, 101, 102, 105, 112, 116, 118, 122, 123, 141, 145, 156
Brumbaugh, Carl — 42, 66
Bucchianieri, Mike — 172, 210, 227, 231
Bucknell University — 22, 121
Buffalo, New York — 111, 124, 127, 186, 205—207, 210, 222
Buhler, Larry — 134, 135, 141, 158, 163, 172
Bultman, Art "Red" — 24, 38, 64
Burnett, Dale — 46, 54
Burke, Paul — 20
Busch, John M. — 74, 75
Butler, Ed — 70
Butler, Frank — 64, 80, 82, 85, 87, 90, 98, 112, 114, 122, 141
Buth, Frank — 75
Butcher, Wendell — 120
Byelene, Mike — 167
Bykowski, Frank — 152
Bystrom, Art — 18, 38, 45, 46, 53, 56, 70

— C —

Cahoon, Ivan "Tiny" — 136, 154, 170
Calhoun, George Whitney — 12, 18, 32, 36, 48, 53, 54, 58, 59, 77, 123, 125, 156, 185, 236
Canadeo, Tony — 167, 172—175, 188, 190, 195, 196, 199, 200, 205, 213
Canton Bulldogs — 115
Cantor, Eddie — 107
Card—Pitt — 208, 211—216, 223
Cardwell, Lloyd — 160, 172
Carlson, Don — 194
Carr, Joe — 26, 27, 29, 31, 57—60, 64, 65, 80, 84, 111, 125, 136, 137, 168
Carroll College — 185
Carson, A.G. — 74, 75
Carter, Joe — 188, 190
Casper, Charley — 64
Cassiano, Dick — 152, 155
Catholic University — 121
Cedar Rapids (Iowa) Crushers — 123
Central State Teachers College [See Wisconsin, Univ. of (Stevens Points)]
Chapman, Dick — 109
Charles, Mary Jane — 173
Charlevoix, Michigan — 185
Chaucer, Geoffrey — 19
Chicago, Illinois — 12, 13, 18, 24, 26, 39, 57, 58, 62, 83, 87, 94, 112, 113, 120, 124, 136, 137, 162, 168, 187, 189, 191, 194, 206, 209, 215, 216, 224, 226, 234
Chicago, University of — 95
Chicago Bears — 13, 17, 18, 20, 26—28, 30—32, 42, 47, 49—56, 59, 61, 63, 65—72, 82—91, 93, 94, 98—106, 110, 111, 114—120, 122, 124, 126—128, 130, 131, 134, 136, 141—148, 158—166, 168, 169, 174—183, 185, 186, 188, 189, 191, 193, 196—198, 200, 201, 208—215, 227—230, 234, 236
Chicago Cardinals — 27, 28, 31, 32, 47, 49, 50, 52—54, 57—59, 67—71, 84—91, 93, 95, 98, 99, 104—106, 110, 114—120, 124—128, 134, 141—144, 158—160, 162, 165, 168—170, 173—180, 182, 185—187, 189, 190, 197, 198, 200, 201, 222, 229, 231, 232
Chicago Cubs — 27, 93, 235
Chicago Stadium — 27
Chicago White Stockings (See Chicago Cubs)
Chippewa Falls, Wisconsin — 13, 83
Chippewa Falls Marines — 13, 83, 84
Cincinnati, Ohio — 26, 47, 186
Cincinnati Bengals — 128, 129, 153
Cincinnati Reds — 29, 31, 47, 49, 50, 52—54, 67—70, 112, 127, 163, 221
Civic Stadium (Buffalo) — 124, 125
Clair, Emmett — 235
Clair, John — 235
Clark, Dutch — 47, 48, 67, 90, 100, 105, 114, 117, 148, 159, 173
Clark, Henry W. — 98
Clark, Potsy — 47, 48, 67, 114, 147, 159, 168, 175
Clemmens, Cal — 97
Cleveland, Ohio — 47, 111, 163, 176
Cleveland Bulldogs — 115, 116
Cleveland Indians — 115, 116
Cleveland Rams (See Los Angeles Rams)
Clifford, Gerald F. — 12, 32, 33, 45, 73, 76, 77, 82, 96, 97
Clintonville, Wisconsin — 13, 44
Clusman, Norman — 75
Cobb, Fred L. — 77
Cohen, Sam — 75
College All—Stars — 112, 113, 156, 226
Colorado, Univ. of — 120, 159
Colorado School of Mines — 47
Colorado State University (Also Colorado A&M) — 197
Columbus, Ohio — 47, 80
Columbus (AFL team) — 158
Columbus Club — 205
Columbus Panhandles — 137
Comiskey Park (Chicago) — 158, 182, 189, 198
Comp, Irv — 194—196, 198—200, 209, 213, 215, 227—230
Comstock, Rudy — 38, 39, 63, 98
Conkey's Bookstore — 13
Conover, Larry — 135
Conrad, Bob — 224

Conzelmann, Jimmy — 158, 175
Cope, Myron — 18, 21—23, 39, 40, 48, 49, 60, 79, 85
Coppoc, Chet — 13
Cordavana, Sam — 207
Cornell University — 152
COWBOY QUARTERBACK, THE — 138, 139
Craig, Larry — 135, 140, 141, 155, 158, 164, 172, 188, 196, 209, 223, 227, 230
Creighton College — 121
Creighton, Milan — 58, 125, 168
Crimmins, Bernie — 228, 232
Croft, Milburn "Tiny" — 188, 196, 210, 227
Croft, William — 97
Crowley, Jimmy — 137, 210
Cruice, Wally — 95
Cuddy, Jack — 218
Custer, Gen. George A. — 166, 199

—D—

Dahlgren, Dick — 109
Daley, Art — 86, 188, 214, 216
Daley, Arthur — 216, 217, 219
Dallas, Texas — 140
Daniell, Averell — 109, 117
Danz, Norman — 75
Davis, Bert — 194
Davis, Corbett — 120
Davis, Russ — 216, 219
Davis, Van — 194
Dayton, Ohio — 47, 137
Dayton (AFL team) — 153
DeGroot, Al — 75
Delafield, Wisconsin — 185
Denver, Colorado — 110
Denver, Univ. of — 194
Denny, Harmer — 50
De Pere, Wisconsin — 121
Detroit, University of — 120
Detroit Lions (Also Portsmouth Spartans) — 17, 20, 26—28, 30, 31, 47—49, 51—55, 57, 59, 60, 64, 66—71, 84, 87—92, 96, 99, 100, 103—105, 114—120, 124, 126, 128, 130—132, 142—149, 159, 160, 162—165, 168, 172, 173, 175, 177, 178, 185, 189, 190, 198—200, 206, 211—215, 222, 228—232
Dettman, Walter — 75
Dietz, William "Lone Star" — 41, 70
Dilweg, Lavvie — 20, 24, 38, 64, 70, 223
Disend, Leo "Moose" — 159
Donelli, Aldo "Buff" — 213, 223
Donkle, S.O. "Sod" — 65
Dorais, Gus — 198, 211
Drake, Johnny — 173
Drum, Ralph — 33
Dubuque (Ia.) College — 140
Duhart, Paul — 210, 215
Duke University — 161
Duluth Eskimos — 23, 141
Dunn, Red — 223

—E—

Earpe, Jug — 20, 24, 46
Eau Claire, Wisconsin — 13
Ebbets Field — 103
Edwards, Bill — 172
Eichler, Vincent — 152
Elks Club — 223
Elmer, Dan — 134
Elson, Bob — 24
Emich, Howard — 138, 139
Engebretsen, Paul "Tiny" — 28, 69, 81, 98—100, 105, 107, 112, 122, 125, 126, 132, 141, 143, 145, 148—150, 157, 172, 173
Englemann, Wuert — 24, 38, 50, 52
Enich, Mike — 167
Evans, Dick "Red" — 155, 157, 196, 197
Evans, Lon — 39, 64, 71, 81, 98, 107, 110, 112, 120, 122, 123
Everson, Jeff — 13

—F—

Fairbairn, Don — 187
Falkenstein, Tony — 121, 196, 197
Famiglietti, Gary — 142, 197
Farkas, Andy — 120, 199
Farris, Tom — 183
Feather, Elvin "Tiny" — 45
Feathers, Beattie — 66, 69, 85, 110, 127, 155, 157
Filchock, Frank — 180
Finley, Jim — 185, 189
Fischer, Emil R. — 77, 82
Fitzgibbons, John — 18
Flaherty, Ray "Red" — 45, 72, 107, 145
Flick, Gene — 183
Florida, Univ. of — 210
Flowers, Bob — 188, 196, 210, 227
FOND DU LAC REPORTER — 86
Ford, Jim — 12, 111, 127
Fordham University — 120, 137, 155
Forrest, Ed — 194
Fort Atkinson Blackhawks — 65
Fort Bliss, Texas — 213
Forte, Aldo — 161, 174
Forte, Bob — 194
Fortmann, Danny — 142, 174, 197
Frank, Harold L. — 76
Frankford Yellowjackets — 29, 51
Frankowski, Ray — 183, 227, 229
Freiberger, John — 167
Friedman, Benny — 46
Fries, Sherwood — 196
Fritsch, Ted — 184, 187, 195, 196, 198, 199, 206, 207, 209—211, 213, 227, 229
Fromhart, Wally — 95
Frutig, Ed — 167, 172, 184, 227

—G—

Gantenbein, Milt — 22, 38, 55, 64, 71, 81, 86, 90, 98—100, 107, 112, 114, 116, 122, 124, 140, 141, 143, 146, 150, 171

Gaspar, Phil — 152
Gatewood, Buddy — 194
Gault, Willie — 13
Gavan, Irish — 109
Gavre, Vincent — 134
Georgetown University — 152, 210
Georgia, Univ. of — 39, 121, 135, 155, 194, 198, 225
Gibson, DeWitt — 109
Gigler, Earl — 75
Gillette, Jim 152, 157
Gish, Lillian — 102
Golden, J.H. — 32
Goldenberg, Charles "Buckets" — 39, 42, 46, 48, 50, 52, 64, 67, 81, 85, 88, 98, 99, 109, 112, 118, 121—123, 141, 157, 158, 188, 196, 210, 223, 227, 230
Gonzaga University — 120, 167
Goodnight, Clyde — 225, 227, 228, 230
Goodwin, Tod — 104
Gordon, Lou — 97, 110, 112, 122
Graass, Judge Henry — 34, 35
Grand Rapids, Michigan — 40
Grange, Harold "Red" — 22—24, 28, 42, 66, 69, 129
Grant, Lou — 199
Gray, Dick — 120
Greeley State College — 121
Green, Bill — 183
Green Bay Association of Commerce — 74, 187
Green Bay Bluejays — 204
Green Bay East High School — 97, 113
Green Bay West High School — 116, 136
Green Bay Whales — 138, 235
Greeney, Norm — 39
Greenfield, Tom — 135, 136, 141, 143, 157, 172, 184
Griffith, Homer — 71
Griffith, Maj. John L. — 207
Grimm, Charley — 204
Grunert, W.H. — 75
Grove, Roger — 24, 26, 38, 41, 48, 53, 58, 64, 66, 68, 81, 97
Gunther, Chester — 135
Guritz, Don — 152
Gustavus Adolphus College — 64, 120
Gutowsky, "Ace" — 28, 173

—H—

Haefs, W.E. — 75
Halas, George — 12, 18, 27, 29, 30, 32, 42, 51, 64, 68, 69, 95, 97, 101, 102, 130, 137, 139, 142, 143, 146, 147, 158, 166, 169, 174, 177—179, 182, 186, 187, 193, 197, 206, 209, 221, 222, 235, 236
Hall, Johnny — 135
Hall, Parker — 173
Halloran, Bill — 154
Halsey, Adm. William F. — 137
Handler, Phil — 211, 223
Hanson, "Swede" — 65

Hardin—Simmons University — 161, 194
Hare, Ray — 180
Harris, George M. 153, 154
Haskell Institute — 41
Hauptmann, Bruno — 102
Hawaii, Univ. of — 17, 20, 21
Hayes, Robert — 167
Hefferman, Ed — 167
Hein, Mel — 45, 104
Heisman Trophy — 95
Henry, "Fats" — 97
Herber, Arnold — 20,24, 39—42,48, 49, 51, 53, 55—57, 62, 64, 66, 70, 80, 81, 84, 85, 87, 89, 98—100, 102—104, 106, 107, 110—112, 114—116, 118, 122—124, 126, 127, 132, 140, 141, 143, 146, 150, 157—159, 161, 172, 215
Hermansville, Michigan — 121
Hershey, Pennsylvania — 183
Hewitt, Bill — 42, 66, 100, 101
Hiemenz, Paul — 167
Hinkle, Carl — 122
Hinkle, Clarke — 18, 20—22, 39, 41, 46, 48—50, 53, 57, 64, 66, 68, 70, 71, 78, 81, 84, 85, 89—91, 98—100, 104—107, 110, 112, 114, 116—118, 120—122, 124, 125, 128, 130—132, 140, 141, 143—145, 147, 149, 155, 157, 162, 164, 165, 167, 171—181, 202, 223
Hinte, Hale — 188
Hiram, Ohio — 185
Hoeffel, Joe — 235
Hofer, Willard — 135
Hollywood, California — 17, 19, 24, 25, 111, 219, 236, 237
Hollywood Light Horsemen — 96
Holovak, Mike — 194
Holtermann, J.A. — 75
Holy Cross College — 109, 167
Honolulu, Territory of Hawaii — 19, 20, 22, 24
HONOLULU STAR—BULLETIN — 17
Hoover, J. Edgar — 107
Hornung, Paul — 191
Houston, Texas — 135
Houston Astros — 235
Hovland, Lynn — 134
Howell, John — 121
Hubbard, Cal — 18, 20, 38, 39, 52, 57—60, 63, 69, 78, 81, 86, 87, 98, 99, 104, 204, 223
Hutson, Donald — 11, 19, 79, 80, 85, 86, 88—90, 92, 94, 96, 98—100, 102—105, 107, 110, 112, 116—118, 120, 122, 123, 125, 128, 130, 140, 141, 143—146, 148, 155, 157—161, 164, 165, 172—175, 177, 179, 180, 188—192, 194—196, 198—205, 210—212, 215—217, 219, 223—230, 232, 234, 237

—I—

Idaho, Univ. of — 95
Illinois, Univ. of — 97, 152
Indian Packing Corporation — 12
Indiana University — 63, 120, 136, 172, 183, 210
Ingalls, Bob — 183
Iowa, Univ. of — 63, 81, 112, 134, 136, 152, 155, 167, 183, 206, 207, 210
Iowa City, Iowa — 136
Ironwood, Michigan — 123
Isbell, Cecil — 120, 125, 126, 129, 131, 135, 140, 141, 143, 146, 148, 150, 152, 155, 157, 159, 164, 172—178, 180, 188—190, 192, 194, 199, 216—219, 223

—J—

Jacunski, Harry — 137, 141, 146, 148, 172, 178, 188, 196, 198, 209
Jankowski, Ed — 109, 115, 117, 118, 122, 124, 130, 141—143, 150, 155, 158, 164, 172, 173, 184
Joannes, Leland H. — 17, 18, 27, 32—37, 44, 68, 73—77, 82, 123, 138, 149, 150, 156, 170, 171, 176
Joannes Brothers Wholesale Grocers — 149
Johnson, Chuck — 12
Johnson, Howard "Smiley" — 155, 157, 172, 184
Johnson, Kermit — 208
Johnson, Preston — 183
Johnsos, Luke — 42, 51, 66, 110, 197, 210
Johnston, Chester "Swede" — 64, 68, 81, 82, 98, 99, 112, 121, 122
Jolson, Al — 110, 191
Jones, Bob — 63
Jones, Dr. David — 59
Jones, Ralph — 42, 136, 209
Jones, Tom "Potsy" — 121
Jonet, Frank J. — 34—36, 73, 77, 82, 123, 156, 171, 185
Jorgensen, Carl — 64

—K—

Kahler, Bob — 186, 189, 196, 210
Kahler, Royal — 189
Kamehameha School — 21
Kansas City, Missouri — 39
Kansas State University — 81
Karamatic, George — 120
Kassel, Chuck — 58
Katalinas, Leo — 121, 127, 141
Kaukauna, Wisconsin — 98
Kavanaugh, Ken — 174
Kell, Paul — 135, 140, 141, 155, 157, 164
Kelly, John "Shipwreck" — 79, 80
Kelly, Leslie J. — 76, 77, 195
Kelly, Dr. W.W. — 32, 73, 77, 115 146, 148, 150, 152, 155, 157, 159, 164, 172—178, 180, 188—190, 192, 194, 199, 216—219, 223
Kenneally, George — 65
Kennedy, Myrna — 25
Kenosha, Wisconsin — 179
Kenosha Cardinals — 145, 153, 157, 179
Kentucky, Univ. of — 167
Kercher, Bob — 210
Kerr, Bill — 152
Kersten, S.M. — 75
Keuper, Ken — 227
Kezar Stadium — 23
Kieppe, Dick — 194
Kiesling, Walt — 66, 81, 98, 112, 113, 129, 211, 223, 224, 226
Kilbourne, Warren — 140, 141, 145, 156
King, Ray — 121
Kinkade, Tom — 183
Kirksville (Mo.) Teachers College — 121
Knights of Columbus — 17, 23
Kodros, Archie — 152
Kostka, Stanley — 94
Kotal, Eddie — 184, 203
Kovatch, John — 121
Kresky, Joe — 65
Krivonak, Joe — 183
Krueger, Franklin W. — 75
Kuechle, Oliver E. — 43, 44
Kurth, Joe — 39, 64, 69
Kuusisto,, Bill — 172, 188, 196, 209, 227

—L—

La Crosse Old Style Lagers — 83, 84
Lafayette College — 98
La Guardia Airport — 163
Lake Forest College — 136
Lambeau, Donald — 137
Lambeau, Earl J. "Curly" — 11, 14, 17—25, 29, 30, 37—40. 47, 48, 55—65, 68, 69, 73, 76, 78—87, 89, 92, 95—99, 102—104, 106, 109—115, 117—123, 125—131, 134—145, 147—149, 151—153, 155—159, 161, 162, 167, 168, 170—174, 176, 178—181, 183—187, 189, 191, 194—205, 207—210, 213, 215—219, 222—226, 229—236
Lambeau, Marcel — 33
Langdale, Phil — 183
Lankas, Jim — 196, 197
Lassaro, Louis — 56
Lawrence, College — 203
Lawrence, Jimmy — 143, 155—157
Lawrie, George — 58, 59
Laws, Joe — 63, 68, 81, 98—100, 104, 112, 116, 122, 128, 140, 141, 143—146, 148, 150, 158, 172, 174, 188, 190, 196, 199, 209, 213, 215, 227, 237
Layden, Elmer — 167, 168, 170, 181—183, 206, 209
Lee, Bill — 117, 122, 141, 155, 157, 158, 172, 188, 189
Lee, George — 24
Leemans, "Tuffy" — 104
Leicht, Fred C. — 77, 82, 123, 156, 185
Leicht, Ray — 76

The Lambeau Years — Part Two 245

Lester, Darrell — 95, 112, 122, 141
Letlow, Russ — 95, 97, 112, 118, 122, 141, 157, 178, 188
Lewellen, Verne — 18, 24, 38, 39, 43, 61, 110, 171, 185, 223
Lewis, Lloyd — 101, 103
Lhost, Harvey — 77
Lincoln, Nebraska — 135
Lincoln, Abraham — 102
Lipscomb, Paul — 227
LITTLE CAESAR — 24
Lodl, Lee F. — 195
Lombardi, Vince — 21, 78
Long Island Indians — 171, 172, 185, 186
Los Angeles, California — 18, 23—25, 205—207, 222
Los Angeles Bulldogs — 81, 110, 153, 189
Los Angeles Coliseum — 153
Los Angeles Rams (Also Cleveland Rams) — 111, 114—120, 122, 123, 126, 128—130, 136, 137, 143, 144, 148, 159, 160, 162, 163, 165, 169, 173—178, 185, 186, 190, 191, 193, 194, 201, 206, 212—215, 222, 228—232, 234, 237
Louisiana State University — 109
Louisiana Tech — 41
Louisville (AFL team) — 153
Luckman, Sid — 142, 146, 174, 178, 181, 197, 211, 228
Luebcke, Henry — 152
Luhn, Nolan — 225, 227, 229
Lyman, Dell — 167, 172
Lynch, R.G. — 43, 44

—M—

Maddox, George — 81
Madison, Wisconsin — 159
Madison Cardinals — 98
Malinowski, Bruno — 167
Maloney, Pat — 75
Maniaci, Joe — 142
Manchester (Ind.) College — 112
Manders, Jack "Automatic" — 42, 51, 66, 89, 100, 142
Manhattan College — 171
Manitowoc, Wisconsin — 13, 44, 185
Manley, J. R. — 152
Mara, Tim — 30, 32, 95, 169, 221, 222, 225
March, Dr. Henry — 64
Mare Island Marines — 41
Marinette, Wisconsin — 44, 65
MARIPOSA, S.S. — 18, 20
Marquette University — 64, 97, 101, 121, 127, 159, 183, 210
Marshall, George Preston — 30—32, 95, 106, 111, 154, 155, 166, 169, 199, 223
Marshall University — 155
Marshman, Homer — 111
Mason, Joel — 186, 196, 198, 209, 227
Masse, Henry — 195
Masterson, Bernie — 142, 143
Masterson, Bob — 180

Mathys, Charles — 32, 73, 77
Mattos, Harry — 97, 116
Matuza, Al — 152
MAUI, S.S. — 22
Maznicki, Frank — 188
McAfee, George — 161, 174, 188
McCarty, Pat — 121
McCrary, Hurdis — 32, 73, 77
McDonald, Jim — 120
McGuire, Dan — 195
McHale, John — 36
McKay, Roy — 194, 210, 227—230
McKinley High School (Honolulu, Hawaii) — 21, 22
McLaglen, Victor — 96, 110
McLaughlin, Lee — 172, 184
McLean, Scooter — 197
McNally, John (See Johnny Blood)
McPartland, Bill — 208
McPherson, Forrest — 196, 210, 227, 231
Menasha, Wisconsin — 56
Merrill Fromm Foxes — 83
MGM Studios — 111, 153
Miami, Florida — 207
Michalske, August "Mike" — 20, 24, 38, 39, 41, 57, 64, 71, 78, 81, 85, 86, 88, 90, 98, 112, 117, 118, 122, 204, 223
Michigan, Univ. of — 46, 135, 137, 140, 152, 167, 183, 207, 227
Michigan State University — 39, 64, 80, 109, 185
Midler, Lou — 156
Miketinac, Nick — 121, 141
Miles, C.P. — 29
Miller, Abe — 75
Miller, Charles "Ookie" —
Miller, Don — 186, 189
Miller, Paul — 97, 99, 100, 112, 114, 118, 122, 127, 141
Milwaukee, Wisconsin — 12, 13, 43—46, 66, 68—70, 72, 74, 86—88, 98, 115, 124, 127, 138, 144, 145, 149, 150—154, 156—158, 160, 169—176, 179, 186, 187, 189, 190, 199, 200, 210, 228, 229, 233, 234
Milwaukee Brewers — 13, 204
Milwaukee Chiefs — 153, 154, 170, 176, 186, 197
MILWAUKEE JOURNAL — 43
Minneapolis, Minnesota — 111, 137, 222
Minnesota, Univ. of — 81, 94, 109, 121, 134, 135, 137, 140, 152, 154—156, 167, 172, 183, 194
Mississippi State University — 208
Moana Hotel (Honolulu, Hawaii) — 21
Moffett, John — 77
Molenda, Bo — 46
Molesworth, Keith — 28, 66
Monahan, Regis — 126
Monnett, Bob — 39, 42, 46, 50, 52—54, 64, 66, 81, 85—87, 90, 98, 99, 107, 112, 114, 116, 118, 122, 125, 130, 141
Moore, Allen — 140, 141
Moore, Frank — 75
Morabita, Anthony — 207

Morrison, Ray — 122
Mosely, Russ — 227
Mott, Buster — 39, 51
Mulleneaux, Carl — 112, 122, 127, 132, 141, 142, 157, 159, 164, 172, 176, 177, 184, 227
Mulleneaux, Lee "Brute" — 112, 127, 141
Municipal Stadium (Cleveland) — 148
Murphy, C.M. — 12
Murphy, Neil M. — 12
Murray, Charlie — 124
Musick, Jim — 54
Musso, George — 66, 142, 161, 197

—N—

Nagurski, Bronko — 28, 42, 66, 69, 197
Nash, Tom — 18, 20, 69
Nashville, Tennessee — 122, 212
National Broadcasting Company — 107
Neal, Ed — 227
Neale, Greasy — 223
Nebraska, Univ. of — 81, 95, 121, 134, 152, 155, 160, 167, 183, 186, 189
Nesbitt, Dick — 58
Nevers, Ernie — 23, 141, 168, 207
Newman, Harry — 46, 63, 70
New Richmond, Wisconsin — 39
New York Giants (baseball) — 203
New York Giants — 30—32, 44—47, 49, 50, 52—56, 60, 65—72, 83, 84, 86—95, 99, 100, 103—106, 112, 114—121, 126—128, 130—134, 136, 144—152, 159, 160, 162, 163, 168, 169, 172, 175, 177, 179, 180, 185, 191, 200, 205, 212—216, 218, 219, 225, 230, 232
New York Jets — 235
New York University — 114
Nichols, H.J. "Ham" — 225
Nolting, Ray — 142, 174
Norgard, Al — 64
North Carolina State University — 155
North Dakota State University — 112
Northwestern University — 69, 95, 109, 121, 152, 167, 173, 183
Notre Dame University — 39, 42, 64, 81, 95, 121, 135, 137, 140, 152, 167, 168, 194, 198, 203, 208, 209, 228, 234

—O—

O'Brien, Davey — 157
O'Connor, Bob — 81
O'Connor, C.J. — 32
Odson, Urban — 183
Ohio State University — 109, 120, 152, 167, 183
Ohlgren, Earl — 188
Oklahoma, Univ. of — 39, 95, 109, 152
Oklahoma State (A&M) University — 63, 194
Oldfield, Barney — 24
Olson, Glenn — 157
Orange, New Jersey — 204

Orangeburg, New York — 103
Oregon, Univ. of — 135, 136
Oregon State University — 63, 120
Oshkosh, Wisconsin — 44, 63
Osmanski, Bill — 142, 146, 174, 197
Owen, Steve — 72, 131, 205, 215

—P—

Pacific Coast All—Stars — 23, 96
Paeps, J.E. — 77
Paffrath, Robert — 167
Pagel, Ray — 86, 179, 185, 190
Palmer House (Chicago) — 194
Pannell, Ernie — 167, 172, 180, 188, 228
Parker, Duke — 127
Parkyakarkas — 107
Paskvan, George — 167, 172, 173
Paterson, New Jersey — 61
Paulekas, Tony — 97, 113
Peal, Lewis E. — 32
Perkins, Don — 197, 197, 210, 212, 227, 231
Perry, Claude — 24, 38, 64, 81, 98
Peterson, Les — 38, 64
Peterson, Nelson — 123
Peterson, Ray — 112, 115
Phil—Pitt — 194, 196, 201, 223
Philadelphia, Pennsylvania — 94, 201
Philadelphia Eagles — 29, 31, 32, 47, 49—54, 56, 65, 67—71, 84, 87—91, 94, 95, 99, 103, 105, 110, 115, 118, 120, 125, 126, 128, 132, 141, 147, 155, 157, 159, 160, 162, 163, 169, 172, 175, 177, 179, 180, 185, 191, 194, 196, 197, 206, 208, 212—215, 218, 226, 230
Pickens, Champ — 24
Pine Bluff, Arkansas — 79, 196
Pinewood Lodge — 83
Pinkert, Ernie — 41
Pinkerton, D.V. — 76
Pittsburgh, Pennsylvania — 29, 30
Pittsburgh, Univ. of — 109, 152
Pittsburgh Americans — 98
Pittsburgh Steelers (Pirates) — 29, 31, 32, 47, 49—54, 61, 67—71, 84, 87, 89, 90, 99, 100, 103—106, 110, 112—115, 120—123, 125—130, 134, 140, 141, 156, 159—163, 169, 173, 175—177, 179, 180, 185, 186, 189, 191, 194, 203, 206, 222—224, 226
Platteville State Teachers College — See Wisconsin, Univ. of (Platteville)
Polo Grounds (New York) — 54, 72, 106, 119, 131, 132, 149, 163, 169, 171, 200, 215, 232
Pool, Hampton — 197
Portsmouth Spartans — See Detroit Lions
Powers, James — 194
Pregulaman, Mervin — 207
Prescott, Harold — 194
Presnell, Glenn — 67
Preston, Fred — 183
Price, Charley — 164
Princeton, New Jersey — 185
Pukema, Helge — 167
Purdue University — 41, 120—122, 152, 155, 167, 194

Pyle, C.C. — 129

—Q—

Quatse, Jesse — 39, 60
Quincy, Illinois — 157
Quinn, J.H. — 75

—R—

Raasch, Charles A. — 74, 75, 77, 113
Racine Legion — 12
Ragazzo, Phil — 121
Ranspot, Keith — 189
Ray, Buford "Baby" — 122, 125, 141, 149, 155, 157, 172, 188, 196, 209, 223, 227
Reeder, Jim — 152
Reeves, Dan — 193, 194
Reimer, A.A. — 113
Remick Trucking Co. — 56
Reynolds, Bob — 95
Rhinelander, Wisconsin — 83
Rice Institute — 135, 225
Richards, George A. — 64, 84
Richardson, Jimmy — 183
Rickey, Branch — 225
Riddick, Ray — 155, 157, 172
Ripon College — 63, 64
Robbins, John — 120
Robbins, Walter — 195
Rockne, Knute — 167, 168, 198, 203, 209
Rogers, Joe — 183
Rohrig, Herman — 167, 172, 174
Rondou, Lee — 40
Ronzani, Gene — 42, 66, 85
Rooney, Art — 32, 49, 50, 84, 128, 129, 160, 169, 208, 211, 223, 224
Roosevelt, Franklin Delano — 52, 138, 182, 225
Rose, Al — 38, 41, 64, 81, 87, 98
Rossi, Angelo — 22
Ryan, Bill — 235

—S—

Saggau, Bob — 167
St. Benedictine College — 194
St. Edward's College — 39
St. John's Military Academy — 185
St. Louis, Missouri — 186
St. Louis Cardinals (baseball) — 135
St. Louis Gunners — 56, 64, 68, 70, 71, 84, 112, 121, 127, 144, 153
St. Mary's College — 64, 97, 121, 167, 185, 194, 197, 208
St. Norbert's College — 21, 121
St. Paul, Minnesota — 135
Salem, Oregon — 121
Salinas Iceberg (Lettuce) Packers — 110
Sample, Chuck — 185, 189, 190, 231
San Diego, California — 96, 185
San Francisco, California — 17, 22, 24, 78, 81, 96, 199, 206, 207

San Francisco, Univ. of — 95, 112, 167
San Pedro, California — 18
Santa Clara College — 135, 194
Sarafiny, Al — 39
Sarkkinen, Esco — 152
Sauer, George — 81, 84, 85, 89, 90, 96—98, 100, 102, 105, 106
Schammel, Francis "Zud" — 112, 116, 117, 122, 123
Scherer, Bernard — 95, 97, 99, 112, 118, 122, 128, 141
Schindler, Ambrose — 152
Schlinkman, Walt — 225
Schneidman, Herm — 81, 87, 96, 98, 104, 112, 116, 117, 122, 141, 157
Schoemann, Leroy "Bunny" — 121, 127, 141
Schreyer, Martin — 121
Schultz, Charles — 135, 137, 141, 157, 172, 184
Schumacher, Arthur E. — 77
Schuster, Ed — 32, 77
Schwammel, Adolph "Ade" "Tar" — 63, 66, 81, 88, 89, 98, 113, 119, 209
Schweger, Ed — 32
Seemann, George — 152, 155, 157
Seibold, Champ — 63. 64, 68, 81, 98, 112, 122
Servotte, William — 187
Seton Hall College — 203
SEVENTY THOUSAND WITNESSES — 24
Seymour, Bob — 180
Shaffer, Lee — 163
Shakespeare, William — 19
Shaughnessy, Hubert — 75
Shepherd, Bill — 90, 105, 126
Shepherd, Jim — 194
Sherman, Willard — 135
Sherman Hotel (Chicago) — 120
Shibe Park (Philadelphia) — 201
Shirey, Fred — 155, 157, 159
Sinkwich, Frankie — 198
Slater, Art — 75
Smith, Ben — 39
Smith, Bruce — 183
Smith, Cecil — 56
Smith, Ed — 114, 115
Smith, Ernie — 81, 89, 96, 98—100, 104, 105, 107, 110, 112, 116—118, 122, 141, 145, 150, 157
Smith, Kate — 107
Smith, Pete — 111, 153
Smith, Ralph C. — 190, 227
Smith, Richard "Red" — 97, 101—103, 110, 127, 140, 158, 203—205, 215—219, 224
Smith, Riley — 95
Snelling, Ken — 194
Snyder, Bob — 174
Snyder, Harry — 26
Soldier Field — 113, 156, 226
Sorenson, Glen — 196, 197, 210, 227
South Bend, Indiana — 42, 203
South Carolina, Univ. of — 135, 140, 172, 183
South Dakota State University — 97

Southern California, Univ. of — 23, 81, 97, 152, 194, 210
Southern Conference — 29
Southern Methodist University — 95, 135, 183, 189, 225
Southern Surety Co. — 33
Southwest All—Stars — 140
Spachmann, E.A. "Spike" — 82, 144, 173
Spears, Dr. Clarence W. 204
Spencer, Wisconsin — 187
Spencer, William H. — 197
Sprague, Charles — 135
Stahlman, Dick — 20
Standlee, Norman — 174, 188
Stanford University — 41, 64, 78, 79, 81, 95
Starrett, Ben — 185, 195, 196, 210, 212, 213, 227
State Fair Park (Milwaukee) — 66, 68, 124, 145, 149, 150, 153, 169, 176, 187, 199
Staten Island Stapletons — 29, 56
Stathas, James — 75, 76
Steen, Frank — 135, 141, 143
Stevens Point, Wisconsin — 39, 83
Stewart, Rodney — 195
Stiefel, Jack — 74, 75
Stolz, H.J. — 77, 123
Stonebraker, John — 188
Storck, Carl — 64, 137, 154, 168
Stork Club (New York) — 61
Strasbaugh, James — 167
Strickler, George — 147, 206, 207
Strong, Ken — 45, 46, 136
Sturgeon, Lyle — 112, 122, 123
Sturgeon Bay, Wisconsin — 44
Stydahar, Joe — 110, 111, 142
Superior, Wisconsin — 185
Susseof, Nick — 194
Sutherland, Jock — 175
Svendsen, Earl "Bud" — 109, 121, 141, 148, 155
Svendsen, George — 81, 96, 98, 112, 121, 172
Sweeney, Chuck — 121
Swisher, Bob — 188
Syracuse, Univ. of — 109

—T—

Tate, Bob — 194
Taylor, "Tarzan" — 101, 102
Telesmanic, Bill — 188
Temple, Shirley — 102
Tenner, Bob — 81, 96
Texas, Univ. of — 194, 210, 228
Texas A&M University — 63, 140, 167
Texas Christian University — 39, 64, 95, 112, 134, 145, 183
Texas Tech — 225
Thomas, Ron — 194
Thompson, Clarence "Tuffy" — 141, 144
Thorpe, Jim — 41
Tinsley, Pete — 121, 141, 172, 178, 184, 188, 196, 209, 227

Titan Stadium (Detroit) — 105, 149
Toledo, Ohio — 47, 186
Toledo, Univ. of — 167, 185
Tollefson, Charley — 210, 227
Topping, Dan — 169, 210, 225
Torinus, John — 12, 45, 86, 89
Trafton, George — 208, 209, 214, 224
Travers Island, New York — 148
Trimble, Tiny — 183
Tulane University — 152
Tulsa University — 109, 225
Turnbull, Andrew B. — 18, 32, 36, 48, 73, 74, 77, 82, 188, 189, 219, 226
Turner, Clyde "Bulldog" — 161, 174, 197
Tuscaloosa, Alabama — 80
Twedell, Francis — 134, 140, 141, 143
Two Rivers, Wisconsin — 140, 185
Tyson, W.F. — 74, 75

—U—

UCLA (University of California at Los Angeles) — 135, 167, 194
Ukiah, California — 12
United Airlines — 163, 176
United Press International — 91, 218
Upton, Francis — 51
Uram, Andy — 121, 122, 128, 141, 145, 147, 158, 159, 164, 165, 172, 175, 188—190, 196, 198
Urban, Alex — 227, 229
Utah, Univ. of — 97, 112, 227
Utah State University — 197

—V—

"Vagabond Halfback" — See Johnny Blood
Vairo, Dominic — 81
Valparaiso, Florida — 75
Vanderbilt University — 122, 152
Van Every, Hal — 152, 155, 158, 164, 165, 172, 180, 184
Van Sickle, Clyde — 38
Vant Hull, Fred — 188
Veeck, Bill, Sr. — 27
Verry, Norm — 194
Victoria Hotel (New York) — 106
Virginia, Univ. of — 152, 172
Virginia Polytechnic Institute — 29

—W—

Waikiki Beach — 21
Waldenbooks — 13
Walker, Frank — 75, 77
Walkers Cleaners and Tailors — 21, 24
Wall, Norm — 195
Walsh, Charles F. "Chili" — 230
Walter, John — 82, 87, 99, 113, 114, 124, 126, 128, 138, 157, 167, 185
Warburton, Cotton — 96
Ward, Arch — 12, 111, 154, 237
Ward, Earl, S. — 187
Ward, Theron — 95

Warner, Glenn "Pop" — 41
Washington, D.C. — 30, 167
Washington, George — 80
Washington, Univ. of — 183, 227
Washington & Jefferson College — 97
Washington Redskins (Also Boston Redskins) — 30—32, 41, 47, 49, 50, 52—54, 60, 67—71, 84, 87—90, 95, 99, 100, 103, 105—107, 111, 114—120, 126, 128, 130—132, 134, 143—149, 156, 157, 159, 160, 162, 165, 166, 169, 171, 175, 177, 179—181, 185, 187, 196, 197, 199—201, 210, 212—215, 218, 222, 223, 226, 230
Washington State University — 41, 121, 194
Waterfield, Bob — 228, 231
Wattner, Abe — 207
Waukesha, Wisconsin — 185
Weeman, King — 75
Wehba, Ray — 210
Weisgerber, Dick — 121, 141, 158, 165, 188
Welch, Mike — 194
Wells, Don — 225
Wendt, Merle — 109
Werblin, Sonny — 235
West Coast All—Stars — 17
West De Pere, Wisconsin — 21
Western Michigan University — 186
Western Reserve College — 121
Wetzel, J.C. "Ironman" — 95
WGN radio — 24
WHBY radio — 21, 24
Wheeler, Bob — 95, 139
White, Byron "Whizzer" — 120, 129, 159, 160, 164, 172
White, Millard — 152, 155
Wildung, Dick — 194
Wilkinson, Bud — 109, 112
Willamette College — 121
Wilmington Clippers — 186
Wilson, Donald "Weenie" — 140, 141
Wilson, George — 142, 174, 197
Winchell, Walter — 107
Winona, Minnesota — 40
Winters, Arnold — 189
Wintgens, H.J. — 77
Wisconsin, Univ. of (Madison) — 39, 63, 65, 109, 134, 159, 167, 183, 186, 204, 206, 207
Wisconsin, Univ. of (Plattesville) — 197
Wisconsin, Univ. of (Stevens Point) — 184
Wisconsin, Univ. of (Whitewater) — 135
Wisocnsin State League — 204
Wisconsin Supreme Court — 33
Witte, Earl — 64
WMAQ radio — 13
Wochenske, Ed — 75
Wojciechowicz, Alex — 120
Wood, L.G. — 77, 113
Woodin, Whitey — 38, 39
Woodward, Dave — 154
Woronicz, Henry — 183
Wray, Lud — 52, 65
Wrigley Field (Chicago) — 26, 71, 88, 100, 106, 117, 119, 120, 146, 161, 169, 178, 181, 230
Wrigley Field (Los Angeles) — 23
WTMJ radio — 13, 44
Wunsch, Harry — 64
Wyoming, Univ. of — 41
Wyrick, "Slats" — 135

—Y—

Yankee Stadium — 225
Yerby, John — 135, 136
Young, Horace — 183
Young, Paul — 39

—Z—

Zarnas, Gus — 144, 157
Zeller, Joe — 20
Ziegfield Follies —
Ziebell, L.P. — 32
Zoll, Carl — 116, 136
Zoll, Dick — 116, 123, 136, 141
Zoll, Frank — 116
Zoll, Martin — 116, 136